China's Trapped Transition

China's Trapped Transition

THE LIMITS OF DEVELOPMENTAL AUTOCRACY

❖   ❖   ❖

Minxin Pei

HARVARD UNIVERSITY PRESS

Cambridge, Massachusetts

London, England

2006

Library of Congress Cataloging-in-Publication Data

Pei, Minxin.
China's trapped transition : the limits of developmental autocracy / Minxin Pei.
p. cm.
Includes bibliographical references and index.
ISBN 0-674-02195-9 alk. paper
1. Democracy—China.   2. China—Politics and government—1976–2002.
3. China—Economic policy—1976–2000.   4. China—Economic policy—2000–   I. Title
JQ1516.P44 2006
320.951—dc22
2005052762

To Samuel P. Huntington

Contents

Abbreviations

ABC	Agricultural Bank of China
ADB	Agricultural Development Bank
AMC	Asset Management Company
BOC	Bank of China
BSSPIN	Bureau for Supervising the Security of Public Information Networks
BYTNB	*Banyuetan (neibuban)* (Semi-Monthly Forum, internal edition)
CASS	Chinese Academy of Social Sciences
CCB	China Construction Bank
CCP	Chinese Communist Party
CDIC	Central Discipline Inspection Commission
COD	Central Organization Department
COE	Collectively Owned Enterprises
CPPCC	Chinese People's Political Consultative Conference
CPS	Central Party School
DRC	Development Research Center of the State Council
FCC	Federal Communications Commission (U.S.)
FDI	Foreign Direct Investment
GDP	Gross Domestic Product
GGBRS	Governors' Grain-Bag Responsibility System
ICBC	Industrial and Commercial Bank of China
IMF	International Monetary Fund
IPO	Initial Public Offering
ISP	Internet Service Provider
LPC	Local People's Congress
MEI	Ministry of Electronic Industry

MEP	Ministry of Electric Power
MII	Ministry of Information Industry
MOF	Ministry of Finance
MPS	Ministry of Public Security
MPT	Ministry of Post and Telecommunications
MR	Ministry of Railways
NFZM	*Nanfang zhoumo* (Southern Weekend)
NIC	Newly Industrializing Countries
NGO	Nongovernmental Organization
NPC	National People's Congress
NPL	Nonperforming Loans
OECD	Organisation for Economic Co-operation and Development
PBOC	People's Bank of China
POD	Provincial Organization Department
RCC	Rural Credit Cooperative
SARS	Severe Acute Respiratory Syndrome
SCB	State Commercial Banks
SHLPS	*Shehui lanpishu* (Social Bluebook)
SOE	State-owned Enterprises
SPC	Supreme People's Court
TVE	Township-and-Village Enterprise
UNDP	UN Development Programme
WHO	World Health Organization
WTO	World Trade Organization
ZGFLNJ	*Zhongguo falü nianjian* (Law Yearbook of China)
ZGTJNJ	*Zhongguo tongji nianjian* (Statistical Yearbook of China)
ZGTJZY	*Zhongguo tongji zhaiyao* (Statistical Abstract of China)
ZGYW	*Zuzhi gongzuo yanjiu wenxuan* (Selected Essays on Organizational Work)

China's Trapped Transition

Introduction

THE ECONOMIC MODERNIZATION DRIVE that China launched at the end of the 1970s ranks as one of the most dramatic episodes of social and economic transformation in history. This process occurred in a unique political and economic context: a simultaneous transition from a state-socialist economic system and a quasi-totalitarian political system. Despite temporary setbacks, brief periods of high political tension, episodes of economic instability, and numerous conservative counterattacks, the two-decade-old, and ongoing, transition has dramatically altered the Chinese economic, social, and political landscapes.

In measurable terms of economic development and social change, China's achievement has been unprecedented in speed, scale, and scope.[1] Rapid economic growth has not only vastly improved the economic well-being of the country's 1.3 billion people, but also has fundamentally altered the structure of Chinese society. Additionally, as market-oriented reforms have made the Chinese economy less state-centered and more decentralized, economic development has turned Chinese society from one that was once tightly controlled by the state, into one that is increasingly autonomous, pluralistic, and complex. During this period, China's integration with the international community proceeded along several fronts. Trade and investment spearheaded this integration as China ascended from a negligible player in the world economy prior to reform, to a leading trading state and one of the most favored destinations for foreign direct investment (FDI). China's integration with the outside world has also taken place in other important areas, such as membership and participation in various international institutions, advancement in key bilateral ties, and educational and cultural exchanges with the West.

Most of these momentous changes have been captured by statistics measuring various aspects of Chinese society and economy. The aggregate size of the Chinese economy in 2002 was more than eight times the size it was in 1978.[2] In twenty-five years per capita income rose more than 600 percent, from $151 in 1978 to $1,097 in 2003.[3] Rapid economic growth accelerated social change as well. The rate of urbanization, 18 percent in 1978, had reached 39 percent by 2002.[4] A different measure, used by the United Nations, put China's urbanization in 1998 at 50 percent.[5]

Rapid economic growth has greatly expanded Chinese citizens' access to information and increased their physical mobility. About two thousand Chinese people shared a telephone line in 1978; in 2002, a fixed telephone line was available for roughly every six people and, in addition, about one mobile telephone was available for every six people. In 1978, three out of one thousand households owned a black-and-white television set. In 2002, there were 126 color television sets in every 100 urban households and 60 color sets in every 100 rural households. In 1978, on average, only 180 million domestic long-distance calls were made (about one for every five people); in 2001, 22 billion such calls were made—17 calls per capita. From 1978 to 2002, the number of newspaper copies printed tripled, and the number of titles of books published had risen eleven-fold. Internet users, barely 160,000 in 1997, numbered 79 million in 2003.[6] Such data suggest that access to information for average Chinese citizens has risen by several orders of magnitude on a per capita basis within a quarter century.

The rise in physical mobility is equally impressive. Passengers transported by various means rose 533 percent in this period, from 2.54 billion in 1978 to 16 billion in 2002. Measured in per capita terms, increase in physical mobility was close to 500 percent. Significantly, an increasingly large number of Chinese citizens gained the freedom to travel overseas. In 1978, few ordinary citizens were allowed this privilege. In 2002, 16.6 million Chinese traveled abroad.[7]

An important—if not inevitable—by-product of economic reform was the significant decline of the state's role in the economy. In terms of industrial output, the share of state-owned enterprises fell from nearly 78 to 41 percent from 1978 to 2002, while the share of the private sector (including foreign-invested firms) rose from 0.2 to 41 percent.[8] This dramatic relative decline of the state is also reflected in the employment data. In 1978, the state employed nearly 80 percent of workers in urban areas; in 2002, it employed only 29 percent.[9] These figures indicate that the state's control over the economic and social activities of its citizens has greatly eroded as a direct result of its declining presence in the economy.

One of the defining features of China's economic reform is its integration with the world economy.[10] Adopted by Chinese leader Deng Xiaoping as the centerpiece of his reform strategy, the policy of opening the Chinese economy to international trade and investment has produced enormous benefits. During the past twenty-five years, China has become one of the leading trading nations in the world, as well as one of the most popular destinations for FDI. In 1978, China was a closed economy that, relative to the size of its economic system, conducted a small amount of foreign trade and had token FDI. After a quarter century of reform, Chinese foreign trade increased, unadjusted for inflation, forty-one-fold—from $20.6 billion in 1978 to $840 billion in 2003—making China the fourth largest trading nation in the world.[11] In relative terms, China's foreign trade grew almost six times faster than its economic output (as gross domestic product, or GDP, rose 700 percent in the same period). The stock FDI, slightly more than $1 billion in 1982, reached $446 billion in twenty years. In 1980, about half a million foreigners, excluding people from Hong Kong and Taiwan, visited China. In 2002, 13.5 million did.[12]

China's integration into the international community has not been limited to trade and investment. Almost equally significant are the extensive educational, social, and cultural links with the West established during the reform period through the training of hundreds of thousands of Chinese students and visiting scholars in Western institutions of high learning, the appointment of tens of thousands of Western experts in Chinese universities, and through tourism and popular culture. Although it is difficult to quantify precisely the impact of such a multifaceted process of integration on Chinese society and politics, it is highly likely that the effects of this transformation have contributed to changes in values, tastes, and lifestyles that have occurred since the late 1970s.

China's Lagging Political Development

Juxtaposed against such massive, and largely positive, economic and social changes, however, is China's political system. Despite more than two decades of rapid socioeconomic changes, the core features of a Leninist party-state remain essentially unchanged.[13] By most conventional standards, the pace of political change has significantly lagged behind that of economic progress. This gap appeared to be expanding toward the end of the 1990s, as the Chinese leadership continued its gradualist economic reform while taking no substantive steps toward political opening. To some extent, the discrepancy between economic progress and political change is captured, however crudely, by polling data in China and several widely followed international indicators of democracy and governance. For example, a survey of 2,723 people across China in 2002 showed that they believed their political rights and ability to influence government decisions, the likelihood of getting equal treatment from the government, and judicial independence had improved only marginally as compared with the prereform era.[14]

In his speech at a small group meeting of the 16th Congress of the Chinese Communist Party (CCP) in November 2002, Li Rui, an outspoken liberal party member and former secretary to Mao Zedong, offered an apt assessment of China's political progress:

> Since China began its transition to a market economy, our national strength has been rising steadily, and we have gained undisputed great progress. But these problems remain: excessively slow pace in the reform of the political system, the lagging development of democracy, the weakness of the rule of law, and the resultant pervasive corruption.[15]

Lagging political development will endanger the CCP's own survival, Li warned:

> Chinese and foreign histories prove that autocracy is the source of political turmoil. As the collapse of the Soviet Union shows, the root cause is autocracy. Modernization is possible only through democratization. This is the trend in the world in the twentieth century, especially since the Second World War. Those who follow this trend will thrive; those who fight against this trend will perish. This rule applies to every country—and every party.[16]

China's lagging political openness is reflected in the low scores the country receives from several widely used international indexes. The Polity IV Project consistently rates China as one of the most authoritarian political systems in the world.[17] Similarly, the Freedom House's survey rates China as almost completely "unfree." In fact, China's ratings for the 1990s were slightly worse than those for the 1980s.[18] Data compiled by Transparency International, a nongovernmental organization (NGO) that surveys perceptions of corruption worldwide, suggest that China is perceived as one of the more corrupt countries.[19] The *International Risk Guide,* which assesses risks stemming from corruption, weak rule of law, bureaucracy, repudiation, and expropriation, has also portrayed China in a mixed light. Its ratings for the period from 1984 to 1997 show that corruption had worsened in China and that the level of bureaucracy remained essentially unchanged. On the positive side, the guide suggests that the legal system may have improved moderately from a very low base, and that the risks of debt repudiation and asset expropriation were considered negligible.[20]

Various measures of governance confirm the underdevelopment of key public institutions in China. In a "quality of governance ranking" compiled by Jeff Huther and Anwar Shah of the World Bank in 1998, China was placed in the bottom third of the eighty countries ranked. China received a score of 39, similar to that given to poorly governed countries such as Egypt, Kenya, Cameroon, Honduras, Indonesia, Pakistan, and Nigeria.[21] Judged by another set of measurements used by the World Bank's Daniel Kaufmann, Aart Kraay, and Massimo Mastruzzi to track governance in 199 countries from 1996 to 2002, China was grouped among the countries commonly associated with weak states.[22]

On "voice and accountability," China was ranked 186, ahead only of failed states and the most repressive countries; it was comparable to Angola, Belarus, Vietnam, Saudi Arabia, and Afghanistan. China was behind most former Soviet-bloc states and major developing countries, including Russia, Ukraine, India, and Mexico. In terms of "regulatory quality," China was placed at 116, in the company of Nicaragua, Cambodia, Papua New Guinea, Egypt, and Mali. China's ranking was below India, Mexico, and Russia, three countries normally known for weak regulatory regimes. On "control of corruption," China was ranked 111, along with Colombia, Ethiopia, Iran, and Romania. Although China fared better than Russia, it was judged to be less capable of controlling corruption than India, Brazil, and Mexico. China did better on the other three governance indicators. In terms of "government effectiveness," China was placed at 71, in the company of Namibia, Croatia, Kuwait, and Mexico; it was slightly ahead of Russia and India. On "political stability," China was ranked 87, comparable to Belarus, Mexico, Tunisia, and Cuba. China scored higher than India, Russia, the Philippines, and Indonesia. In terms of "rule of law," China was ranked at 94, comparable to Mexico, Madagascar, and Lebanon, and better than Russia but worse than India.[23]

Such ratings, however, should not completely negate the substantial—and in many aspects, positive—changes that have taken place in the Chinese political system since the late 1970s, particularly in the areas of elite politics, institutional development, and state-society relations. Some of these changes have been forced on the ruling regime by the necessity of economic reform, while others were the products of regime-initiated policies or societal pressures. As a result, politics in China following two decades of economic reform exhibits tentative signs of institutional pluralism, tolerance of limited public space, and emergence of democratic grassroots participation.

On the positive side, the post-Mao regime has put an end to mass terror and significantly curtailed the reach of the state into society. Personal freedom and social mobility have both expanded substantially; limited alternative channels of political participation have been opened; and autonomous civic organizations are allowed to exist and function outside the political sphere.[24] At the elite level, the post-Mao leadership has also restored the most basic institutional norms and procedures required of a stable government, thus contributing to relative elite cohesiveness and political stability during the reform era.[25] The need to promote economic reform and social stability has motivated the regime to implement a limited program of legal reform that has begun to have some impact on political, economic, and social behavior in China.[26]

Another trend in the development of incipient institutional pluralism is the growing role of the National People's Congress (the national legislature) and local legislatures in policy-making. Originally conceived as a necessary step to restore the constitutional order devastated by the Cultural Revolution, the strengthening of the legislative branch of the government has acquired a political momentum of its own. Consequently, China's legislature has become increasingly assertive of its constitutional prerogatives and gained considerable political stature.[27] Modest progress has been made even in the area of democratic participation. Although the post-Mao regime has suppressed the demands of systematic democratic reforms, it was forced, by the political necessity of maintaining order in rural areas, to permit the election of village committees as de facto governments of the basic administrative units in the countryside. As a new political institution that began as a limited experiment in the late 1980s, village elections had become an established practice by the end of the 1990s and received full official sanction. Although village elections have not produced effective local democratic governance in many areas where they have been held, they represent the first step, however small and tentative, toward expanded political participation in an authoritarian regime.[28]

These signs of limited political opening, unfortunately, have yet to alter the defining characteristics of the post-Mao regime as a one-party autocracy. In many ways, these changes have been tolerated largely because they do not represent a direct challenge to the monopoly of power of the CCP. Indeed, these changes are compatible with the short-term objectives of the party. Thus, political reform under the rule of the CCP can occur only within the strict limits imposed by the party. In practical terms, these limits have stunted the development of an effective legal system, constrained the constitutional role of the legislative branch, obstructed the growth of rural self-government, and restricted the emergence of a civil society. Thus, to most outside observers, post-Mao political reform is, at worst, an oxymoron and, at best, a series of tentative, partial, and superficial measures most likely to fail because they in no way challenge, limit, or undermine the Communist Party's political monopoly. A democratic transition under the rule of the CCP thus seems a distant, or even unrealistic, prospect.[29]

Transition Trapped?

The combination of market reforms and preservation of a one-party state creates contradictions and paradoxes, the implications of which the ruling elites have either chosen to ignore or are reluctant to face directly. For example, the market-oriented economic policies, pursued in a context of exclusionary politics and predatory practices, make the

CCP increasingly resemble a self-serving ruling elite, and not a proletarian party serving the interests of the working people.

Commenting on the CCP's transformation, the deposed former general secretary of the CCP, Zhao Ziyang, perceptively observed:

> The problem is, the CCP is a party built on the basis of Leninism. It controls all the resources of the country . . . under a market economy, after property becomes legitimate and legal, the CCP inevitably becomes corrupt. Those with power will certainly use their control of the resources to turn society's wealth into their private wealth. These people have become a huge entrenched interest group . . . What China has now is the worst form of capitalism. Western capitalism in its early phase was also bad, but it could gradually become more progressive. But the worst form of capitalism in China today is incapable of becoming more progressive.[30]

Of course, there are other irreconcilable conflicts between the self-interest of the CCP and its declared goals of reform, such as building a socialist market economy and ruling the country according to law. To the extent that a market economy requires a minimum degree of the rule of law, which in turn demands institutionalized curbs on the power of the government, these two goals run counter to the CCP's professed determination to maintain political supremacy. The CCP's ambition to modernize Chinese society also leaves unanswered the question of how the new autonomy of society is to be respected by the state and protected from the caprice of the government. The CCP's perennial fear of independently organized social interests does not prepare it well for the likely emergence of such forces, which a more industrialized society inevitably creates.

These unresolved contradictions, fundamental to China's transition away from communism, are the source of rising tensions in the Chinese polity, economy, and society. At the intellectual level, the intensification of these contradictions raises doubts about whether China could, as many of its East Asian neighbors, evolve along a neoauthoritarian development path, eventually perhaps toward a more open society.[31] In terms of policy, these tensions make the political and economic strategies adopted by post-Mao rulers appear increasingly unsustainable. China's transition to a market economy and, perhaps potentially, to some form of democratic polity, risks getting trapped in a "partial reform equilibrium," where partially reformed economic and political institutions support a hybrid neoauthoritarian order that caters mostly to the needs of a small ruling elite.[32] Under this order, the power of the state is used to defend the privileges of the ruling elite and to suppress societal challenges to those privileges, instead of advancing broad developmental goals. Notably, opinion polls conducted in China since the late 1990s reveal that the Chinese public, including both the intelligentsia and the masses, increasingly believe that members of the ruling elites have gained the most from economic reform while ordinary people, such as workers and peasants, have benefited the least. Such a perception of a self-serving elite supports the hypothesis of a partial reform equilibrium trap.[33]

Indeed, symptoms of a trapped transition have become highly visible or even pervasive. Some keen observers of Chinese politics have warned of the "death of reform" because the political and ideological forces that initially energized China's reform have dissipated.[34] On the economic front, important reform measures have encountered strong resistance.[35] The sense that economic reform has stalled is widely shared by Chinese corporate executives, many of whom are members of the CCP. A poll of 3,539 senior corporate executives across the country conducted by the State Council's Development Research Center in late 2002 found that only a minority was satisfied with the progress of key reforms. For example, about a third rated as "satisfactory" the progress in establishing a modern corporate system, in reforming the foreign trade system, and in healthcare reform. Between 25 and 28 percent of the executives were satisfied with the results of the reforms of the financial system, the fiscal system, and state-owned enterprises (SOEs). Nineteen percent were satisfied with the reform of the investment system.[36]

In the financial sector, reforms that would have transformed China's dominant state-owned banks into commercial banks have made little progress. Despite the legacy of huge nonperforming loans in these banks, the government continues to use them to support unprofitable and even bankrupt SOEs and fund large fixed-asset investments that can inflate growth.[37] As a result, mounting bad loans in state-owned banks, equivalent to more than 40 percent of GDP, threaten the country's entire financial sector.[38] The government's reform of SOEs has also entered a difficult period.[39] The rising level of unemployment, a direct result of SOE reforms, has forced the government to slow down the restructuring of SOEs out of fear of exacerbating incipient social unrest.[40] Although many small and medium-sized SOEs were privatized in the late 1990s, the state maintained its ownership stakes in almost all large SOEs and is obliged to maintain their life support, thus causing further deterioration in China's fiscal health.[41] Genuine privatization of these large SOEs has yet to occur.

In addition, a quarter century of reform has not succeeded in breaking down state-owned monopolies in most key industries, such as banking, telecommunications, civil aviation, energy, rail transportation, tobacco, and wholesale trade on agricultural inputs and products. These markets remain distorted and inefficient. Barriers to market entry continue to be high because of political interference from local governments, which rely on the obstacles to protect their vested interests in local industries that constitute sources of local fiscal revenue and political patronage.

Toward the end of the 1990s, despite the proreform rhetoric and publicly announced ambitious goals of the Chinese government, the costs of the lagging institutional and structural reforms began to be reflected in the performance of the Chinese economy. In a wide-ranging study of the Chinese economy conducted in 2002, the Organisation for Economic Co-operation and Development (OECD) warned that "the important engines that have driven China's growth in the past are losing their dynamism" because "China's economy has become badly fragmented and segmented, and this has led to increasing under and inefficient utilisation of resources."[42] Among the critical weaknesses cited by the OECD study were anemic growth in the rural sector, inefficiency in SOEs, and weakness in the financial system. Such structural weaknesses contributed to the considerable slowdown of the Chinese economy in the late 1990s.[43] An International Monetary Fund (IMF) study of the economy in 2003 found similar structural weaknesses and warned that, because the one-off productivity gains from earlier reforms had already been realized, China's continual growth would depend on new and more difficult structural reforms.[44]

Even official Chinese statistics, which tend to be inflated, show that the double-digit growth in the early 1990s fell to the 7- to 8-percent range in the late 1990s. The real rate of growth is likely to have been even lower.[45] Although China's growth accelerated in 2002–2004, it was driven primarily by state-led fixed-asset investment.[46] Such growth, occurring in a context of a lack of structural reforms, would likely exacerbate the distortions in the economy. Wu Jinglian, China's most respected economist, repeatedly warned in 2004 that, because economic growth was driven by excessively high investment rates (more than 40 percent of GDP), this type of growth was low quality and unsustainable and would create new problems.[47]

The Lack of Political Reform

Signs of a trapped transition also permeate Chinese politics. It is worth noting that all the important institutional reforms in the political system—such as mandatory retirement of government officials, the strengthening of the National People's Congress, legal reform, experiments in rural self-government, and loosening control of civil society groups—were all conceived and implemented in the 1980s—before China's economic take-off. In the 1990s, although incremental reforms continued in these areas, albeit at a slower pace in most instances, the CCP leadership under Jiang Zemin did not launch any new or significant institutional reform initiatives. In addition, whereas internal and, sometimes, public discussion and debate on political reform was tolerated and even sanctioned during the Deng era, similar discourse was practically banned during Jiang's tenure in office.

Among leading Chinese academics was a widely shared consensus that the political system had lagged behind the economic system and that the failure of political reform was the most serious constraint on China's development. In their judgment, however, the imbalance between an increasingly open economic system and China's current political system was unlikely to improve. Half of the academics interviewed by the researchers from the Chinese Academy of Social Sciences in 2003 thought the imbalance would persist, and a third said it would worsen.[48] Even many officials shared the view that such an imbalance existed and was likely to grow worse.[49] Four polls of officials being trained at the Central Party School (CPS) between 2000 and 2003 show consistently that the issue they were most concerned with was political reform, an implicit admission of their recognition of the political system's relative stagnation.[50] Like leading academics, 80 percent of the 133 cadres polled in the CPS survey in 2002 said that lack of progress in political reform would be the most important factor in constraining China's development—even more important than economic reform.[51]

The lack of progress in political reform in the 1990s not only high-lighted the stagnation of China's autocratic polity vis-à-vis its fast-changing economy and society, but undermined the regime's ability to maintain effective governance and to address three critical challenges.

Rampant Official Corruption

Partially reformed economic and political institutions provide a fertile environment for official corruption because institutional rules are ei-ther unclear or politically unenforceable in such environments. The ruling elite are unaccountable and immune from punishment for wrongdoing. Consequently, it is unconstrained from adopting preda-tory policies and practices. In the Chinese case, corruption by the rul-ing elite reached endemic proportions in the late 1990s.[52] Public opinion surveys in this period consistently ranked official corruption as one of the top political issues facing China.[53] High-profile scandals in-volving senior government officials, from members of the Politburo to provincial governors, to chief executives of large SOEs, have become a staple of the Chinese media. Invariably, these ruling elite members were found to have engaged in illegal real estate deals, accepted huge bribes, sanctioned large-scale smuggling operations, participated in fi-nancial fraud, provided protection for organized crime, and sold gov-ernment appointments for personal gains.

The costs of uncontrolled corruption are enormous, both economi-cally and politically. Rough estimates of the total costs of corruption range from 4 to 17 percent of GDP—a substantial amount of resources diverted from public coffers into private pockets.[54] The political effects of corruption perpetrated by the ruling elite are difficult to estimate, but are likely to be even more harmful than pure economic losses. Cor-ruption by government officials undermines the integrity of many key institutions that enforce laws, maintain rule and order in the market-place, and deliver crucial public services. Corrupt practices adopted by government officials—such as taking bribes, rigging bids, insider deal-ing, selling government offices, fraudulent accounting, and large-scale theft—inevitably reduce the effectiveness of the affected state agen-cies, increase the costs of market transactions, and raise the level of systemic risks, especially in the financial sector. Thus, state capacity of countries governed by corrupt regimes is always found to be weak. More important, official corruption in a transition economy, as one Chinese social critic observed, allows the ruling elite to use their political power to amass large private wealth through theft and market manipulation, thus directly contributing to rising socioeconomic inequality and resulting in levels of social discontent.[55]

Erosion of State Capacity

The erosion of state capacity in China is epitomized by the Chinese government's deteriorating performance in maintaining several critical functions that are generally considered central to the effectiveness of a state: the extraction of revenues, the provision of key public goods, the collection of information, and the enforcement of laws and rules.[56] To some extent, the decline of state capacity in China is captured by the paradox of power and ineffectiveness. Although the Chinese state appears to be institutionally unconstrained, centralized, and omnipresent, its ability to implement policy and enforce rules is severely limited by its incoherence, internal tensions, and weaknesses. The phenomenon of *zhengling buchang*—or ineffectual government directives—is widely reported in the Chinese press. It includes the defiance of central government laws and policies by local authorities, the willful violation of laws and regulations by government officials, and the practice of local protectionism that has plagued the enforcement of contracts, court judgments, and national laws.[57] This unique characteristic of Chinese politics is appropriately labeled fragmented authoritarianism.[58]

To be sure, market and regime transitions unleash forces that contribute to the erosion of state capacity, as experiences from other countries in transition show. Since a reversion to the status quo ante is not feasible, the rejuvenation of the state is likely only through institutional reforms designed to adapt the organizational structure and functions of the state to meet the new economic and political challenges. Thus, the erosion of state capacity most likely results from a failure to reform the political system. China's runaway official corruption is an apt example. The ruling elite's unwillingness to reform flawed state institutions creates conditions for systemic corruption, which in turn further undermine the effectiveness of the state.

Factors other than corruption are also at work in explaining the erosion, however. The most important is the distortion, uncertainty, and instability built into three sets of relationships that define the nature and boundary of the authority of the state: party-state, central-local, and state-market. The indeterminacy of these critical relationships directly compromises the effectiveness of the state. The supremacy of the ruling party over the state, for example, weakens the authority of the state apparatus at all levels and limits its capacity for performing routine administrative functions. The fluidity in central-local relations creates enormous commitment, information, and coordination problems within the state as the central and local state agencies constantly engage in opportunistic behavior because no credible institutions exist to reward cooperation and punish cheating. The net effect is the concurrent excessive provision of private goods that benefit favored jurisdictions and sectors and the inadequate provision of public goods, such as public health, education, and research and development. Similarly, the poorly defined boundaries between the state and the market create an environment in which the state is incapable of effectively performing its basic functions—such as enforcing contracts, protecting property rights, and policing the marketplace—while simultaneously overreaching into areas it does not belong, such as investing in and operating businesses, and selling its administrative services under different guises.

Growing Imbalances in Society and Polity

The idea that severe structural imbalances have accumulated in China's society and political system has gained currency within China.[59] Specifically, such imbalances refer to the rising inequality (socioeconomic, regional, and urban-rural), the growing tensions between the ruling elite and the masses, the erosion of values, and the simultaneous consolidation of an elite-based exclusivist ruling coalition and the increasing marginalization of weak groups, such as workers, peasants, and migrant laborers.[60] Because of these imbalances, some Chinese social scientists warn that enormous risks have built up in Chinese society. Citing rising public dissatisfaction, growing unemployment, and increasing inequality, Wang Shaoguang, Hu Angang, and Ding Yuanzhu argue that China has entered a new period of social instability.[61] Sun Liping, a sociologist, has identified such imbalances as contributing to destabilizing social divisions in Chinese society.[62] Unavoidably, such imbalances are reflected in rising tensions in state-society relations. Both aggregate-level data and press reports indicate a sharp rise in the number of incidents of collective protests, violent confrontations, and various forms of defiance and resistance against state authorities.[63]

Obviously, as expressions of social discontent, such acts of protest are likely the product of the hardships suffered by groups hurt by economic transition, such as peasants and urban SOE workers. (Indeed, protests from these two social groups account for the majority of collective riots.) The rising frequency, scale, and intensity of collective protest and individual resistance also reveal the flaws in the Chinese political institutions that give rise to the buildup of such stress during transition. The breakdown of the system of political accountability governing agents of the state is likely one of the key causes of rising state-society tensions in the Chinese context. State agents who routinely abuse their power and perpetrate acts of petty despotism create victims every day, personify state predation, and bring ordinary citizens into direct contact with state oppression. Private grievances accumulated in such a system are more likely to find violent expressions when institutional mechanisms for resolving them—such as the courts, the press, and government bureaucracies—are unresponsive, inadequate, or dysfunctional.

Additionally, the CCP's resistance to democratic reforms results in the lack of effective channels for political participation and interest representation, creating an environment in which groups unable to defend their interests are forced to take high-risk options of collective protest to voice their demands and hope for compensatory policies. The totality of such institutional flaws contributes to a systemic propensity toward violent collective protests even in the absence of organized social interests.[64] The accumulation and increase of state-society tensions bode ill for political stability in China, especially because the dynamics that generate such tensions trap the ruling CCP in an almost hopeless dilemma. As the CCP's initial resistance to political reform has aggravated state-society tensions, rising tensions increase the risks that any such reform could get out of control, thus deterring the CCP from undertaking it. This political paralysis further fuels state-society tensions as individual and collective grievances continue to accumulate, compounding risks of future reform.

These difficult challenges and deeply embedded structural problems in China's closed political system and partially reformed economy further cast into doubt whether China can sustain its dynamic economic modernization. To address this question in this book, I will first explore, at the theoretical level, the causes and dynamics of a trapped transition. The theoretical framework developed will then guide the four empirical chapters that examine the pathologies created by partial political and economic reforms in China.

In developing this framework in Chapter 1, I will draw on the theories on the relationship between economic development and democratization, economic transitions from state-socialism, and the predatory state. Chapter 2 analyzes the ruling elite's conception of and approach to political reform, and assesses the effects of the various institutional reforms that have occurred since the late 1970s. Chapter 3 critically evaluates the economic legacy of gradualism and seeks to demonstrate the hidden costs of piecemeal reforms in the Chinese context and the political logic behind them. Chapter 4 traces the decentralization of state predation in post-Mao China and probes the underlying institutional causes responsible for the runaway corruption symptomatic of a decentralized predatory state. Chapter 5 focuses on the consequences of a trapped transition and highlights the three difficult challenges facing China's one-party regime that epitomize a trapped transition: declining state capacity, eroding mobilization capacity of the ruling party, and rising state-society tensions. In the concluding chapter, I discuss the theoretical and policy implications of the Chinese transition experience.

ONE

Why Transitions Get Trapped:
A Theoretical Framework

IN PROBING the underlying causes and dynamics that have contributed to the emergence of a partial reform equilibrium that exhibits,
metaphorically speaking, the distinct characteristics of a trapped transition, we now turn to three sets of theoretical literature: democratization, economic reform, and the state. By applying the theoretical insights
from the literature, we can better understand the logic of trapped
transitions and the political and institutional mechanisms through
which market and political transitions under autocratic rule lose momentum and direction.

Economic Development and Political Change

Most studies of the impact of economic development on political
change suggest a robust link between rising levels of economic well-
being and the openness of the political system, and between changing
social structures and the emergence of political competition.[1] Historical examples of democratization and more recent cases of democratic
transition in several fast-growing East Asian societies (South Korea,
Taiwan, and Thailand) further bolster the hope that China could follow
a similar evolutionary path toward political openness. The absence of substantive movement toward such openness in China—even after twenty-
five years of economic reform that have produced one of the economic
miracles in history—does not necessarily negate the key theoretical assumptions of the relationship between economic development and

17

democracy. For one, China's rapid economic growth started on a relatively low base. The per capita GDP was US$151 in 1978 and US$769 in 1999, based on the exchange rate. It is likely that despite more than two decades of sustained high growth, China's economic development may not have reached a level sufficiently high enough for democratic transition to occur. This makes China lie outside the "democratic transition zone" hypothesized by Samuel Huntington, who found that non-democratic countries with per capita GDP of US$1,000 to $3,000 were more likely to liberalize or democratize.[2] Judging by per capita GDP on a purchasing power parity basis, however, China may have entered the transition zone in the late 1980s.[3]

In addition, several factors unique to China may also explain why a movement toward democratic transition has failed to materialize. China's huge size and enormous regional disparities in economic development constitute an extra hurdle because the growth of social forces, considered essential for the emergence of democracy, is uneven across regions. The costs of organizing and coordinating countrywide collective action can be prohibitive, especially in the context of authoritarian repression and underdeveloped communications infrastructure. The institutions, practices, and collective mentality of China's quasi-totalitarian regime pose another, and definitely tougher, obstacle to progress toward democracy. In all former communist countries, transition toward democracy has occurred only after a sudden breakdown of the old regime. Historically, no communist regime has ever completed an evolutionary process of democratic transition. This suggests that transitions from communist regimes to democracy *gradually managed by the old regime itself* may be infeasible because the overwhelming advantages possessed by the regime over potential opposition groups would give the ruling elites no incentives to exit power, even through a negotiated process. The growth of autonomous, organized social forces is more difficult in such a system even when economic development may have created a large number of individuals with middle-class socioeconomic attributes. Democratic transition can occur most likely as a result of regime collapse because when the ruling elites are eventually forced to undertake even limited political reforms, the regime may have become so enfeebled by misrule and politically delegitimized that it no longer possesses the capacity to manage a gradual opening.

The slow progress in democratic reform in China may thus be better explained by theories of democratic transition that focus on the political choices made by the ruling elites as the immediate and direct causes of regime change. After all, theories based on economic development and social structures may best explain the social and economic contexts in which democratic institutions may emerge and function, but are not helpful in identifying the timing and exigencies of the transition. Proponents of the crucial role of the decisions made by the ruling elites in the authoritarian regime maintain that democratic transitions per se have little to do with the social structure or levels of economic development.[4] Rather, such transitions take place only when the ruling elites make the crucial decision to withdraw from power, even though the political contexts in which such decisions are made vary from regime to regime.[5] From the perspective of choice-based theories, we may even posit a perverse short-run negative relationship between rising levels of economic development and democratic transition: everything else being equal, the ruling elites may have less incentive to withdraw from power because rising prosperity makes their political monopoly more valuable.

More important, the authoritarian ruling elites can reap political gains from increasing economic growth because such growth helps legitimize their rule and vindicate their policies. Contrary to the assumption that high economic growth can create more favorable conditions for political opening, rising prosperity can actually remove the pressure for democratization, and frustrations with the slow speed of economic reform may force leaders to seek political reform.[6] Indeed, such appears to be the case with the Chinese experience, as the following chapter on political reform will show. During the reform era, the CCP's senior leadership was most concerned about political reform only when economic reform appeared to have stalled and growth performance was deteriorating. This was the case with Deng's promotion of an agenda of political reform in 1986 when his economic reform initiatives were stymied by bureaucracy and growth began to falter.[7]

A short-term impact of rising economic prosperity on democratization also grants the ruling elites more material resources to strengthen their repressive capacity and co-opt potential opposition groups, especially counterelites. For example, the CCP's efforts to co-opt the intelligentsia and the private entrepreneurs—the former being the leading opposition group in the 1980s and the latter a likely challenger to the party's power in the future—were highly successful in the 1990s mainly because the rapid growth gave the CCP the economic means of political co-optation.

Yet, however salutary to the autocratic regime's rule, rising economic prosperity can provide, at best, a short-time lift to the prospects of such regimes because of the self-destructive political dynamics inherent in an autocracy caught up in rapid socioeconomic change. To an extent, most ruling elites are aware that economic development will result in the emergence of powerful challengers to power and probably the loss of the political monopoly. Such a realization would prompt the agents of the regime to increase their discount rate for future income from the monopoly and, consequently, intensify their efforts to maximize current income while maintaining a high level of repression to deter challengers. In addition, the collapse of a foreign regime with similar characteristics may make fears of losing one's own power even more acute and real. The net effects of the combination of a growing sense of long-term insecurity and the demonstration effects of a fallen fellow autocracy may be those akin to a run on the bank, with agents rushing to cash in their political investments in the regime, quickening the collapse of the regime's authority.[8]

Intriguingly, one can find some evidence of a rising discount rate in the behavior of China's ruling elites. In Chinese press stories of officials punished for corruption, many officials openly admit that they have lost faith in communism and in the CCP, and that their corrupt actions were prompted by their fear of the future. Some high-ranking officials have even resorted to superstition to help them predict the future. Hu Changqing, a deputy governor of Jiangxi executed for corruption, reportedly told his son (who had already immigrated to North America) that "one day China will be no more . . . But with two nationalities, we will have insurance." (Hu got every member of his family false identity papers and passports.) Hu Jianxue, the party secretary of the city of Tai'an in Shandong, privately told his subordinates that "Socialism is a dead-end."[9]

Li Zhen, the head of the provincial tax bureau in Hebei province who was executed in 2003 for accepting tens of millions of yuan in bribes, confessed to his interrogators:

After the collapse of the Soviet Union, many former senior Soviet officials had to work as security guards and peddle pancakes on the street. I wrongly thought that, rather than losing everything once the party's power is gone, I should start making economic preparations [accumulating wealth] when I still have power—just to be ready for the worst.

Li's worries were shared by another official, a deputy county party secretary in an unnamed province, who said:

The disintegration of the Soviet Union at the end of 1991 made me lose my faith. I thought it was hard to say whether the CCP could survive and avoid the same fate! Two months later, Deng Xiaoping's speech on his southern tour was published, I wrongly thought that the market economy China was going to build was the same as the free economy that followed the Soviet disintegration. Free economy means freely grabbing money. So I used my power to grab money aggressively.[10]

Empirically, the rising discount rate for future gains from membership in the ruling elite is reflected in the corruption by younger officials. If the discount rate remains constant, fewer younger officials will run the risk of getting caught for corruption because they can afford to wait and, in return, will probably receive greater total returns on their political investments. Prior to the 1990s, official corruption was frequently associated with the so-called fifty-nine phenomenon (officials approaching the mandatory retirement age of sixty were more tempted to break the law). But in recent years, government statistics show that increasingly younger officials were caught for corruption. In 2002, for example, 19.3 percent of the officials prosecuted for bribery were younger than thirty-five; 29 percent of the officials prosecuted for abuse of power were younger than thirty-five. This percentage is higher than that of the CCP officials of the same age group.[11] Among the top local officials and government agency chiefs (the so-called *yibashou*, or number-one leaders) caught for corruption in Henan province in 2003, 1,773 (or 43 percent) were ages forty to fifty, compared with 1,320 (or 32 percent) in the over-fifty age group.[12]

These two hypotheses—rising prosperity tends to blunt the pressures for political reform but also fuels official corruption—are, in fact, consistent with the developments in China in the 1990s. During that decade, amid unprecedented economic prosperity, the ruling CCP's resistance to democratic reform grew more determined just as official corruption became increasingly virulent.

Theories of Economic Reform

Economic reform in countries in the former Soviet bloc, China, and Vietnam has proceeded along two distinct routes. In the former Soviet bloc, the pace of economic transition was unusually fast, as was the scope of such transition. Thus, such transitions have often been characterized as "big bang."[13] In contrast, economic reform in China and Vietnam has taken a more gradual and deliberate pace, and the scope of such reform was initially limited. In the literature on economic and regime transitions in communist systems, whether one approach is superior to another remains a heated and unsettled controversy.

Proponents of gradualism maintain that gradual reform has three principal advantages.

LOWER INITIAL COSTS AND GREATER SUSTAINABILITY: The big-bang approach may create too many losers at the same time. In addition, a big-bang approach entails enormous compensation costs, which the government may have no credible means to pay. As a result, losers from big-bang reforms tend to oppose them fiercely, making them politically less sustainable. By comparison, gradual reform, through improving efficiency in certain sectors first, can produce more overall social benefits. Since the number of losers from partial reform is limited and the costs of compensation are manageable, the government has greater credibility in its commitment to compensating the losers, which can enhance the political sustainability of reform.[14]

GREATER FLEXIBILITY: As captured by Deng's alleged axiom, "crossing the river by feeling for the stones," the essence of gradualism is "learning by doing" and reform through experiments. Reformers may not find the best policy mix, but they may seek "second-best" solutions that yield immediate efficiency gains.[15] Gradualism allows decision makers to target certain sectors for breakthrough reforms and acquire valuable knowledge for applying reform to other sectors. Most important, gradualism allows reformers to make—and correct—policy errors and avoid costly mistakes that can fatally undermine the support for reform. Over time, market forces can gain strength and become dominant in influencing decision making and the allocation of resources.[16]

CONSTITUENCY OF REFORM: Gradualist reformers can use the classic strategy of divide and rule by creating beneficiaries of reform first and using them as constituencies for further reform.[17]

Gradualism has many risks, however. First, its record in reforming state-socialist economies is dismal. In Eastern Europe, the gradualist approach to reform in the 1970s and 1980s was generally considered a failure. Most scholars of Soviet-style planned economies argue that only a comprehensive, not a piecemeal, approach could transform such economies.[18] Second, a gradualist approach suffers from the lack of complementarity among various reform measures. Some reform measures that are implemented cannot be fully effective without other accompanying reforms. János Kornai argues, for example, that implementing some reforms over others in a piecemeal fashion could backfire and discredit the entire process of economic liberalization. Initial reforms that are carried out sluggishly and inconsistently would likely preclude the success of future reforms.[19]

The lack of complementarity can distort markets.[20] Gradual or partial reforms also create new rent-seeking opportunities for the politically connected groups to double-dip by taking advantage of both the new opportunities offered by the market and the rents provided by the old unreformed system. These groups typically rely on their administrative power to create new monopolies and barriers to trade, resulting in lower output, efficiency losses, and fragmented markets.[21]

Finally, the ultimate economic costs of transition can be very high if gradualism allows the ruling elites to make selective withdrawals, initially from sectors with low rents while holding on to sectors with high rents. Allocation of resources will remain inefficient. By concealing the information from the public, rulers can often hide the costs of such gradualist reforms, especially through hidden public obligations and bad debts in state-controlled banking systems. (Such concealment is much easier if the country begins the reform with practically no debt load, as China did in 1979.) China's approach to reforming state-owned enterprises is an apt example. The CCP treated SOEs as its last bastion of rents and patronage, and maintained them on life-support through fiscal subsidies and bank credits during the reform era. As a result, the allocation of China's scarcest resource—capital—was severely distorted. Although SOEs contributed to only a third of China's GDP toward the end of the 1990s, they consumed two-thirds of the domestic investment capital.[22] In addition, two decades of massive subsidies to loss-making SOEs saddled Chinese public finance with huge hidden obligations.[23]

Gradualism in economic reform may be more likely to fail when it is undertaken without accompanying reforms that restructure the key political institutions that define power relations and enforce the rules essential to the functioning of markets, such as security of property rights, transparency of government, and accountability of leaders. An implicit, but vital, assumption of gradualism is that reformers are expected to build political coalitions to push for such institutional changes to safeguard the fruits of economic reform as well as to sustain its progress. In reality, however, the feasibility of building such coalitions is rarely assured. This assumption is particularly problematic when gradualism is undertaken by a regime that possesses overwhelming initial advantages vis-à-vis societal forces, such as private capital and organized civic interests. In such a system, proreform coalitions are more likely to emerge *within* the regime, rather than *between* the regime and society, because either organized societal interests were practically nonexistent after years of quasi-totalitarian rule or the neoauthoritarian regime does not allow the emergence of such groups out of fear of their potential threat.

The low feasibility of forming and sustaining a grand proreform coalition encompassing both progressive elements inside the regime and organized societal interests not only increases the uncertainty of gradualist reforms, but also provides the entrenched interests inside the regime an inherent advantage. Such interests can always invoke the threat of further reform to the viability of the regime to block initiatives designed to institutionalize the rules and norms of the market, further liberalize the economy, and curb the predatory power of the state. Since reformers within the regime are unable to form alliances with societal groups—which would benefit from such institutional reforms—they often experience great difficulty in overcoming such opposition to reform that is phrased by their opponents in terms of regime survival, rather than economic or policy rationality. Moreover, antireform elements within the regime can use private deals to co-opt members of newly influential social groups, such as private entrepreneurs, thereby creating a government-business collusive network that makes participation in the antireform coalition far more attractive than an uncertain alliance with the proreform forces.[24]

Due to such a balance of political power, which favors the ruling elites, gradual political opening under a postcommunist autocratic regime is likely to be highly uncertain and subject to frequent reversals. In sum, three unfavorable factors are set against a process of gradual political opening that parallels gradual economic reform. First, the initial conditions provide the ruling elites an overwhelming advantage in political organization, patronage, and coercive power. Second, the process of selective withdrawal creates strong incentives for the ruling elites to defend their last strongholds of economic and political privileges. Third, gradualism allows the ruling elites to co-opt new social elites and form an exclusionary network that divides the opposition, while creating an incentive structure that rewards cooperation with the antireform elements and penalizes opposition to such elements.

Gradualism, Chinese Style

Despite the potential pitfalls of gradualism, the experience of China's economic transition seems to suggest the opposite: gradualism has been a resounding success in China. In fact, the consensus view has so overwhelmingly endorsed China's gradualism that Thomas Rawski claimed in 1999 that "We are all gradualists now."[25] Such an assessment is mainly based on the consistently high output growth the country has achieved since it began economic reform in the late 1970s. Compared with the large fall in output in the transition economies in Eastern Europe and the former Soviet Union, China's rapid output growth seems to vindicate its gradual approach to economic reform. A leading textbook on economic transition, which cites the Chinese experience as the most robust example of the gradualist model, claims that such a model is "more complete and adequate" than the big-bang approach, otherwise known as the "Washington consensus."[26] Specifically, economists who have given high marks to China's gradualist approach have singled out several key incremental institutional reforms as reasons for its success in introducing market forces and incentives without causing disruptions in output.[27] One such reform was the use of dual prices for the same goods; one price was set by the government and the other determined by market forces. This measure of limited market liberalization was deemed, economically, "Pareto-improving" and, politically, palatable to opponents of economic reform. It was "reform without losers."[28]

Another important example of gradualist institutional innovations cited was the township-and-village enterprises (TVEs). By Western standards, the property rights of the TVEs were poorly defined because they were owned by local governments. Political constraints in China, including both ideological prejudices against private property and the absence of the rule of law, prevented the emergence of purely private firms at the initial stage of the transition. Rural township governments, rather than the central state, managed to overcome these political constraints and established TVEs that performed more efficiently than state-owned firms because the interests of the TVE managers and local politicians were more closely aligned, and because TVEs contributed significantly to the budgets of township governments.[29]

In addition, China's gradualist approach has had several unique features. First, it has allowed Chinese leaders fully to exploit the structural advantages provided by favorable initial conditions. These included a relatively decentralized economic decision-making system; a political structure conducive to regional competition; a relatively small proportion of the labor force employed in the state sector; a less distorted industrial structure compared with the former Soviet bloc; and a significant nonstate sector.[30]

Second, Chinese reformers quickly responded to peasant demands to dismantle the communes and implemented breakthrough reforms in the country's most critical economic sector: agriculture. The initial success of the rural reforms built a crucial proreform constituency. The surpluses generated by the reform allowed rural governments to invest in new manufacturing businesses, which eventually became a critical source of local public finance.[31] Thus, while China's overall pace of reform may be gradual, its rural reform was decidedly big-bang.

Third, perhaps the most important feature of China's approach is the strategy of "growing out of the plan," the main thrust of which was to grow a nonstate sector rapidly along the side of the state sector.[32] Unlike the former Soviet bloc countries that experienced sharp falls of output after adopting the big-bang approach, this strategy allowed China to increase its output rapidly, thus increasing overall social benefits and generating the financial means to compensate the losers of reform. More critically, the same strategy avoided making immediate losers of those groups with entrenched interests in the state sector (state bureaucracy and workers). This would have led to a potentially debilitating political battle and undermined support for reform.

Of course, China's gradualist approach has its critics. Some believe that the success of China's reform has been overstated, especially given the hidden costs of deteriorating public finance, the slow pace of structural reform, and the inefficient allocation of capital.[33] Others argue that China's superior economic performance during transition is largely due to the country's structural factors or initial conditions—such as a less distorted industrial structure, smaller state subsidies, and a more restrictive state-socialist welfare system—and not to better policies or institutional innovation.[34] In addition, skeptics believe that economic distortions tend to increase in a partially reformed economy, citing China's well-known problem of local protectionism and the fragmentation of internal markets as examples of massive economic distortions.[35]

Implicit in the arguments presented by the skeptics of China's gradualist approach is their belief that gradualism will ultimately fail. They reason that China will eventually exhaust the advantages generated by its favorable initial conditions, and the market distortions embedded in an incremental approach will slow down economic growth. In the absence of constitutional transition (or democratic transition) in China, the same skeptics worry that the process of economic transition can be "hijacked by state opportunism" and be exploited by the ruling elites to consolidate their hold on power, at the expense of the long-term interests of society.[36]

The assessment of China's economic performance by its own economists shows a surprising degree of nuance and demonstrates a deep understanding of the benefits and limits of gradualism. Two themes dominate the discussion by Chinese economists concerning the country's reform strategy. First, like their Western counterparts, Chinese economists clearly recognize the country's achievement in output growth during the reform era, and a majority of them share the belief that this gradualist strategy is a more appropriate approach for China. They point to the rapid improvement in the standard of living, the pace of industrialization, the growing links with the world economy, and the increasing influence of market forces as evidence of the success of the gradualist strategy.[37] Second, they also understand the limits of gradualism in transforming the deeply embedded institutions of a planned economy. In particular, they are acutely aware of the so-called salient systems contradictions—or the constant frictions and incompatibilities between the emerging market institutions and the powerful influence of the old system.

To use the blunt language of an official assessment, "markets in capital, land, technology, and labor" are underdeveloped; the government has only "incomplete capabilities in macroeconomic management" and has failed to "form a system of public finance . . . and transform fundamentally the management mechanisms of state-owned enterprises." Reform is threatened by the "emergence of special interest groups within certain government departments and the weakening of the state's capacity" and by "the influence of local protectionism."[38] Wu Jinglian argues that, judged by the changes in the allocation of economic resources, China has not yet passed its reform test. He believes that the state-owned economy has not been fundamentally reformed or restructured and that capital is, to a very large extent, allocated by the government via administrative means.[39] Fan Gang, a well-known proponent of gradualism, admits that gradualism carries huge costs, especially in terms of efficiency losses, continuing price distortions (due to the controls imposed by the government on key inputs), soft budget constraints, and monopoly.[40]

Even the CCP Central Committee's assessment of China's progress in economic reform in late 2003 painted a picture full of difficult challenges ahead. According to the communiqué of the third plenum of the CCP's 16th Central Committee, "China's economic structure is not rational, the redistributional relationships have not been smoothed, peasants' income growth remains slow, contradictions of employment are growing salient, resource and environmental pressures are increasing, and the aggregate competitiveness of the Chinese economy is not strong."[41]

The most serious threat to the viability of China's gradualist approach, however, is the weakness of the institutions critical to the functioning of a market economy. Such institutions include, among other things, a modern legal system and a constitutional order that can protect private property rights and enforce contracts, as well as a political system that enforces accountability and limits state opportunism. A quarter century after China began its transition to a market economy, these institutions remain relatively underdeveloped. It is worth noting that, starting in 2001, Wu Jinglian began to emphasize the rule of law, rather than market forces, as the key to China's future success. He publicly declared that, without completing the necessary political reforms, which would be required to strengthen the institutional foundations of a market economy, China risked falling into the "trap of crony capitalism."[42] Reflecting on the evolution of his own thinking, Wu admitted that Chinese economists like him were naïve at the beginning of reform. They thought that "once the practices of a planned economy were jettisoned and a set of market-based relationships was established, everything would be smooth-sailing." But the problems that emerged twenty-five years into China's transition cannot be solved by "pure economics." "Although a market economy is gradually emerging in China, problems such as social anomie, rising inequality, and rampant corruption are getting worse." Wu concluded that a "good market economy should be built on the foundations of the rule of law."[43]

Why No Autocracy Has Opted for the Big Bang

The focus on output growth, incremental institutional change, and the merits and flaws of the gradualist approach misses a key issue: the connection between an authoritarian regime and the type of economic strategy it is forced to adopt. To be sure, most researchers recognize the role played by political constraints on the course of economic reform. Gérard Roland, for example, identified two such constraining factors. First, the uncertainty of outcomes, especially in terms of the distribution of costs and benefits of reform, constrain policymakers and hamper their ability to build proreform coalitions. Second, "complementarities and interactions among reforms" also matter because individual reform measures rarely produce their intended effects without other complementary measures. In political terms, implementing a reform package deemed, at least economically, as having a higher degree of complementarity (so that various components of the reform work better with each other) may actually undermine reformers. Such a package can hurt more entrenched interests and, at the same time, galvanize their opposition to change.[44] Implicit in the complementarity constraint is the assumption that this type of constraint forces reformers to adopt a gradualist or incremental approach to divide and conquer the opposition.

Proponents of gradualism seem to have overlooked the greatest political constraint on economic reform: an authoritarian regime's fear of losing power during reform most likely far outweighs its worries about encountering opposition to such reform. The most important political logic that drives economic reform under autocracy is not one based on a Machiavellian calculation of coalition-building, but one that is centered on regime survival. According to this perspective, authoritarian regimes facing the choice between reform and a crisis-ridden status quo—as was the case in the immediate aftermath of the Cultural Revolution in China—must choose between two unpalatable options. Maintaining a deteriorating status quo will most likely threaten the regime's survival both in the short term and for the long run.

However, to the extent that complete market-oriented reforms will eventually deprive the regime of the resources it needs to buy support from interest groups, an authoritarian regime's long-term survival will also be at risk—even though its short-term prospects may brighten as a result of economic reform. In addition to status-quo bias, which threatens regime survival, and gradualist reform, which increases risks to the regime's long-term survival should it truly succeed, there is a third threat: a big-bang reform.[45] A big-bang approach may not only mobilize opposition from various quarters simultaneously, but it could also force the authoritarian regime to relinquish its control over vital economic resources so quickly that it would also lose its grip on political power.

This is why all authoritarian regimes in history, including the most promarket Pinochet regime in Chile, have shunned the big-bang approach to economic reform.[46] Instead, all authoritarian regimes that have been forced to undertake economic reform have opted for the gradualist strategy, with the state maintaining tight control in vital sectors (Vietnam in the 1990s, Indonesia under Suharto, Taiwan under the Kuomintang, South Korea in the 1960s, and Mexico under the PRI [revolutionary party]). Revealingly, the big-bang approach was embraced only in those countries where the authoritarian regimes had been overthrown, including the former communist regimes in Eastern Europe that had tried various forms of gradualism before.

What makes gradualism a favored strategy for authoritarian regimes embarking on economic reform? The political logic of gradualism is both compelling and straightforward. Few authoritarian regimes can rely on coercion alone to maintain power. Most autocracies mix coercion with patronage to secure support from key constituencies, such as the bureaucracy, the military, and business groups. In the Chinese case, for example, the state controlled more than 260,000 enterprises, with total assets valued at 16.7 trillion yuan in 2001 (or 177 percent of GDP).[47] The patronage that the control of these assets can underwrite is the key to the CCP's survival. The centerpiece of such a vast patronage system is the regime's ability to secure the loyalty of supporters and allocate rents to favored groups. The CCP appoints 81 percent of the managers of SOEs and 56 percent of all enterprise managers. The corporate governance reforms implemented since the late 1990s did little to change this patronage system. In the restructured large and medium-sized SOEs—which were ostensibly transformed into share-holding companies—the party secretaries and the chairmen of the board were the same person in about half the firms. In the 6,275 large and medium-sized SOEs that had been classified as restructured as of 2001, the party committee members of the prerestructured firms became the board of directors in 70 percent of the restructured firms. Altogether, the CCP had 5.3 million officials—about 8 percent of its total membership and 16 percent of its urban members—who held executive positions in SOEs in 2003.[48]

To the extent that a big-bang strategy reduces economic distortion and hence an authoritarian regime's ability to create and allocate rents, that regime's ability to retain political support will be undermined drastically. Under the logic of political survival, the advantages of gradualism appear self-evident to authoritarian regimes. Unlike the big bang, gradualism allows the ruling elites to protect their rents in vital sectors and use retained rents to maintain political support among key constituencies. Under gradualism, the regime is assured of its ability to decide where it wants to surrender rents and to whom such rents will be given. Retaining this ability is of paramount political importance. If a regime can choose the sectors to liberalize, the same political logic dictates that it should first liberalize sectors where rents are relatively low and less concentrated. Giving up low-rent sectors means that the regime suffers, at most, minor loss of patronage. Liberalizing sectors in which rents are not highly concentrated is unlikely to encounter determined opposition. In the Chinese case, reforms in agriculture, consumer retail, and light industry fit this logic very well.

It is a more tricky issue to decide to whom the regime should turn over the rents from these liberalized areas, if we assume partial reform and residual rents in these sectors, as is often the case. It is possible that, once liberalizing reforms are implemented fully, rents may disappear completely. As a result, rent reallocation is no longer an issue. But as residual rents are a common feature of transition economies, an authoritarian regime engaged in economic reform must decide which groups should have access to the residual rents. Again, based on the political logic of survival, authoritarian regimes tend to favor nonthreatening groups and groups that can be co-opted. Foreign investors, for example, can be a nonthreatening group because their primary motive is profit, not power. Domestic private entrepreneurs, however, may pose more direct long-term threats.

That is perhaps why, as of 2003, indigenous private Chinese firms still faced high, if not impossible, barriers to entering about thirty sectors, such as banking, insurance, securities, telecommunication services, petro-chemicals, automobiles, and other industries deemed critical by the government.[49] In contrast, the Chinese government welcomed foreign firms to enter many of the same industrial sectors. China has favored foreign investors not solely because they can supply capital and technology, but also because of the CCP's fear of domestic private capital.[50] Indeed, as Yasheng Huang's groundbreaking research shows, foreign direct investment surged into China mainly thanks to the Chinese state's discrimination against domestic private firms.[51]

The regime's ability to protect and reallocate rents under gradualism allows the ruling elites to retain the resources to co-opt new social elites and groups that may threaten their authority. Under gradualism, market reforms tend to be incremental and create imperfect competition in the interim. Because of this, the government maintains significant residual control even in areas where liberalization has already taken place. The ruling elites can parcel out the residual rents in these areas to new groups targeted for co-optation. Politically, such co-optations can help shore up the social base of support for the regime even as it alienates its traditional allies. In the Chinese case, gradualism has apparently generated political dividends not only in growth-enhanced legitimacy, but also in the CCP's success in co-opting emerging private entrepreneurs and a large segment of the new urban middle class, such as professionals and select members of the intelligentsia who have been recruited into the government.[52]

However, gradualism ultimately becomes untenable because of rent dissipation by insiders. At the aggregate level, an authoritarian regime that is successful in protecting the major sources of its rent should be able to extend its longevity. It can use the rent to maintain its base of support, provided that it keeps rent dissipation by insiders at a manageable level. But both theory and experience show that rent protection and dissipation go together. Few regimes are capable of protecting their rents for long, while preventing their insiders from dissipating the same rents. In a transitional environment marked by high uncertainty for the members of the ruling elites, weak enforcement of rules, and low accountability, rent dissipation by insiders is likely to increase because insiders have both the means (monopolistic political power) to appropriate the rent to themselves and the motivations to do so (fear of an uncertain future).

The combined effect of rent protection and dissipation is the coexistence of aggregate inefficiency, financial deterioration, and insider corruption, as illustrated by the three case studies in Chapter 3. In other words, a self-destructive logic is embedded in a gradualist reform strategy adopted by an authoritarian regime obsessed with survival. As proponents of gradualism have argued, such a strategy may make a lot of sense, especially given the historical contexts marking the transition to a market economy in former socialist countries. Such a strategy assumes, however, that agent opportunism will be held in check, although literature on gradualism has not specified how. In reality, agent opportunism—the main reason for rent dissipation by insiders—is a common problem in transition economies. In the context of gradualism under autocratic rule, state or regime opportunism further encourages agent opportunism as the policies of the authoritarian regime provide its agents with the chances to appropriate rents. Because the authoritarian regime relies on the same agents to maintain its power, it becomes almost powerless in combating agent opportunism and containing rent dissipation.

A Question of the State: Developmental or Predatory

The sustained economic development achieved under authoritarian rule in Singapore, Taiwan, Hong Kong, and South Korea from the 1960s to 1980s has provided the factual basis for the claim that a neoauthoritarian mode of development—state-guided rapid economic growth under authoritarian rule—is a superior and proven strategy.[53] To be sure, in the Western academic community, the concept of an East Asian model is a subject of debate, especially because of the controversy over the efficacy and degree of state intervention in East Asian countries. For some scholars, the East Asian experience is proof of the centrality of state intervention in the rapid growth of late-developers.[54] For others, right public policies were the key to East Asian success.[55]

Unfortunately, most leading scholars of East Asian political economy have skirted the issue of regime and development. Only Robert Wade, author of one of the most influential studies on the role of the state in East Asia's economic development, explicitly identified the development "of effective institutions of political authority before the system is democratized" as a key to East Asia's success.[56] Within the Chinese political and intellectual elite, the East Asian model has been essentially reduced to a simple formula: strong government authority + pro-market policies = superior economic performance. It has further been argued that strong government authority would be difficult to obtain under democratic political systems.[57] In fact, when asked about his views on neoauthoritarianism by Zhao Ziyang in a private conversation in 1988, Deng admitted that such a strategy, "relying on a political strongman to maintain stability and develop the economy," was exactly what he was advocating even though "it is not necessary to use the term (neoauthoritarianism)."[58]

Such a preoccupation with the efficacy of the state in the context of economic development overlooks one crucial issue: the relationship between economic growth and the predatory behavior of the state. In other words, the real East Asian puzzle is not how sustained rapid economic development occurred under strong states, but why and how the *predatory* practices of the state were held in check. Based on the assumption of the state as a "helping hand," much of the literature on the political economy of development in East Asia has all but ignored the possibility that a strong state can also be a "grabbing hand."[59] Peter Evans's influential *Embedded Autonomy: States and Industrial Transformation* may be the only exception. By identifying the nature of the state as *the* critical variable in explaining the variations in the success of industrialization in developing countries, Evans shows that a predatory state is incapable of nurturing new engines of growth (in his case, the information industry).[60]

But Evans's explanation of why some states are nurturers while others are predators addresses only part of the puzzle. His formulation of the "embedded autonomy" of the state—the idea that developmental states gain autonomy and efficacy only when they are "immersed in a dense network of ties that bind them to societal allies with transformational goals"—provides a useful answer, but appears to restate the well-known: states counterbalanced by strong societal coalitions are less likely to be predatory.[61] Such explanations, built on the perspective of state-society relations, fail to probe the internal organizational dynamics and norms of the state. While few would deny the desirability and benefits of having strong societal forces committed to economic development, the most important challenge in the real world is that, in the overwhelming majority of developing countries, such forces are extremely weak or absent altogether. The transformative project has to begin inside the state.

Yet, there is another conundrum: as some scholars have argued, no evidence exists to show that institutions can be devised to make the state an effective protector of property rights, but at the same time prevent it from abusing its power. In other words, there is no guarantee that the same helping hand will not become a grabbing hand.[62]

Indeed, as the experience of most developing countries shows, states as helping hands are the exception. Sustained developmental successes probably number fewer than ten, with most of them concentrated in the East Asian region.[63] At the same time, predatory states have caused disastrous failures in a majority of poor countries, the most egregious examples being the Philippines under Marcos, Zaire under Mobutu, and Haiti under the Duvaliers. As the collapse of the Indonesian economy in 1997–1998 demonstrates, without adequate institutional controls imposed on predatory states, even initial successes could end up as catastrophic failures.

The Theory of the Predatory State

In its simplest formulation, the theory of the predatory state is based on a conception of the state as a grabbing hand. It envisions the central role of the state as the expropriation of wealth from society through taxes for the preservation of the state's own power.[64] The recent growing appeal of the theory is due, in large part, to the application of the institutionalist approach to the research on the relationship between political institutions and economic performance.[65] The revival of institutionalism has again elevated the role of the state in economic development.[66]

To be sure, the institutionalist perspective on the state differs from that of the developmental state, which, as popularized by scholars of East Asia, has a direct role in correcting market failures. Institutionalists see the state as the provider and enforcer of rules and norms that underpin market transactions. This distinction is significant because the perspectives on the state behind it are fundamentally different. Unlike the helping hand envisioned in the developmental state perspective, the state is seen by institutionalists as a force both for good and evil. As Douglass North puts it, "The existence of a state is essential for economic growth; the state, however, is the source of man-made economic decline."[67] Although the state may be a helping hand that specifies and protects efficient property rights, it can also be a grabbing hand that expropriates the wealth of its people.[68]

The grabbing-hand perspective appeals to students of development because the theory of the predatory state provides a persuasive explanation for the weakness of the state and the overall poor performance of government. In applying this perspective, however, we need to make the distinction between centralized predation and decentralized predation because such a distinction is crucial to understanding the different dynamics behind a state's institutional performance. In the earlier formulations of the theory of the predatory state, the focus is on the aggregate level of state predation and treats predation as the political imperative of the ruler. There is no distinction between the principal and the agent. As a result, predation is conceived as an act of the principal. This formulation assumes, first, that state predation is universal. Because rulers are monopolists of both violence and public goods, state predation, in the form of taxes, is simply the price private producers of wealth pay for such monopolistic services. Second, the most important factor that limits the level of a ruler's predation is his self-interest. To use Mancur Olson's colorful analogy, a self-interested ruler behaves like a "stationary bandit" who is unlikely to risk his future revenue streams by looting the current stock of wealth of his subjects. He will raise taxation only up to the level that maximizes his tax revenues.[69] Third, rulers are supposed to have an encompassing interest that is akin to the national interest.

In both theory and practice, centralized predation can spiral out of control. The ruler's encompassing interest may diverge fundamentally from that of the state. For example, the ruler's personal greed may become insatiable. He and his close cronies may loot wealth, not to provide public goods, but to line their own pockets, thus creating a kleptocracy.[70] The ruler's encompassing interest may also become too ambitious for his nation's good. Desire to acquire a larger territory (hence tax base) or international prestige may motivate the ruler to extract excessively from society to build a strong military.[71] In addition, the ruler's monopolistic position is always insecure because a domestic or foreign rival can seize his monopoly by force.[72] This structural insecurity affects the ruler's time horizon and the rate of discount on future revenues, incentivizing behaviors that result in short-term gains but long-term revenue losses.[73] Finally, the absence of a third-party enforcer makes the ruler's commitment to self-restrained predation not credible. Temptations for the ruler to break his promise and increase predation always exist, and most rulers have honored their promises in the breach.[74]

In the theoretical literature on decentralized predation, the emphasis is on predation by agents of the state. Although agency costs have been identified as a constraint on the ruler's ability to maintain a desired level of extraction, the effects of such costs on state predation have not been explored until recently.[75] Scholars who focus on the role of agents in state predation see decentralized predation as more harmful to the interest of the state. Andrei Shleifer and Robert Vishny demonstrate that centralized corruption, which is a form of monopolist predation, generates higher aggregate revenue for the state—because the state keeps its rate of extraction at the optimal level—than decentralized corruption (a form of predation by state agents acting as independent monopolists), which not only raises the overall level of theft (that is, making corruption more widespread), but also reduces the aggregate amount of income for the state. Since predatory agents simultaneously compete with one another for the same revenue, they have the incentive to steal everything, behaving essentially like Olson's "roving bandits."[76] The welfare loss from decentralized predation is much greater than that from centralized predation.[77] Decentralized predation, moreover, has emerged as a more prevalent problem today, as regime transition in many countries has restructured some of the key institutions governing principal-agent relations (more on the effects of transition on decentralized predation below).

To be sure, the relationship between centralization and corruption is a subject of scholarly dispute. Some scholars believe that decentralization may actually reduce the level of corruption. For example, decentralization can make local officials more accountable to the public because they can no longer hide behind the actions taken by higher authorities. Greater political accountability would help control corruption.[78] Decentralization may also contribute to lower levels of corruption because local officials are deterred from corrupt activities by a higher likelihood of being caught. Moreover, decentralization deprives the central government of the financial resources that otherwise are routinely squandered on grand corruption schemes (such as white elephant projects), thus reducing the aggregate costs of corruption. Even though decentralization can lead to a short-term increase of petty corruption by local officials, the total costs of petty corruption are likely to be much lower.[79]

Many scholars believe, however, that decentralization can increase corruption for several reasons. Given the low wages paid to local officials, increased political discretion as a result of decentralization is likely to lead to more corruption.[80] If decentralization should lead to the breaking of arm's-length relationships between clients and government agents, it can cause corruption to rise, especially in cultures where interpersonal connections play an important role. Newly empowered local bureaucrats are thus more likely to reward family friends with various forms of rents.[81] Decentralization may exacerbate corruption if it occurs in the context of weak government. When the political authority of the government is weak across the board, decentralization can create independent monopolists who have every incentive to maximize the collection of bribery at the local level.[82] On balance, the argument that decentralization can lead to more corruption is more persuasive because its proponents adequately account for the agency problem, while the same problem is simply assumed away by those who believe that decentralization can reduce corruption.[83]

The distinction between centralized and decentralized predation notwithstanding, the central point of the predatory state perspective is self-evident: without effective political institutions or structural constraints that curb the predatory appetite of the state, a state that is sufficiently strong to promote economic development unhindered by parochial interests is also strong enough to prey upon society without much restraint. The consequences of unrestrained state predation are dire. In such a state, the ruling elites distort markets, create rent-seeking opportunities for self-enrichment, and loot the wealth of society. Sustained economic development under such a state is impossible. The hope that economic development would eventually lead to democratic transition is only wishful thinking because the predatory state and economic development are, logically, mutually exclusive.

Why Decentralized Predation May Emerge during Transition

Research on transitions in the former socialist states indicates a significant increase in decentralized predation immediately following regime changes. Joel Hellman's study of reform in the former Soviet bloc countries suggested that the ruling elites were able to capture the state and reap all the benefits of partial economic reforms.[84] Michael McFaul and Federico Varese found that the communist ruling elites in the former Soviet Union were able to use their institutional privileges and exploit the loopholes in property rights laws to steal public assets in the privatization process.[85] In an insightful analysis of the collapse of the former Soviet Union, Steven Solnick showed that transitions that decentralize authority tend to lead to an increase in the number of thefts of state assets.[86]

Theoretically, the type of post-transition state predation observed by country specialists and journalists is qualitatively different from that which occurred during the pre-transition era. In pre-transition communist countries, state predation was centralized. Two characteristics defined centralized predation under communist rule. First, the aggregate amount of revenues generated was large, reflected in the government revenue as a share of GDP. Second, a significant amount of the revenues was used to provide public goods, mainly national defense, health, and education spending. Consequently, countries ruled by communist regimes enjoyed a higher level of human development relative to their economic development, especially in terms of their literacy rate, infant mortality rate, and life expectancy.[87]

By contrast, posttransition state predation is *decentralized* and manifests itself in various forms of official corruption. Decentralized state predation reduces the aggregate amount of state revenue, as agents divert public money into private pockets. It also causes a fall in the provision of public goods, as state agents convert public resources into private consumption or offshore investments. Although the phenomenon of decentralized state predation in post-transition countries has received enormous attention, the causes of decentralized predation are not well understood.

Centralized predation becomes decentralized when the state, as the principal, loses effective control over its agents. Of course, different types of regime transitions generate different dynamics that affect principal-agent relations. In communist states that saw a quick collapse of the ancien régime, state agents were afforded great advantages by even the temporary decline of the principal's authority. In those societies, the agents' theft of state assets was completed within a relatively short period of time. However, the patterns of post-transition agent predation diverged dramatically in those post-communist states that experienced dual transition. As Hellman's work shows, new regimes with a higher degree of democracy and more complete market reforms tend to restrain such predation, while new regimes with less democracy and partial economic reforms are beset by increased levels of agent-predation.[88]

By comparison, agent-predation followed a different dynamic in post-communist systems that have seen market liberalization but no political transition, such as in China and Vietnam. In these societies, the political authority of the state remains unchallenged. However, the decentralization of decision making, needed to reincentivize state agents, led to a restructuring of the contracts between the state and its agents, which proved to be extremely advantageous to the latter. Therefore, the key to understanding the rise of decentralized predation is to examine both the preexisting and the transition-related institutional changes that have structured and restructured principal-agent relations. Specifically, changes in the control of property rights, mechanisms of monitoring, exit options, and institutional norms are the critical variables responsible for the decentralization of state predation in postcommunist societies.

Decentralization of property rights
In theory, the degree of centralization of property rights is negatively correlated with decentralized predation. In countries with a high level of centralization of property rights, the loss of state money through

agent theft or misappropriation tends to be small. Under the prere-form communist system, despite the lack of clarity of property rights, the high degree of centralization of such rights was the decisive institu-tional factor that limited agent-predation. In practice, the centraliza-tion of property rights prevented large-scale theft of state property. Of course, the mono-property rights regime and the high degree of cen-tralization of property rights caused low efficiency because this system provided few incentives for agents to improve the financial performance of state assets.[89] The decentralization of property rights during the transition phase in most state-socialist systems was originally designed to increase agent incentives so that state assets could become more productive. In some countries, such as China, the decentralization of property rights also involved the transfer of formal ownership of state assets from the central government to local governments. Such de-centralization granted the state's managerial agents more discretion in operating SOEs, especially regarding investment and compensation. Although no evidence shows that decentralization of property rights alone contributes to efficiency gains, the combination of *lack of clarity of property rights* and *decentralization of such rights* has led to widespread asset-stripping and other forms of theft by state agents.[90]

Ineffective monitoring

Given the institutional changes entailed in regime transition, the old sys-tem of monitoring state agents is likely to break down. Rule changes are frequent and confusing during transition, resulting in poor coordina-tion among various state agencies monitoring agent behavior, such as the secret police, tax authorities, auditors, and financial controllers. The breakdown of monitoring becomes even more likely if those state agents in charge of monitoring other state agents detect the latter's theft but de-cide to divide the spoils with the thieving agents, instead of reporting their malfeasance to the principal. (Unsurprisingly, one of the most cor-rupt government bureaucracies in China and Russia is the anticorrup-tion agency.) Transition frequently entails changes in political values and erodes the authority of the principal. Agents face negligible risks in defying the authority of the principal. Erosion of the principal's author-ity makes effective monitoring of agents ineffective. The monitoring of agents has also become more difficult under reform because of an in-crease in transaction channels. As X. L. Ding observed, interfirm trans-actions almost did not exist under the old system, in which ministries directly controlled SOEs' sales and purchase processes. As a result, the monitoring of agents' business deals was easier under the old system. In the transition era, the advent of marketization replaced the firm-ministry-firm transactions chain with the more efficient firm-to-firm transactions chain. Consequently, the number of transactions exploded, making effective government monitoring nearly impossible.[91]

New exit options

Large-scale theft of state assets was made less likely under the old communist system by the *absence* of exit options from the state sector for nearly all agents. Regime transition has opened numerous exits for these agents, including ownership stakes and managerial positions in the new private or semiprivate firms, and overseas investment opportunities.[92] These exits effectively allowed "stationary bandits" under the old system to become "roving bandits" because they can steal and then store their loot safely elsewhere. The time horizon of state agents with lucrative exit options is likely to be short, resulting in more intense theft of state assets.

Erosion of institutional norms

Institutionalists have long recognized the role of institutional norms in constraining agent opportunism and the free-rider problem.[93] As a concept, institutional norms are vague and difficult to define. In practice, institutional norms may derive much of their legitimacy, appeal, and binding power from the prevailing ideology of the political system. In the case of communist systems, it may be controversial to claim that the communist ideology had any appeal. One can point to the widespread cynicism among the ruling elites of the ancien régime. It is nevertheless conceivable that even residual ideological appeals of communism, socialism, or nationalism might have played a role in constraining the predatory instincts of the agents under the old regime. During transition, the total bankruptcy of the communist ideology meant that state agents were under no constraints imposed by institutional norms.

The above theoretical analysis suggests that a temporary partial reform equilibrium, or a transition trapped in semireformed economic and political institutions, is a product of a confluence of factors. The most important among them includes the initial conditions of the transition process in post-totalitarian regimes such as the CCP, which retains unchallenged political supremacy over society and maintains its rule through a mixture of coercion, co-optation, and adaptation. Additional factors contributing to the emergence of such a trap are embedded in the political and economic logic of market transitions and authoritarian politics. Indeed, the Chinese experience provides an intriguing example that demonstrates why gradualist economic reform pursued under a neoauthoritarian regime, even after achieving impressive initial results, may lose momentum. Instead of moving toward an even more open economy and society, such a system may be heading toward long-term stagnation amid widespread symptoms of state incapacitation and deterioration of governance.

At the theoretical level, one can construct an argument that incorporates the insights from the theories of democratization, economic reform, and predatory state to explain the phenomenon of trapped transitions.

Gradual democratic transitions in post-totalitarian regimes face higher hurdles than those in authoritarian regimes. The connection between economic development and political liberalization is likely to be weak in these regimes because the initial conditions are far more adverse. The institutionalized curbs on the power of the ruling elites in a post-totalitarian regime are negligible. The ruling elites thus have far greater ability to defeat societal challenges. The presence of the post-totalitarian ruling party in state bureaucracies, economic entities, the military, and the judiciary provides it with the instant ability to convert political monopoly into economic rents during economic transition. Consequently, economic growth, rather than creating exits for peaceful withdrawal from power and lowering the costs of political transition, may perversely increase the stakes of exiting power because the ruling elites risk losing not only political power, but also economic rents. In addition, such rents become more valuable in an open and fast-growing economy, and, more important, the material wealth accumulated by the ruling elites can be consumed openly, extravagantly, and without fear when the prereform codes of austerity are no longer operative. Therefore, even though economic growth may have a long-run positive impact on democratization, its short-run impact can be decidedly negative.

Gradualist transitions can further help entrench the post-totalitarian party-state and thwart efforts to both deepen market reforms and initiate democratic transition. Gradualism allows the ruling elites to make selective withdrawals and maintain their control in the most lucrative high-rent sectors; this development tends to make the ruling elites even less inclined to give up political power during transition. The control over sectors with rich rents also facilitates the emergence of -political alliances with stakes in a semireformed system but with no interest in political reform, as the ruling elites use such control to co-opt emerging social elites individually, include them in a collusive network of rent-sharing, and preempt potential political challengers. To the extent that initial reform efforts may be successful, gradualist reforms buy the regime a new, albeit temporary, lease on life, removing the pressures for political reform. Gradualism becomes eventually unsustainable because of the problem of dissipation of rents. The regime's strategy of protecting rents in key sectors ultimately fails when such rents are distributed and consumed by the agents of the regime, critically weakening the health of the economy.

However appealing the concept of a developmental state, successful economic development under neoauthoritarianism may be the exception. A self-restrained developmental state can materialize only under rare circumstances that force the ruling elites to choose between curbing their predatory appetite or risking their own survival, a choice that is not always correctly made. In post-totalitarian political systems where the ruling elites possess overwhelming advantages vis-à-vis societal oppositions, operate under ineffective institutional restraints on their power, and face no credible external threat, the state is most likely a grabbing hand, not a helping hand. Thus, despite its promarket rhetoric and policies, a post-totalitarian regime may likely degenerate into a predatory autocracy, rather than evolve into a developmental neoautocracy. Economic development under a predatory autocracy is ultimately unsustainable. Ironically, a democratic opening may emerge in the end, not as a regime-initiated strategy undertaken at its own choosing, but more likely as the result of a sudden crisis brought on by years of corruption, mismanagement, and institutional decay.

TWO

Democratizing China?

PERHAPS THE MOST intriguing question regarding political development in the post-Mao era is why China has not taken significant steps toward democratization despite more than two decades of unprecedented economic modernization. Indeed, during the mid-1980s, with economic reform barely off the ground and encountering strong resistance from conservatives inside the regime, senior CCP leaders appeared more tolerant and permitted more public discussion on sensitive issues such as political reform. In contrast, since the mid-1990s, when economic reform became irreversible and its impact had raised the standard of living several fold, the regime has adopted an even more conservative political stance toward democratization, permitting no public discussion on political reform and maintaining a policy of zero-tolerance toward dissent. On the surface, the CCP's experience with the Tiananmen debacle and the impact of the collapse of the communist regimes in the former Soviet bloc seemed to have hardened the leadership's stance against political reform.[1] But there were deeper causes behind the CCP's renewed resistance to political liberalization. The short-term impact of rapid economic growth on democratization may be negative because such growth increases the value of political power (hence making it harder for the rulers to relinquish it), reduces the pressure for political opening, and provides rulers with more resources to co-opt new social groups and repress the opposition.

In this chapter, this analytical framework will be applied to an examination of the history of political reform during the Mao era. The chapter will first address the question of how the ruling elites viewed the issue of political reform; it then will review and evaluate the three most important institutional reforms—the strengthening of the National People's Congress (NPC), legal reform, and village elections—that have been viewed as essential steps toward democratization. I will finally examine the CCP's strategy of *illiberal adaptation,* which relies both on the state's repressive capacity and the regime's growing economic resources in containing societal challenges and maintaining its political monopoly in a rapidly modernizing society.

Political Reform: The Ruling Elites' Views

Many senior Chinese leaders recognized the need for political reform during the initial phase of economic reform for two reasons. First, as survivors of the Cultural Revolution, they were determined to prevent a similar event from happening. Second, they recognized that restructuring the political system would be needed to ensure the success of economic reform and modernization.[2] To be sure, there was a subtle difference, even among those who viewed political reform as an instrument of advancing economic reform. Deng Xiaoping, for example, understood the benefits of political reform mainly in terms of reducing bureaucracy and increasing efficiency. Zhao Ziyang, however, believed that as Chinese economic reform deepened, the redistribution of power and interests would inevitably trigger conflicts. If such conflicts were not resolved timely, they would accumulate and produce serious consequences. Therefore, Zhao's plan was to use political reform to resolve such conflicts and pave the way for deepening economic reform. Neither Deng nor Zhao sufficiently appreciated that political reform itself would initiate new conflict because the power to block economic reforms was entrenched within the political system itself.[3]

Political Reform According to Deng Xiaoping

Deng articulated the most consistent—and restrictive—views on political reform. He was the first to raise the issue of political reform in a famous speech on August 18, 1980; six years later, Deng's call for political reform as a means to speed up economic reform led to the most serious and systematic examination of political reform as a strategy by the top Chinese leadership.[4] In Deng's diagnosis, China's political system had four major flaws: bureaucraticism, overcentralization of power in the CCP's leaders, lifetime tenure of cadres, and (official) privileges. To deal with bureaucraticism, official privileges, and lifetime tenure, Deng called for some of the party's routine administrative power to be divested, a younger and more professional generation of officials to be cultivated, and a discipline inspection committee to be established within the party.

Apparently, Deng was most concerned about the dangers of over-centralization of power within the party, as this could lead to another Cultural Revolution. His solution was to introduce constitutional reforms, which he did not specify, and strengthen collective leadership within the party, a prescription he himself failed to follow later.[5] But Deng left no doubt about the ultimate objective of political reform. In the same speech, he declared,

> The purpose of reforming the system of the Party and state leadership is precisely to maintain and further strengthen Party leadership and discipline, and not to weaken or relax them. In a big country like ours, it is inconceivable that unity of thinking could be achieved among several hundred million people . . . In the absence of a Party whose members have a spirit of sacrifice and a high level of political awareness and discipline . . . Without such a Party, our country would split up and accomplish nothing.[6]

Deng's fear of political chaos that may arise as a result of democracy and his resolve to maintain the party's supremacy have since then remained the two constant refrains in his—and the CCP's—views on political reform.

After the success of agricultural decollectivization provided Deng with the momentum he needed to launch further economic reform, he stopped talking about the need for political reform. Deng put political reform on the agenda only in mid-1986 when economic reform in the urban areas, especially in the state-owned sector, encountered resistance. Deng's numerous speeches on political reform from June to November 1986 revealed his increasing appreciation of the complementary role of political reform in the implementation of his economic reform strategy. His views, however, were remarkably consistent in that his concept of political reform was restricted to efficiency-boosting administrative streamlining because he believed that "China's fundamental flaw is bureaucraticism."[7] This perspective led Deng to maintain his firm opposition to institutional checks and balances and to the dilution of the CCP's power. This is clear in his speech in June 1986—the first time Deng mentioned political reform in almost six years. While being briefed on the economic situation, he said:

> As it stands, our political structure is not adapted to the current situation. Political restructuring should be included in the reform—indeed, it should be regarded as the hallmark of progress in the reform as a whole. We must streamline the administration, delegate real powers to lower levels and broaden the scope of socialist democracy, so as to bring into play the initiative of the masses and the grass-roots organizations.[8]

Deng followed up his call for political reform with similar public pronouncements during the September–November 1986 period. In his remarks, Deng expressed his frustrations with the resistance to economic reform coming from within the party and warned that economic reform would fail without accompanying political reform.

> Our reform of the economic structure is going smoothly on the whole. Nevertheless, as it proceeds we shall inevitably encounter obstacles. It is true that there are people, both inside and outside our Party, who are not in favour of the reform, but there are not many who strongly oppose it. The important thing is that our political structure does not meet the needs of the economic reform.
>
> When we first raised the question of reform we had in mind, among other things, reform of the political structure. Whenever we move a step forward in economic reform, we are made keenly aware of the need to change the political structure. If we fail to do that, we shall be unable to preserve, and build, the gains we have made in the economic reform. The growth of the productive forces will be stunted and our drive for modernization will be impeded.[9]

Deng was also aware of the risks posed by political reform. He cautioned:

> The content of the political reform is still under discussion, because this is a very difficult question. Since every reform measure will involve

a wide range of people, have profound repercussions in many areas and affect the interests of countless individuals, we are bound to run into obstacles, so it is important for us to proceed with caution. First of all we have to determine the scope of the political restructuring and decide where to begin. We shall start with one or two reforms and try not to do everything at once, because we don't want to make a mess of things. In a country as vast and complex as ours, reform is no easy task. We must be very cautious about setting policies and make no decision until we are quite sure it is the right one.[10]

However, Deng left no doubt that political reform would be narrowly defined and not be allowed to weaken the dominance of the party.

The first objective is to ensure the continuing vitality of the Party and the state . . . The second objective of political structural reform is to eliminate bureaucratism and increase efficiency . . . The third objective of political reform is to stimulate the initiative of grass-roots units and of workers, peasants and intellectuals . . . We must uphold leadership by the Party and never abandon it, but the Party should exercise its leadership effectively.[11]

To be sure, Deng himself also talked about democracy, but his views were colored by his traumatic experience during the Cultural Revolution and by his belief that democracy was an instrument to promote economic development. For example, in December 1978, shortly after he consolidated his power, he said, "During the current period, we especially need to stress democracy because for quite a long period of time in the past, the system of democratic centralism was not really implemented . . . There was too little democracy" within the party. He put special emphasis on "economic democracy," which he defined as decentralization to promote incentives. Politically, democracy has to be institutionalized and written into law, so as to make sure that institutions and laws do not change whenever the leadership changes, or whenever the leaders change their views or shift the focus of their attention. Moreover, in promoting democracy and a legal system, we must concentrate on enacting criminal and civil codes, procedural laws and other necessary laws concerning factories, people's communes, forests, grasslands and environmental protection, as well as labour laws and a law on investment by foreigners.[12]

Political Reform: A Liberal Alternative

In retrospect, the most comprehensive and sustained examination of political reform was conducted by a task force set up by Zhao under Deng's direct orders. Led by Zhao's trusted aide, Bao Tong, the task force, called "zhongyang zhengzhi tizhi gaige yantao xiaozu bangong-shi" (the office of the central small group for studying and discussing the reform of the political system), consisted of mostly young and middle-aged liberal intellectuals and officials. It convened more than thirty seminars on various aspects of political reform from October 1986 to August 1987, including seven attended by Zhao, Hu Qili, Bo Yibo, Tian Jiyun, and Peng Chong, the five members of the small group.[13] At that time, Deng was committed to implementing some form of political reform to overcome the systemic obstacles to his economic reform. He told the party's central secretariat to "spend about a year to investigate and study [political reform], think through the issues, make up our mind, and then implement" the plan.[14]

The sense that China's economic reform could not move forward without complementary political reform was widely shared by the ruling elites, especially among those associated with the liberal wing. Hu Qili, a member of the Politburo Standing Committee who was later purged during the Tiananmen crisis in 1989 along with Zhao, said in April 1986 that "economic reform cannot make progress without political and cultural reforms . . . We should not cede the ideas of freedom, democracy, and human rights to capitalism." Wang Zhaoguo, a protégé of Deng, declared, "When we implement the reform of the economic system, we must adopt accompanying reforms targeting some aspects of the political system." Wan Li, a vice premier known for spearheading the agricultural reform in Anhui in 1979, echoed the same view. Zhao himself was even more blunt in his criticism of the existing system. "Fundamentally speaking," he said, "we do not have a tradition of the rule of law . . . We want discretion but no constraints; China overemphasizes the role of the core leadership; this type of system cannot guarantee stability."[15]

Many provincial-level leaders invited by the task force to participate in these discussions expressed similar views on the flaws of the Chinese political system and the necessity of reform. Wen Shizhen, deputy governor of Liaoning, pointed out that the main flaw of the political system was "feudalism and the lack of democracy and rule by law . . . Democratization should be the principal direction of reform. The focus of the reform should be on the redistribution of the power of the state." He called for ending the party's control of all decision making, strengthening the NPC, and making the state administration more efficient. Wang Jiangong, a deputy party secretary of Shanxi, concurred: "The flaws of the current system are the overcentralization of power, the duplication of functions between the party and the state, the lack of rule by law and democracy, and the unscientific management of cadres." Some also considered political reform as absolutely necessary to push forward economic reform. Xu Shijie, party chief of Guangzhou, said, "Political reform must work in concert with economic reform and promote economic development." Sheng Shuren, deputy commissioner of the State Economic Commission, believed that the time was ripe for political reform. In his view, without political reform, economic reform could not proceed.[16]

On the issue of democracy, a consensus emerged among the more liberal officials as well. Wang Jiangong proposed to redistribute power between the party and the state; strengthen the Standing Committee of the NPC; change how the deputies are elected; and institute checks and balances among the legislative, judicial, and executive branches. Xu argued that the key to political reform was "the gradual improvement in democracy and the legal system" and that "the greatest democracy is election." Liao Bokang, party secretary of Chongqing, agreed: "The mechanism for people to participate in politics is the key measure of a country's democratization." He suggested introducing direct popular nominations of candidates for the People's Congress as one step to democratize political participation. Wen Shizhen thought that democratization should be the principal direction of political reform and that its focus should be on the redistribution of the power of the state.[17]

The task force identified six major aspects of political reform: the separation of the party from the state (*dangzheng fenkai*); inner-party democracy (*dangnei minzhu*); decentralization and administrative reforms; personnel system reform; socialist democracy; and legal reform.[18] Of these, the task force focused on three: separating the party from the state, establishing inner-party democracy, and the development of socialist democracy.

Political Reform: Content, Goals, and Dilemmas

The deliberations on political reform by the Chinese elites of all ideological stripes showed that they all recognized the fundamental source of the inefficiency of the existing political system: the party-state in general, and the overcentralization of administrative power in the party in particular. In Zhao's vision, the first and most crucial step of political reform was the separation of the party from the state. This would be followed by inner-party democracy, which should be implemented at the very top of the party's leadership (the Politburo Standing Committee and the Politburo). For the task force, dominated by the liberals, *dangzheng fenkai,* the separation of the party from the state, meant divesting some of the party's power to the state, thus strengthening the state while improving the authority and leadership of the party.[19] Zhao believed *dangzheng fenkai* would solve the problem of *yidang daizheng,* or "replacing the government with the party." In practical terms, Zhao thought *dangzheng fenkai* meant that the party would cease to issue orders or handle administrative affairs directly.[20] Implicitly, the separation would most likely create institutional checks and balances because the divestiture of the party's power would lead to a limited form of separation of powers in a one-party regime—a view shared by Zhao himself, who affirmed *dangzheng fenkai* as "division of power between the party and the government." Indeed, institutionally, *dangzheng fenkai* would consist, according to Zhao, of three aspects: separating the party from the government, separating the party from the NPC, and separating the NPC from the government.[21]

Despite the lofty expectations the liberals had for *dangzheng fenkai* and the importance they attributed to it, only a small number of specific institutional reforms were proposed. Wen Jiabao, the director of the Central Committee's General Office who became the premier in 2003, was asked to head a separate group to work on the issue of *dangzheng fenkai.* But the report he produced was described by Zhao as "empty" and lacking specific measures. Even for Bao, the most liberal member of the group, the only specific measures of *dangzheng fenkai* were abolishing the positions of the deputy party secretaries responsible for specific policy areas, reforming the party's organization departments and propaganda departments, and separating the party's disciplinary committee from the procuratorate and courts. Another measure of *dangzheng fenkai* was the strengthening of the NPC. Bao thought that the key was to strengthen the NPC Standing Committee by raising the number of committee members to more than 250 and by establishing specialized committees within the Standing Committee.[22]

Promoting inner-party democracy was considered a crucial step of political reform. Zhao believed that instituting inner-party democracy would be the key to establishing social democracy. He called for more inner-party democracy at the central level, perhaps reflecting his own difficult political position as a result of the concentration of decision-making power in the hands of Deng. Zhao would have liked to give the full Central Committee more power.[23] Other measures proposed by the task force to democratize the party included instituting a majority rule in decision making; increasing the transparency of the party's activities; strengthening collective leadership; holding competitive elections within the party; and protecting the freedom of speech within the party. Institutionally, the task force recommended reforming the party congress by establishing a system of permanent party deputies and convening the party congress annually, instead of once every five years.[24]

Another sensitive issue discussed by the task force was how to undertake democratic reforms under the slogan of "building socialist democracy." Zhao believed that democratization was inevitable, although he thought that Mikhail Gorbachev's *glasnost* and *perestroika* were "very risky" strategies. In implementing democratic reforms, Zhao said, China should "talk less but do more. Do not make that many promises. But in practice give people more freedom. Democracy is not something socialism can avoid." He warned that "the people's demand for democracy is a trend. We must meet their demand to the fullest extent." For Zhao, socialist democracy consisted of grassroots democracy, dialogue among various social groups (including the CCP and labor unions), and protection of civil liberties, the key of which is the freedom of speech. Specifically, Zhao emphasized the need to hold elections as a means of expanding democracy. He argued that "to build a highly democratic socialist society, we must put on the agenda the issues of grassroots democracy, people's participation in administration, and people's self-administration, especially in the cities." And "the electoral system must also be improved."[25]

Although Zhao thought it was premature to hold direct elections for the NPC, he suggested that competitive elections for the deputies to the provincial People's Congress should be held. He saw no reason why "we cannot open up the elections for the chairman, vice chairmen, provincial governor, and vice governors." Bao shared the same view and insisted that elections could increase political accountability for cadres, and that the democratic elections of government officials would be the prerequisite for instituting "democracy in other areas."[26]

Even among the liberal-leaning senior officials, there were divergent views about the ultimate goal of political reform. Zhao, for example, believed that such reform would strengthen the party and enable it to maintain power. He pointed out, "we must solve not the problem of whether the CCP will rule, but how it will rule." Hu Qili expressed the same thinking even more explicitly. "The goal for us is to have it both ways. We want both a high level of democracy and a high level of efficiency. The first and foremost principle is to maintain the party's leadership and improve it. Political reform must strengthen the authority of the party, not undermine it."[27]

Other participants in the discussions thought differently, however. Liao Gailong, an eminent party historian, envisioned a set of goals that were more radical. He said that political reform should lead to judicial independence and equality under law; a more powerful role of the NPC; an autonomous civil society; the separation of the party from the state; and inner-party democracy.[28] Bao presented perhaps the most articulate argument on the objectives of political reform and a strategy to accomplish them. The short-term goal of political reform was institutionalization (*zhiduhua*). The long-term goal was democratization. Institutionalization, mainly through restructuring the party's leadership system and the administrative system of the government, would create a more pluralist, though not necessarily democratic, system of interest representation under the current political order. Introducing inner-party democracy would create favorable conditions for political democracy. Additionally, with legal reforms, China could build "a normal political order."[29]

It was also clear from the debate among the Chinese elites in the late 1980s that they were acutely aware of the risks and dilemmas of experimenting with political reform. First, they were worried about both an unsustainable status quo and the possibility that the existing system was too fragile to withstand reform, especially at the initial stage. Zhao cautioned, "If the status quo is not changed, it won't do; but if the steps are too big, that won't do either. To ensure the smooth and healthy process of democratization, no problem must occur at the beginning. If there is a problem, we must step back."[30]

The second practical dilemma for the liberals was how to deal with the difficulties created by institutional checks and balances that would inevitably result from the reforms. Zhao openly worried about how strengthening the NPC would reduce the party's control and the government's ability to make policy. "If the NPC grows more powerful and really becomes the supreme organ of power, it will be very difficult for the government to run things," Zhao mused. "There ought to be checks and balances, but how to let the NPC play its role" without tying up the governing process? Zhao did not have an answer to the question he raised.[31] Citing examples of Western democracies, he said, "In capitalist countries, the government must spend a lot of energy dealing with the parliament. We cannot go down this path and spend a lot of energy and time internally."[32]

Political Reform: A Stillborn Plan

After almost a year of deliberations, the task force submitted its final report, titled "Zhengzhi tizhi gaige zongti shexiang" (A General Outline on the Reform of the Political System), to the Politburo and laid out its case for political reform. The report included a discussion on the necessity and urgency of political reform and set the goals and principles for such reform. It recommended the separation of the party from the state; reform of the People's Congress; administrative reform; reform of the legal system; the establishment of a civil service system; the development of socialist democracy; and reform of the CCP. However, the report failed to provide a detailed action plan. Zhao complained that "there is not enough of a sense of action" in the report. For different reasons, Deng was not entirely satisfied with the report, even though he endorsed it at the end of September 1987. He thought the proposals of reform copied "some elements of checks and balances" and he reiterated his mantra that "the main goal [of political reform] is to ensure that the administrative branch can work efficiently; there cannot be too much interference. We cannot abandon our dictatorship. We must not accommodate the sentiments of democratization." In a meeting with Zhao toward the end of the task force's work, Deng emphasized, "You have a bit of checks and balances [in your proposal]. The Western type of checks and balances must never be practiced. We must not be influenced by that kind of thinking. Efficiency must be guaranteed."[33] It was very clear that Deng's notion of political reform was fundamentally different from that of the liberal vision.

Nevertheless, the Central Committee approved the "outline" in October 1987. Shortly afterward, the CCP's 13th Congress officially endorsed the essence of the task force's report and declared that the goal of political reform was to "build socialist democratic politics." But few specific measures were taken to follow up on the party's declarations. Zhao implemented one symbolic reform—announcing the convening of each Politburo meeting in the media. The party's control on the media was relaxed as well, making 1988 a year of lively debate about Chinese culture. But as the economic conditions deteriorated in the summer of 1988, mainly as a result of surging inflation caused by Deng's premature plan to lift price controls, the regime's focus shifted to economic stabilization. Political reform was put on hold. After the outbreak and suppression of the prodemocracy Tiananmen Square movement from April to June 1989, the regime imposed a ban on political reform discussions. Although the official pronouncements kept mentioning "socialist democracy," "reforming the political system," and "ruling the country according to law," none of the reforms proposed in principle by the task force was adopted. Bao, the head of the task force, was imprisoned for seven years following the Tiananmen crackdown—a tragic, but perhaps fitting metaphor for the political reform attempted by the party's liberal wing.

To the extent that the aftermath of the Tiananmen crisis determined the course of political evolution in China after 1989, as Joseph Fewsmith shows in his study of the policies of the Chinese leadership in the decade following the crackdown, one is tempted to ask: What if the 1989 political crisis had not happened or had been resolved in a different way?[34] Few would dispute that the near-death experience of the CCP during the crisis and its bloody aftermath had turned the Chinese leadership toward a more conservative direction. In the context of the collapse of the communist regimes in Eastern Europe in 1989 and the disintegration of the Soviet Union in 1991, it would be hard to envision the CCP leadership—besieged, insecure, and isolated—to have favored a strategy of political liberalization for survival. In addition, the Tiananmen crisis gravely weakened the liberal wing inside the CCP, as top leaders such as Zhao Ziyang and Hu Qili were purged. Needless to say, the limited political reform program they had planned to implement never came to fruition. Had the crisis been resolved peacefully and the liberal leaders triumphed, China's post-1989 history would have been different, and it most probably would have made more progress in political liberalization. Even then, however, the strong conservative forces within the CCP, Deng's own hostility toward democracy (if he himself had retained power under this scenario), and the CCP's institutional interest in maintaining its political monopoly would have made a dramatic democratic breakthrough unlikely, if not impossible.

This also appears to be the assessment of Zhao Ziyang. When a friend asked Zhao in 2004 whether he "could have pushed political reform had June 4 not occurred," Zhao reportedly paused and then said he could not because he "did not have enough power." Because "there was such a large government, there was such a huge number of cadres, and so many people's interests were involved, I did not have the power," Zhao repeated. The only person who had the power and ability to do so, said Zhao, was Deng himself. But while Deng would give free reign to economic reforms, he was "very vigilant against the reform of the political system," Zhao commented. When pressed to elaborate further what he would have done had June 4 not happened, Zhao said that he "would have practiced enlightened politics. I had thought about allowing democratic parties to grow . . . If I were to have started political reform, I would have pushed democratic politics slowly."[35] Even without Tiananmen, China would have been much more liberal than it is today, but not necessarily as fully democratic as one might hope.

Institutional Reforms: Promise and Disappointment

The emergence of the NPC and, to a lesser extent, Local People's Congresses (LPCs), as major actors in decision making in China in the reform era have been hailed by many scholars as a sign of political institutionalization or even pluralization.[36] Based on Western experience, a stronger legislature can constrain the power of the executive branch and create institutional checks and balances conducive to democracy and the rule of law. Yet, in a political system dominated by the CCP, China's legislative branch has long been regarded as no more than a rubber stamp, whose sole function is to provide pro forma legitimacy for the decisions already made by the ruling party.[37] Therefore, the extent to which the NPC and LPCs assert their constitutional authority and influence in decision making should be a key measurement of political reform. This section will assess the institutional development and political empowerment of the NPC and LPCs.

The growth of the NPC as one of the most important political institutions in China has been extensively documented. But major studies
of the growth of the NPC reached different conclusions regarding the
institution's influence during the reform era. In his study of the institutional development of the NPC during the 1980s, Kevin O'Brien argues
that NPC reforms during the decade did little to increase competition
or institutionalize responsiveness. Through procedural rationalization,
the legislators of the NPC sought to improve one-party rule, instead of
pursuing genuine political liberalization. As a result, NPC reforms
were limited to the organizational changes in the NPC that strengthened the Standing Committee, increased specialization and procedural regularity, and improved internal organization.[38]

In a major study of the passage of administrative laws, several leading
Chinese legal scholars also found that the executive branch dominated
the legislative process. Because the executive branch does not want to
have legal constraints, "the legislation on administrative law in China, especially since the 1980s, is marked by a strong pro-administration bias."

> The administrative branch is the biggest beneficiary of the passage of ad-
> ministrative laws in the last twenty years. The administrative branch
> ceaselessly uses the legislative process to expand its power and, through
> this process, legalizes certain illegitimate powers. This has resulted in im-
> balances between the rights of citizens and the power of the administra-
> tive branch . . . This problem also stems from the lack of democracy in
> the legislative process; there is not enough participation by the people.[39]

Such criticism is shared by Stanley Lubman, who believes that the language of Chinese legislation and rules is intentionally designed to maximize flexibility and discretion. As a result, arbitrariness is embedded
in Chinese laws and rules.[40]

In *The Politics of Lawmaking in Post-Mao China,* Murray Scot Tanner
tries to provide a more positive assessment of the NPC's institutional
development. In his case study of the passage of several laws, Tanner
suggests that the political monopoly of the CCP in policy-making was
waning and that the NPC was gaining influence as a player in China's
decision-making process. However, Tanner does not believe that the
NPC's emergence as a key institutional actor necessarily signals the arrival
of democratic politics or pluralism. Instead, the NPC should be viewed
as a political arena where bureaucratic and factional politics are played

out as different bureaucratic and interest groups within the CCP seize the political forum provided by the NPC to express policy preferences.

Tanner identifies several positive trends indicative of the NPC's growing influence. Using the data on dissenting votes and the number of motions put forth by delegates during NPC plenary sessions, he argues that NPC delegates have continued to shed their rubber-stamp reputation and become more assertive. The NPC has increased in power and authority through the leadership of powerful individual politicians, such as Peng Zhen. In many cases, nominally retired CCP elders were able to assert their influence through the NPC Standing Committee or the body's plenary sessions. Tanner believes that, with the expansion of the NPC's professional staff and committee system, the legislative branch has become more capable of forcing the executive bureaucracy to share policy-making power.

Tanner concedes, however, that the CCP continues to wield enormous authority in the lawmaking process. For example, the CCP Politburo must approve the candidate list for the NPC Standing Committee. Through appointments to the chairmen's group, the party controls agenda-setting privileges. Additionally, party groups within the NPC, including the Standing Committee CCP group, communicate legislative activities to the party Secretariat. CCP Politburo and Secretariat approval is required for almost all draft laws promulgated by the NPC. Consequently, Tanner remains uncertain whether reforms in the lawmaking process will affect China's democratic prospects.[41]

Despite such divergent assessments of NPC reforms, it is possible to apply several critical tests to measure whether the NPC and LPCs have gained real institutional autonomy since the late 1970s.

Legislative Output

The most important achievement of the NPC was its enormous legislative output (Table 2.1). The several hundred laws and resolutions passed by the NPC since 1978 have provided the legal framework for economic reform and rationalized administrative procedures. For example, of all the laws and resolutions that were enacted by the NPC from 1978 to 2002, ninety-five, or about a third, were economic laws.[42] Of the 216 new laws passed from June 1979 to August 2000, 126 were classified as administrative laws.[43]

But these numbers should not be taken at face value. In the passage of most laws, the NPC has largely played a secondary role, endorsing the bills drafted by the executive branch. On a few rare occasions, the NPC Standing Committee showed its autonomy by rejecting the bills proposed by the government, such as the Law on Residents' Committees in 1989 and the Highway Law in April 1999, which was later approved. In 1987, the Draft Law on the Bankruptcy of State-Owned Enterprises almost failed to pass due to strong opposition within the NPC. Like the NPC, LPCs rarely reject bills proposed by local governments. When they do, it becomes national news, as in the case of the People's Congress of Shenzhen, which voted down, in 2004, a law on auditing and supervising the local government's investment, an unprecedented act of political independence.[44] Official figures also indicate that individual legislators play an insignificant role in lawmaking. Not a single bill proposed by NPC delegates has been enacted into law. For example, from 1983 to 1995, more than 5,000 bills were proposed by delegates, but only 933 (18 percent) of them were referred to committees. There is no record that any of the proposed bills ever became law.[45]

Constitutional Oversight Power

On paper, the constitutional oversight power of the NPC has expanded significantly. The NPC supervises the courts and appoints and removes officials. It also investigates and oversees the work of the executive branch; approves the work reports of the State Council, the Supreme People's Court, and the Supreme People's Procuratorate; reviews and approves budgets; and provides legislative interpretations. The NPC

Table 2.1. Legislative Output of the NPC, 1978–2003

Years	Laws Passed	Resolutions Passed
5th NPC (1978–1983)	41	19
6th NPC (1983–1988)	47	16
7th NPC (1988–1993)	60	27
8th NPC (1993–1998)	85	33
9th NPC (1998–2003)	74	N/A

Sources: Zhongguo falü nianjian (Law Yearbook of China), various years; www.chinanews.com.cn, February 20, 2003.

can review the constitutionality of laws; inspect the implementation of specific laws by supervising individual court cases; hold hearings; conduct special investigations; and impeach and dismiss government officials.[46] But in reality, the NPC has seldom asserted its formal oversight power. For example, the NPC has never declared a law unconstitutional or rejected a work report by the State Council, the Supreme People's Court, or the Supreme People's Procuratorate. It has never refused to approve a budget, and has never launched its own special investigations or initiated proceedings of dismissal against a single government official. The NPC's inspection tours or hearings do not appear to have had any impact on policy, either. The most visible expression of the NPC's oversight power is rather symbolic: each year, about 20 percent of the NPC delegates vote against the work reports of the Supreme People's Court and the Supreme People's Procuratorate.[47]

By comparison, in some provinces, cities, and counties, the LPCs occasionally have tried to be more assertive.[48] Playing what O'Brien called the role of remonstrators, LPC members sometimes take local bureaucracies to task for poor performance and corruption.[49] In 2000, in a well-publicized case, the Guangdong Provincial People's Congress held a hearing on the work of the provincial environmental protection agency. Unhappy with the agency's work, the deputies voted, 23 to 5, on a resolution to express dissatisfaction with the agency's response given at the hearing and demanded a second hearing. Even after agency officials gave an improved performance at the second hearing, the deputies remained unsatisfied, although such expressions of dissatisfaction did not appear to have any substantive political effects.[50]

LPC deputies have demanded audits of the expenditures of local governments and criticized local governments' commercial deals and corrupt activities.[51] In 2002, members of the Guangdong Provincial People's Congress aggressively questioned the provincial government about its 22 billion yuan budget and demanded explanations for many line-item expenditures. Afterward, the Guangdong provincial government became more forthcoming in providing more detailed budgetary information to the congress.[52] In wielding one of its most controversial oversight powers, LPCs also began to monitor judicial proceedings, mainly as a response to rampant corruption in the judicial system. LPCs' oversight of judicial proceedings in both civil and criminal cases can force courts to conduct trials with greater transparency and integrity.

Typically, LPC delegates would review files, interview witnesses, and sit in on trial proceedings. In one instance, such intervention helped free a peasant wrongly convicted of drug trafficking.[53]

For many NPC delegates, the passage of a "supervision law" (*jiandu fa*), which would explicitly grant the legislative branch broad-ranged oversight power, attracted a great deal of interest even though legislative intervention in judicial proceedings is considered harmful to judicial independence. From 1993 to 1999, more than 1,600 NPC delegates proposed 51 pieces of legislation to legalize judicial oversight.[54] While the NPC insists that such oversight, in cases involving major violations of law, does not constitute interference in legal proceedings, however, it has yet to enact a law formally granting itself and LPCs the power of judicial and executive oversight.

Power of Appointment and Removal

Another noteworthy development is that LPCs have become an arena in which bureaucratic and factional politics begin to influence, in a very limited way, the appointment of local officials. Because Chinese law mandates "competitive elections" (*cha'e xuanju*) for senior local officials, LPC delegates have an opportunity to use such indirect "elections" to foil the appointment of official candidates and elect their own choices. Under Chinese law, an official candidate cannot be appointed if he or she fails to gain half the votes of the delegates. LPC delegates can also write in their nominees. In Liaoning in the late 1990s, for example, the CCP's provincial organization department (POD) reported that an increasing number of official candidates could not be confirmed by LPCs due to factionalism, poor lobbying by the party, and unattractive nominees. Local legislators occasionally were successful in nominating and electing their own candidates to local offices. In five cities in Liaoning, twelve independent candidates were elected to local offices.[55] Similar incidents occurred in Hangzhou's twelve counties in the 1990s. Each time the county LPC appointed officials nominated by the party, an average of six to nine official nominees would fail to be appointed, while the same number of unofficial candidates nominated by the delegates themselves would get elected. In the counties where the LPC delegates were the most assertive, about 10 to 15 percent of the official nominees would fail to get elected.[56]

In practice, however, such revolts by LPC delegates are rare, and nearly all the candidates nominated by the CCP are appointed. According to a senior NPC official, Qiao Xiaoyang, from the mid-1980s to the mid-1990s, only 2 percent of the candidates nominated by the provincial CCP Committee failed to win elections at the provincial People's Congress.[57] Nevertheless, the CCP has taken numerous measures to prevent such procedural setbacks. For example, the CCP's POD in Liaoning proposed a set of measures to ensure the appointment of the party's candidates. They include making local party chiefs the chairmen of the LPC Standing Committee, appointing the local CCP organization department chiefs to be the heads of the personnel committee of the LPCs, packing the presidium of the LPCs with loyalists, and appointing loyalists to be the heads of local delegations to the LPCs.[58] In Hangzhou, the provincial party committee took similar steps prior to the convening of the municipal People's Congress in 1996. These tactics were so effective that 98 percent of the official nominees won.[59] Nationally, similar measures, some illegal or questionable, contributed to the dominance of the CCP over the LPCs. In 1997 and 1998, the election of the chairmen of the provincial People's Congress Standing Committee was not competitive, contrary to law.[60] By 2003, in twenty-three of the thirty-one provinces, the party chief was also the chairman of the provincial People's Congress Standing Committee. This shows that the CCP has maintained almost complete control over the legislative branch in the provinces.

Organizational Growth

Organizationally, the NPC has grown considerably as well. The body had only fifty-four full-time staffers in 1979. By the mid-1990s, the number had risen to about two thousand.[61] The NPC's committee system grew as well. From 1983 to 2003, the number of specialized committees in the NPC Standing Committee rose from six to nine. Nationwide, the number of staffers in the People's Congress system at and above the county-level reached 70,000 by 1997.[62] As a whole, however, the membership of the NPC and LPCs does not mirror Chinese society. Rather, it appears to better represent the bureaucratic interests of the Chinese state and the ruling CCP. For example, nearly all of the 134 members of the 9th NPC Standing Committee (average age 63.4) were retired government and party officials.[63]

CCP members make up about two-thirds of the delegates to the NPC and LPCs. In the NPC, the percentage of delegates who were CCP members was 73 in 1981 and 72 in 1998. The situation is similar in LPCs. In 1998, 72 percent of the delegates to provincial people's congresses and 75 percent of the delegates to municipal people's congresses were CCP members. In fact, the party's presence in the NPC and LPCs was less domineering during the early years of the People's Republic. In 1954, for example, 55 percent of the NPC delegates were CCP members, and 58 percent of the delegates to the provincial people's congresses were CCP members.[64]

As a group, members of the NPC and LPCs are among China's political and social elites, based on their educational attainment and occupations. Seventy-three percent of the NPC delegates and 62 percent of the delegates to municipal people's congresses in 1998 had college degrees or college-equivalent education, compared to the average of the national population of about 3 percent. Twenty-one percent of the NPC delegates were "intellectuals" and professionals. In addition, while the percentage of peasants and workers declined steadily from the 1980s, the share of officials rose significantly. In 1983, workers and peasants made up 27 percent of NPC delegates. By 1999, their combined share had fallen to 19 percent. By comparison, the share of officials among NPC delegates increased from 21 percent in 1983 to 33 percent in 1999. Together with the military (9 percent), representatives of the Chinese party-state accounted for 42 percent of NPC delegates. The share of officials in the delegates to provincial people's congresses was even higher. From 1983 to 1999, it rose from 24 percent to 43 percent, while the combined share of workers and peasants fell from 33 percent to 24 percent.[65]

In retrospect, the failure of the Chinese NPC and LPCs to grow into genuine autonomous legislative institutions capable of checking the power of the CCP and the Chinese state is fully predictable. It is clear, both from elite-level discussions and the CCP's actual policy, that the party has never intended for the legislative branch to acquire its own institutional identity or power because the CCP recognizes the huge risks that an autonomous legislative branch would entail. As Barrett McCormick argues, genuine institutional pluralism embodied in an autonomous legislative branch such as the NPC would fundamentally endanger the survivability of Leninist states. The fear of such a danger led Chinese leaders to restrict the power of the NPC, even as they tried to make the institution an instrument of popular legitimization.[66]

Consequently, the NPC and LPCs, which are not directly elected through competitive elections, lack their own power base and popular legitimacy and must depend on the support of the executive branch—the Chinese party-state—for their institutional existence and relevance.[67]

Legal Reform

The efforts by the Chinese government to develop a modern legal system in the post-Mao era are viewed as crucial steps toward political reform.[68] To the extent that a modern legal system will foster the rule of law and constrain the power of the ruling CCP, such reforms constitute one of the most basic requirements of the commitments of the post-Mao regime to genuine political reform. Yet, the record in legal reform since the late 1970s has been mixed. While the Chinese government has made unprecedented progress in many areas of legal reform, the Chinese legal system remains structurally flawed and ineffective because the CCP is fundamentally unwilling to allow real judicial constraints on the exercise of its power. In his survey of China's legal reform, Randall Peerenboom observes:

> There is considerable direct and indirect evidence that China is in the midst of a transition toward some version of rule of law that measures up favorably to the requirements of a thin theory . . . but the reach of the law is still clearly limited. The party's actual role in governing the country is at odds with or not reflected in the Constitution or other legal documents.

As a result, one can see "little evidence of a shift toward a rule of law understood to entail democracy and a liberal version of human rights that gives priority to civil and political rights."[69]

Another comprehensive review of China's legal reform reached a similar conclusion. "In general, the reform of the judicial system has not kept pace with the rapid economic reforms and social changes in China" because the Chinese government adopted a piecemeal approach to law reform and lacked full commitment to real reform.[70] This section will briefly review the major achievements in China's legal reform and analyze the political factors that lie behind the limits of such reform.

The motivations to undertake even limited legal reform were compelling for the CCP in the post-Mao era. To restore political order and create a new legal framework for economic reforms, reforming and strengthening the legal system was a top priority for the Deng regime. In the speech that marked his return to power in December 1978, Deng called for the strengthening of the legal system and identified, as the new leadership's top priority, the passage of a criminal code, a civil code, procedure laws, as well as laws on enterprises, foreign investment, labor, and environmental protection.[71] As William Alford observed:

> The [Chinese] leadership's principal objective in initiating and supporting law reform has not been to foster a rule of law. Rather it has been to legitimate the leadership's own power while erecting the edifice of technical guidelines believed necessary to facilitate economic reform and reassure anxious prospective foreign transferrers of sorely needed capital and technology.[72]

Indeed, China's legal system, developed under a planned economy and wrecked by a decade of political turmoil during the Cultural Revolution, was inadequate, outdated, and ill-suited for a transition economy. Economic reform would have been inconceivable without reforming the legal system.[73] Thus, the CCP's need for survival through economic reform overlapped with the practical necessities of legal reform. Legal reform, however, as in the case of other major political and economic reforms, can also produce spillover effects and unintended consequences. Such reforms, in Alford's words, can be a "double-edged sword"—it may bolster the regime's legitimacy and help gain investor confidence, but it can also spark the political liberalization feared by the regime.[74] This political dilemma provides the overall context for China's legal reform and limits the extent to which such reform can be achieved.

Nevertheless, the progress in legal reform since the end of the Mao era has been unprecedented in Chinese history, as reflected in the passage of a large number of new laws; the increasing use of the courts to resolve economic disputes; social and state-society conflicts; the development of a professional legal community; and improvements in judicial procedures. Stanley Lubman captures both the achievements and limitations of China's legal reform in his assessment: "The accomplishments of China's legal reformers have been impressive despite the limitations set by policy on the role of law itself, the flux of China's ongoing social and economic transformations since 1979, and the continuing strength of traditional legal culture."[75]

Specifically, the most important progress that China has made in legal reform is threefold: "law has been made a major instrument of governance, a legal framework for a marketizing economy has been created, and a judicial system has been constructed."[76] As a result, legal reform has greatly increased the role of courts in adjudicating civil, commercial, and administrative disputes. As indicated by the data on the rapid growth of commercial, civil, and administrative litigation, Chinese courts have assumed an indispensable role in resolving economic, social, and, to a limited extent, political conflicts (Table 2.2). A number of empirical studies on commercial and administrative litigation show that, despite its flaws, China's legal system is capable of providing limited protection of property and personal rights.[77] In addition, China's legal profession, including judges and lawyers, has expanded rapidly during the reform era. The number of lawyers rose from a few thousand in the early 1980s to more than 100,000 in 2002. The number of judges nearly doubled from the late 1980s to the late 1990s. As measured by educational attainment, the qualifications of the legal profession have risen dramatically as well. The percentage of judges with a college or associate degree rose from seventeen in 1987 to forty in 2003.[78] Of the 100,000 lawyers in 2002, 70 percent had undergraduate degrees and higher and 30 percent had only *dazhuan* (equivalent to an associate degree) or lower. The overall level of professional legal qualifications remains relatively low, however, especially when measured by Western standards.[79]

But behind these numbers lies a different political reality. For all the progress in reform, China's legal system remains politically hobbled by the ruling party's restrictions. Legal reform was apparently losing momentum in the late 1990s. For example, the growth of civil and

Table 2.2. Growth of Litigation, 1986–2002
        (cases accepted by courts of first instance)

Year	Commercial	Civil	Administrative
1986	308,393	989,409	632
1990	598,314	1,851,897	13,006
1996	1,519,793	3,093,995	79,966
1999	1,535,613	3,519,244	97,569
2000	1,297,843	3,412,259	85,760
2002		4,420,123[a]	80,728

Sources: Zhongguo falü nianjian, various years.
[a]Including both commercial and civil cases.

administrative litigation slowed in the late 1990s, peaked by 1999, and began to decrease afterward (Table 2.2). The total number of civil and commercial cases fell from more than 5 million in 1999 to about 4.4 million in 2002, a 12 percent decline in three years. Administrative litigation cases registered even more dramatic declines. After peaking in 2001, with 100,921 cases filed, the number of administrative lawsuits fell to about 80,000 in 2002, back to the level of 1996. Such broad and large declines in litigation may be indicative of the poor performance of the court system and the consequent erosion of the public's confidence in the courts' ability to adjudicate justly.

Although there are no data available about the trial outcomes of civil cases, the trend of administrative litigation suggests that the decline in the number of lawsuits filed against the government may be directly related to the increasing difficulty with which plaintiffs were winning these cases in courts, which in turn reflects the courts' progovernment bias. For example, plaintiffs suing the government had an effective winning rate of 38.3 percent in 1993 (including favorable court judgments and settlements). This rate rose to 41 percent in 1996, but fell to 32 percent in 1999. By 2002, the rate plummeted to 20.6 percent, half the level reached in 1996.[80] It is likely that the decreasing probability of receiving judicial relief through the administrative litigation process has discouraged many citizens from taking their cases to the courts.

The rapid growth of the legal profession has not led to the emergence of a genuinely independent bar or a well-trained judiciary. The government maintains tight restrictions on lawyers in their representation of their clients. The Lawyers' Law (1996) provides for inadequate protection of lawyers' rights, leaving lawyers vulnerable to harassment and persecution by local officials.[81] According to the president of the Chinese Lawyers Association, the number of incidents in which lawyers were mistreated was large. Law enforcement officers frequently assaulted, detained, and verbally abused lawyers. Many lawyers were wrongfully convicted and sentenced to jail. Lawyers' rights to defend their clients in court were restricted. Some lawyers were ejected from courts without justification. But local governments, in most cases, refused to cooperate with lawyers' associations in investigating such cases of abuse.[82]

Despite a massive effort to raise the qualifications of judges, the overall level of professionalism of the judiciary is very low. For example, 60 percent of the judges in 2003 had not received a college or college-equivalent education.[83] A large number of sitting judges, many of whom are former officers in the People's Liberation Army (PLA), have dubious legal qualifications. For example, in one midsized city in 1998, of the 1,354 judges in the city's courts, 500 (37 percent) were former PLA officers, and 733 (more than half) were transferred from other government agencies and presumably had received little formal legal education. Only 87 had college degrees and 96 had associate degrees, and 364 judges had a high school education or less.[84]

Perhaps the most revealing evidence that the rule of law is fundamentally incompatible with a one-party regime is the CCP's steadfast refusal to undertake the necessary reforms to correct the two following well-known institutional and structural flaws in the Chinese legal system—even though they have long been identified and numerous remedies have been proposed. For example, in a study commissioned by the Supreme People's Court to amend the "People's Court Organic Law," He Weifang and Zhang Ziming, two leading academics, detailed a long list of the symptoms that manifested these flaws. What is remarkable about the proposal by He and Zhang is that similar proposals had been floated before but were never acted upon by the CCP.[85] To the extent that reforms are adopted to address the critical weaknesses in the legal system, the measures implemented by the government tend to be piecemeal and technical. They try to remedy the less controversial procedural flaws while avoiding the most sensitive political issues.[86]

Politicization of the Courts and Lack of Judicial Independence

As a judicial institution, Chinese courts are heavily politicized and deprived of the independence crucial to their role as guardians of justice and adjudicators of disputes.[87] The politicization of the courts is reflected in the control exercised by the CCP over the various aspects of the courts' operations. For example, each level of the CCP organization, down to the county level, has a special political and legal committee (*zhengfa weiyuanhui*) headed by a senior party official. The committee directly makes decisions on important policies and issues related to the courts and law enforcement. In many cases, this committee even determines the outcomes of major court cases.

In terms of judicial appointments, the CCP's organization department would nominate candidates for the presidents and vice presidents of courts, often regardless of their judicial training or the lack thereof. A former vice president of the Supreme People's Court (SPC), Wang Huai'an, admitted that the CCP's nomenclatural system (*dang guan ganbu*) controls the appointment of key personnel in the court system. In the case of the SPC, the members of the SPC party committee, who are the most senior judge-officials of the court, are appointed and supervised by the CCP Central Committee, and members of the party committee of provincial high courts are jointly supervised by the SPC party committee and the provincial party committees. The members of the party committees of intermediate courts are under the direct supervision of the party committees of the provincial high courts. The CCP's control of the most senior judicial appointments profoundly affects how judgments are determined by the courts because, as Wang said, "in the last fifty years, the system of giving the ultimate trial authority to the presidents of the courts has remained basically unchanged."[88]

Additionally, judicial independence is compromised by local governments that wield enormous influence over the courts through their control of judicial appointments and court finances.[89] Dependent on the local governments for funding, services, and political support, Chinese courts find it hard to try cases fairly where the economic and political interests of the local governments and officials are at stake. In the most crucial respects, Chinese courts are run like other government bureaucracies and follow a similar modus operandi. Administrative ranking or seniority, not judicial qualifications and experience, determine the hierarchical structure in the courts. For example, trial committees, which have the ultimate authority in determining judgments, are composed of individuals with the most senior administrative ranks, rather than the best judicial qualifications.[90]

Trials in courts are conducted like planned production drives. Typically, during the first half of the year, the pace of trials falls below average, leading to a backlog of untried cases. Backlogs force courts to try cases in a typical "campaign style," contributing to higher error rates. In 1998, for example, 13 percent of the cases were tried in the first quarter (which includes the Spring Festival), 26 percent in the second, 25 percent in the third, and 30 percent in the fourth quarter. Mistakes abound in the cases hastily tried at the end of the year. Of the economic cases tried in December 1997, a third of the judgments were revised or ordered to be retried on appeal, a much higher percentage than the cases tried in other quarters.[91] Similarly, the courts' enforcement of judgments is performed through campaign-style drives. Under the direction of the SPC, Chinese courts often designate a certain period for such campaigns to clear up backlogs of unenforced judgments.[92]

Inevitably, the politicization and administrative control of the courts corrupts judicial integrity.[93] In public perception, the Chinese judiciary is one of the most corrupt government institutions. A survey of 12,000 people in ten provinces commissioned by the CCP's Central Discipline Inspection Commission in late 2003 found that the courts, along with the police and the procuratorate, were considered among the five most corrupt public institutions; 39 percent of the respondents said corruption in these three institutions was "quite serious."[94] The Chinese press frequently reports corruption scandals involving judges. In Hubei province, from 2002 to mid-2003, ninety-one judges were charged with corruption. The accused included one vice president of the provincial high court, two presidents of the intermediate court, four vice presidents of the intermediate court, and two presidents of the basic-level court. In 2003 alone, 794 judges in the country were investigated and punished (*chachu*).[95]

Corruption by senior provincial judges was reported in many other jurisdictions. The presidents of the provincial high courts in Guangdong and Hunan provinces were convicted of corruption in 2003 and 2004. In Heilongjiang, the president, a vice president of the provincial high court, and the head of the provincial judicial department were removed from office in late 2004 for corruption. In Hainan, a vice president of the provincial high court, along with the head of the enforcement department of the court, a vice president of an intermediate court, and a president of a district court, were sentenced in 2004 to long jail terms for corruption.[96]

Fragmentation of Judicial Authority

The control by the party and local governments of the judiciary has contributed to the fragmentation of judicial authority and undermined its effectiveness. In addition to the weakening of the judiciary as a result of the CCP's control of judicial appointments, the enormous power wielded by local governments over the judiciary undercuts the courts' authority. Because judicial jurisdictions and administrative jurisdictions completely overlap one another, the dominance of the administrative authorities in effect creates what Chinese observers call judicial "independent kingdoms," in which local political interests, instead of national law, hold sway. Under these conditions, laws made by the central government cannot be implemented or enforced, leading to the widespread problem of "local protectionism"—the phenomenon of local authorities providing political protection to local interests in violation of national laws. Consequently, enforcement of court judgments is extremely difficult when judicial authority is fragmented.[97] One study finds that, despite official rhetoric about strengthening the legal system, court judgments became even more difficult to enforce in the late 1990s. In some cases, court judgments could not be executed without the explicit political backing from CCP officials.[98]

To remedy the structural weaknesses caused by such a fragmentation of judicial authority, Chinese scholars have offered several proposals for institutional reform. These proposals include the establishment of two separate judicial systems: a central system and a local system (similar to the American federal system); the formation of cross-regional courts; and the use of the central government's appropriations to fund courts.[99] The government has adopted none of them, however. Such a failure to implement crucial reforms led to a growing sense among China's legal community that the court system had become so dysfunctional that more radical measures—or "major surgery," to use a colorful phrase—would be required.[100]

In summary, the dominance of the party-state over the judiciary is the fundamental cause of the limitation of legal reform in China. The CCP's goals in allowing legal reform are tactical in nature: such reform must serve the party's overall strategy of maintaining its political monopoly through economic reform. Measures of legal reform must not threaten its authority or the institutional structure upon which its political supremacy is based. As long as the CCP places its own political interests above China's need for the rule of law, legal reform will remain confined to the tactical realm.

Village Elections

The emergence of village elections in rural China since the late 1980s marks an important step toward democratization. Even though these elections produce, technically, a self-governing civic organization, not a local government, the advent of village elections has led some analysts to praise them as an example of political liberalization in China.[101] Based on his field research in 1999, Lianjiang Li argued that such elections politically empowered peasants and increased local political accountability.[102] According to Kevin O'Brien, the introduction of elections into the villages would eventually lead to full citizenship status to rural residents, who have been denied many of the rights enjoyed by urban residents.[103] Allen Choate, who oversaw the Asia Foundation's democracy-assistance program in China, believes that village elections increased transparency in village governance and offered rural residents more choices of representation and avenues of appeal.[104] Some Chinese social scientists hold similarly positive views of this democratic experiment, arguing that such elections have contributed to rising political consciousness among the peasantry and broken the balance of power in villages in favor of the villagers.[105]

Other scholars, however, were skeptical about the democratizing impact of village elections. Jean Oi and Scott Rozelle found in their study of elections in thirty-two villages that the elections did little to change the power balance and decision-making authority in these villages because the village communist party secretary retained political dominance.[106] Based on his fieldwork in Hebei in 1997, Bjorn Alpermann concluded that township government and party organizations maintained dominant advantages while elected committees exercised only limited "self-administration."[107]

In all likelihood, the diversity of socioeconomic conditions in China, the unevenness with which local officials implement village elections, and the dearth of reliable data make it almost impossible to assess the role and impact of village elections in the expansion of democratization in rural China. In this section, we will review the evolution of village elections and focus on the most contentious, and unresolved, political issues surrounding this limited democratic experiment.

Villagers' committees, averaging five to seven members who serve three-year terms, first emerged as an administrative replacement of the production brigade almost as soon as the agricultural decollectivization began. With the dismantling of the people's communes, alternative institutions of grassroots governance in rural areas were needed. Similar to agricultural decollectivization, the movement toward self-government in the villages began as a spontaneous response by the peasantry to the deterioration of local governance following the disappearance of the communes. The Chinese government tentatively endorsed this democratic experiment because the authorities believed that such self-governing civic organizations would help maintain rural stability. The strongest proponent for legalizing village elections was Peng Zhen, chairman of the NPC's Standing Committee and a political hardliner. Peng was credited with the passage of the draft Organic Law on Village Committees in 1987 and its initial implementation, despite the conservative backlash in the aftermath of the Tiananmen tragedy in June 1989.[108]

Judging by the speed of implementation, village elections appeared to be a considerable success. Although only half the provinces had instituted village elections by 1990, the experiment quickly gathered momentum. In the early 1990s, the Chinese government promoted the use of "demonstration sites"—villages to which local officials were dispatched to develop and enforce proper election procedures. By the late 1990s, more than three hundred counties (or 15 percent of the total in the country) were designated as "demonstration counties," and the number of villages as "demonstration sites" reached 164,000, about 18 percent of the total number of villages.[109] The effect of using "demonstration sites" to improve village elections appeared to be limited, however. In Wang Zhenyao's view, the procedures for village elections improved mostly as a result of pressures and initiatives from the peasantry. The popularization of competitive primaries (*haixuan*) was credited to village residents rather than to local officials. Indeed, when the Organic Law was revised in 1998, many of the electoral procedures invented and used by village residents were formally adopted and codified.

By the end of the 1990s, village elections had spread to nearly all Chinese provinces. In several provinces that led the nation in the implementation of village elections, four rounds of such elections had been held between 1988 and 2000. In eighteen provinces, three rounds had occurred. A survey conducted by Tianjian Shi in 2002 showed that 83 percent of the villagers polled reported elections in their villages in 2002, compared with 76 percent in 1993. The voter turnout rate had increased as well. In 1993, 63 percent of the respondents of a similar poll said that they had voted in the village elections. In the 2002 poll, 69 percent had voted.[110] In some parts of China, village elections seem to have become more organized, and candidates are engaged in various campaign activities to seek voters' support. In Fujian, for example, one study finds that 43 percent of the villagers reported that candidates visited their homes; 37 percent said that candidates asked their relatives for help with the campaign; 30 percent said that candidates called on their clan leaders to rally support; and 24 percent reported that candidates provided free meals to earn goodwill from the villagers. In addition, village elections offered opportunities for voters to pick the candidates offering attractive policy choices. In Fujian, 25 percent of the voters recalled that candidates pledged to improve village infrastructure; 24 percent reported that candidates promised better economic performance; 10 percent said that candidates vowed to investigate corruption by their predecessors; and 7 percent reported that candidates campaigned on cutting or even abolishing taxes.[111]

In evaluating the impact of village elections on rural democratization, one of the most disputed issues is how competitive such elections are. Given the political dominance of the CCP, the likelihood that the party would permit genuinely competitive elections may be small. The findings from various surveys and field research, however, show a mixed picture. One indicator of competitiveness—whether elections have a single candidate or multiple candidates for the chairmanship of the villagers' committee—appears to have improved. Shi reports that, in 1993, 53 percent of the villagers surveyed said that had multicandidate elections. In 2002, 70 percent reported multicandidate elections.[112] But this measure may misrepresent the political reality in Chinese villages because the competitiveness of village elections depends not on how many formal candidates appear on the ballot, but on how such candidates are nominated.

Local party and township officials can manipulate the nomination process to ensure that their preferred candidates win positions on the villagers' committees. Such manipulation is relatively easy to carry out because, like primaries, only a small percentage of the village voters normally attend nomination meetings. One study of forty villages in Fujian in 2001 found that only 12 percent of villagers attended nomination meetings.[113] Indeed, Shi's survey showed that in about a quarter of the villages, the party, the township government, and the previous villagers' committees picked the members of the "village election leading group," which organizes village elections and exerts decisive influence on the nomination process. Only about 43 percent of the villages formed their village election leading groups through an election by the village assembly or villagers' small groups, as required by the revised Organic Law. Partly as a result of the influence of the party and local governments, only 43 percent of the villages used *haixuan,* the most democratic method of nomination, and 35 percent of villages used methods deemed illegal under the Organic Law.[114]

Applying the most stringent standard of competitiveness, Shi finds that only 11 percent of village elections held in China could meet all four requirements.[115] If the legal requirements stipulated by the Organic Law are applied, Shi argues that only 31 percent of the villages in China are in compliance with the law.[116] Case studies conducted by other researchers offer additional confirmation that elections in many, if not the majority, of villages do not follow proper procedures. A study of forty villages in Jiangxi in 1999 found that in one county, only one in five villages complied with the law, while in another county, one in two complied. In the same study, 61 percent of the villagers reported that the county and township "election guidance group" played the most important role in the election process; 31 percent said that village party secretaries wielded significant influence. The legally mandated village election committees played only a negligible role, with 60 percent of the villagers reporting that such committees had no influence.[117] The interference in the electoral process by the party and the government contributed to the peasants' disillusionment with village elections. According to Xiao Tangbiao, while 79 percent of rural residents hoped to participate in real democratic elections, only 32 percent thought that such elections would be held. More important, in villages where elections were manipulated by local officials, elections had no visible or significant impact on village governance.[118]

A study of thirty-four villages in Shaanxi province in 2000 by John Kennedy reached similar conclusions. Of all the formal candidates, only 35 percent were nominated by villagers, 21 percent were chosen by the village party branches, and 26 percent were nominated by township governments. Kennedy also found that if open nominations, or *haixuan,* were held, nonparty members would more likely win. The nomination process is therefore the most critical link in village elections—the more open the nomination process, the more competitive the elections. Official interference in the election process invariably undermines the legitimacy of village elections because rural residents are politically sophisticated enough to tell real elections from phony ones.[119] The results of Hu Rong's survey of 913 villagers in Fujian in 2001 reinforced the findings reported by Shi, Xiao, and Kennedy. Forty percent of the villagers reported that party and township governments nominated the candidates.[120] A different study of elections in 231 villages in Fujian in 2000 showed that only about 53 percent of the sampled villages had complied with the electoral rules laid out in the Organic Law.[121]

Provincial data provide additional evidence that local ruling elites have decisive influence in the nomination process. During the elections held in 1999 in Jilin, which is considered one of the pioneers in implementing village elections, 49 percent of the members of the village election committees were party members, and 13 percent were incumbents. Sixty-nine percent of the election committee directors were village party secretaries; 16 percent of the election committee directors were incumbent chairmen of the villagers' committees. Only 15 percent of the election committee directors were ordinary villagers.[122] A study of the election results in 2000 in Fujian (another pioneer in village elections) shows similar patterns: 92 percent of the village election committees were headed by CCP village branch secretaries.[123] In examining the election results in forty counties in Hunan in 1999, one researcher found that 55 percent of the members of village election committees were party members and 92 percent of the heads of the election committees were village party chiefs.[124] The ability of the party to control the election process is most likely the direct cause of the dominance of the elected villagers' committees by CCP members (Table 2.3).

Another controversy surrounding village elections is whether they have any substantive effects on local governance, especially on the redistribution of power. Unfortunately, no systematic data are available to shed light on this question. Limited information appears to suggest that under the Organic Law, elected villagers' committees do not have the power legally granted to them.[125] Local authorities, especially unelected township governments and village party branches, infringe on the power of villagers' committees through various means. For example, township governments take away the power of villagers' committees by assuming the accounting responsibility of villages and by centralizing the budgeting and spending of all villages, thus making villagers' committees practically powerless in managing fiscal affairs.[126]

Table 2.3. Dominance of CCP Members in Villagers' Committees

Province	Year of Elections	Elected VC Chairman is a CCP Member (percent)	Elected VC Members are CCP Members (percent)
Hunan	1999	76	N/A
Fujian	2000	66	79
Guangdong	1999	N/A	77
Jilin	1999	70	50

Sources: Liu Xitang, "Hunansheng 1999 niandu 40 ge xian cunweihui xuanju shuju fenxi baogao"; Wu Miao, "Cunweihui xuanju zhiliang de lianghua fenxi: Yi Fujiansheng 9 shi 2000 niandu cunweihui huanjie xuanju tongji shuju wei jiju"; Cao Ying, "Jilinsheng cunweihui xuanju shuju fenxi baogao"; Liu Hong, "Tuijing cunmin zizhi yu jiaqiang jiceng dangzuzhi jianshe de guanxi" (The Relationship between Promoting Villagers' Self-government and Strengthening the Building of the Party at the Grassroots Level), *Neibu canyue (Internal Reference)*, 28 (2001): 11–20.

They can, albeit illegally, remove elected village officials. In Qiangjiang city in Hubei, an investigation by Yao Lifa, a maverick deputy to the municipal People's Congress, found that of the 329 villagers' committee chairmen elected in September 1999, 187 (57 percent) had been illegally dismissed by township governments in the subsequent years before they served out their full terms. In addition, 432 vice chairmen and villagers' committee members had been illegally removed from office in the same period. All the replacements were illegally appointed by the party and local governments. Such illegal removal of elected officials was reported in 269 of the 329 villages within the city's jurisdiction, suggesting that the practice was widespread.[127]

Similar incidents were reported in Shandong. In March 2001, fifty-seven elected villagers' committee officials in four townships in Shandong collectively resigned because the village party committees and township governments did not transfer any power to the elected officials. A year after they were elected, the officials were not able to control the village budget or the official seals. They were also subject to arbitrary dismissals by the party and township officials.[128]

Elected villagers' committees often find their power curtailed by the presence of the CCP branches in the same villages. The tense relationship between the villagers' committees and the CCP branches has been widely reported in the Chinese press and studied by scholars. In a study of five hundred villages in Hunan, two researchers affiliated with the provincial CCP party school reported that in 40 percent of the villages surveyed, the elected villagers' committees were totally powerless, and the village party committees held all the power. The relationship between the party committee and villagers' committee was considered cooperative in only 40 percent of the villages.[129] Another survey in 1999 of 2,600 rural residents in four counties (two in Anhui and two in Heilongjiang) indicated that local government officials and party organizations were perceived as more powerful than the newly elected villagers' committees.[130]

Despite the mixed impact of village elections on rural democratization, the advent of grassroots democracy in the countryside has encouraged small-scale experiments in democratization in urban areas. In 1999, the Ministry of Civil Affairs selected twenty-six cities for experiments in electing urban residents' committees, which are, like villagers' committees, civic groups responsible for providing local services. Experimental elections of urban residents' committees began in June 1996 in Shenyang and were allowed in Beijing, Shanghai, Nanjing, Hangzhou, Wuhan, Hefei, Xi'an, and several other large cities in 2000.[131]

The CCP, however, appeared to have drawn the line on how far it would allow such grassroots democratic experiments to spread. As a result, it blocked elections above the village level. Except for the attention devoted to a few occasional minor experiments in township elections, the government-controlled media did not have much discussion or debate on the desirability or feasibility of township, let alone county-level, elections. It seems that nearly all the experiments in introducing township elections in various forms were initiatives of local officials. The most well-known experiment, a direct competitive election for the township mayor of Buyun in Sichuan, was pushed by a local reformist county official in January 1999. Although the election, considered fair by observers, installed the official candidate, it caused a political furor around the country because no Chinese law permitted direct elections of township mayors. The election was subsequently declared illegal, even though the elected mayor was allowed to remain in office. Notably, while the government used legal technicalities to prohibit the holding of township elections, it has made no attempt to pass a new law to address the legal hurdles to such elections.

Consequently, a few politically sanctioned township elections were confined to a mixture of open primaries and indirect elections so as to comply with the law. Reform-minded local officials used such institutional innovations to skirt the party's ban on direct elections of township mayors. Technically, these innovations allow local residents to recommend nominees for township mayors through a relatively competitive vote. Then the local party organization and People's Congress select the nominee who wins the largest number of "recommendation votes."[132] Dapeng township, in Shenzhen, conducted such an experiment in 1999.

First, township voters recommended candidates who met the criteria set by the local party organization. Then, the five top vote-getters gave campaign speeches at a voters' meeting. Afterward, voters elected one of the five as the formal candidate for the township mayor. These two ballots functioned as popular votes, but had no legal standing or binding power. Finally, the township party organization reviewed the final candidate and nominated him to the township People's Congress for confirmation.[133] A similar method was used by Buyun township in 2002.[134] In 2004, seven townships in Shiping County, Yunnan province, also used a similar method to elect their mayors. It is worth noting that none of these initiatives received the explicit endorsement of the CCP's central leadership. Local reformers took on considerable personal political risks for pushing electoral reforms. For example, a township CCP secretary in a township in Chongqing was suspended for trying to hold a competitive mayoral election.[135]

There is doubt whether such hybrid procedures really advance democracy in the rural areas. Melanie Manion argues that various electoral experiments at the township level were designed to align voter preferences with those of the local party committees. On the one hand, since ordinary people's choices were limited by the party's own preferences for particular candidates, their ability to influence the electoral outcome was limited. On the other hand, the adoption of such a device would enhance the party's own legitimacy at the local level because its own candidates would appear to have received popular endorsement.[136]

Illiberal Adaptation

The survival of the CCP regime does not solely depend on its ability to deliver satisfactory economic growth. An authoritarian regime governing a fast-changing society faces two choices. One is to adopt a strategy of *liberal adaptation*. This addresses the rising tensions between an authoritarian regime and an increasingly pluralist society through political reforms that may strengthen the rule of law; establish institutional checks and balances; gradually expand political participation; and permit more space for civil society. Theoretically, an authoritarian regime that has adopted a strategy of liberal adaptation should have less of a need for repression and co-optation because the ruling elites can rely on newly acquired democratic legitimacy to secure their social support. But for a regime that has opted for only the most restrictive forms of political liberalization, *illiberal adaptation* is a far more attractive strategy for political survival. Instead of favoring far-reaching institutional reforms to restructure regime-society relations, authoritarian regimes that choose illiberal adaptation maximize their control of the state's repressive apparatus and growing economic resources to develop, refine, and implement more subtle and effective means of maintaining political control. Applied skillfully, this strategy can help an authoritarian regime to divide, weaken, and contain the social forces that may threaten its political dominance.

In the Chinese context, the CCP's strategy of illiberal adaptation consists of strictly limited political reform, selective repression, improved technical capacities for dealing with social unrest and emerging technological challenges, and co-optation of new social elites.

Selective Repression

A key feature of a developmental autocracy, as compared with a totalitarian regime, is the selective use of repression. Whereas totalitarian regimes are defined by the indiscriminate use of mass terror in their exercise of power, developmental autocracies tend to be more selective and discriminating in the repression of their political opponents. Indeed, the measurable decline in political repression usually marks the transition from a totalitarian regime to an authoritarian one in general, and to a developmental autocracy in particular.[137] In theory, the replacement of mass terror by selective repression is not hard to explain.

Mass terror is politically and economically costly. Even the most brutal totalitarian regimes—such as the former Soviet Union under Stalin and China during Mao's Cultural Revolution—cannot sustain the reign of mass terror indefinitely.

For developmental autocracies, a strategy of selective repression offers more advantages. It enables the rulers to focus only on those political opponents who are determined to challenge their political monopoly, while allowing those tolerant of the regime's rule a sufficient degree of personal and property security. Domestically, such a strategy alienates fewer people and may even help isolate and weaken the regime's opponents. Selective repression is also less frightening to foreign and domestic investors than mass terror. Although human rights concerns do not always dictate investment decisions, there appears to be a limit to private investors' tolerance of brutality. Historically, few totalitarian regimes have been successful in attracting foreign or domestic private investment because such regimes cannot provide any credible commitment to the personal and property security of the investors.

In the case of China, selective repression replaced mass terror as soon as Deng's economic reforms began. The post-Mao regime immediately ended class struggle, greatly curtailed the scope of repression, and politically rehabilitated millions who had suffered brutally under Mao's rule. The level of repression fell dramatically, as measured by the number of political prisoners.[138] The post-Mao regime's use of selective repression grew increasingly sophisticated as well, especially in the 1990s. Instead of simply brutalizing its opponents through incarceration or worse, the state security apparatus has skillfully employed a wide range of tactics to intimidate, control, and neutralize key political activists. Many leading dissidents were offered a stark choice: either exile or long prison terms. Many, such as Wei Jingsheng, Wang Juntao, and Wang Dan, were forced into exile in the United States. This tactic has successfully decapitated China's fledgling dissident movement and even allowed China's government to deflect international criticisms of its human rights practices by timing the release and exile of key dissidents to important events, such as the annual U.N. Human Rights Commission meeting in Geneva and visits to China by Western leaders.

To prevent the emergence of organized opposition, the security apparatus has also established an extensive network of informants, especially on university campuses and research institutes. These informers receive monthly stipends in exchange for reporting campus political activities to the secret police. In its annual report for 2001, the provincial public security department of Jiangxi disclosed that it recruited sixty-five informants (*qingbao xinxi lianluoyuan*) in fifty SOEs and nonprofit institutions, as well as in fifteen institutions of higher education and "cultural units." These informants collected 256 pieces of information and enabled the authorities effectively to deal with a dozen "unexpected incidents."[139]

Containing Social Unrest

The skillful application of selective repression can also be seen in the regime's handling of the growing social unrest in the countryside and urban areas. In the 1990s, as the number of collective protests increased rapidly as the result of layoffs at bankrupt SOEs and rural tax revolts, the public security apparatus developed and employed effective methods to contain these protests, preventing them from precipitating a political chain reaction and causing greater instability. The most remarkable fact about the tens of thousands of large-scale collective protests that occurred in the 1990s was that none of them, including those that attracted tens of thousands of participants, mushroomed into a sustained antiregime social movement or lasted for more than a few days. The security apparatus's sophisticated methods, which ranged from crowd control to removing leadership, were in large part responsible for containing the effects of growing social unrest.[140] An official directive issued by the Ministry of Public Security (MPS) explicitly demanded that the security forces should emphasize timely intervention through intelligence gathering, crowd control, and containment as the main tactics in dealing with collective protests.[141] An article published in the official MPS magazine in 2002 details the following methods used in containing social protest:

1. A clear division of labor: police units are assigned distinct tasks and functions, such as intelligence collection, traffic control, site security, propaganda and videotaping, arrest, interrogation, and backup.
2. Intelligence collection and analysis: the police recruit activists, establish an extensive network of informers, and gather intelligence.

3. Preventive action: the police are placed on high alert during high-risk periods. Rural collective protest takes place mostly in the fall, when peasants are forced to pay taxes, or in the summer rainy season, when peasants are recruited to fight floods. In the cities, social protest occurs during SOE restructuring, bankruptcy, or forcible removal of urban residents from their housing while political protest becomes more frequent on "sensitive dates."

4. Identification of protest leaders: security officials investigate the protest activities on site, through photos, videotaping, or voice recording, to identify protest leaders and key activists.

5. Ending strikes: the police should arrest the leaders and activists and remove them from the protest site. The timing of the arrest is critical—arrests must take place only after most protest participants are physically tired and when there are fewer onlookers.

6. Quick follow-up action: the police must make decisions on detainees within twenty-four hours of the arrests. Only a few leaders and activists will be punished, while ordinary protest participants should be educated and released.[142]

In addition to its proven record in containing social unrest, the Chinese government has managed to suppress other sources of challenge to its rule. The best example was the crackdown on the quasi-religious group Falun Gong, from 1999 to 2000. Although shocked by Falun Gong's surprise April 1999 siege of Zhongnanhai, the CCP's leadership compound in Beijing, the party resorted, for the first time since 1989, to a massive campaign of repression against this group, which was arguably the most organized social movement that had emerged during the reform era. Within two years, the government had effectively destroyed Falun Gong.[143]

Responding to the Information Revolution

By far the CCP's most successful effort of adaptation was the containment of the threat posed by the advent of the information revolution in the 1990s. With the emergence of the Internet and its rapid spread inside China, many observers assumed that closed authoritarian regimes such as China would find it no longer possible to control the flow of information.[144] One study demonstrated that the arrival of the Internet had a positive impact on the emergence of civil society in China.[145] By mobilizing its security resources, imposing stringent regulations, jailing dissidents, and harnessing new technologies, however, the Chinese government succeeded in minimizing the political impact of the Internet while using the Internet to improve certain aspects of routine administrative functions, such as e-government.[146]

The CCP has received high marks in addressing the threat of the Internet. "Through measures ranging from blunt punitive actions to the subtle manipulation of the private sector, the Chinese state has been largely successful to date in guiding the broad political impact of Internet use . . . the state is effectively controlling the overarching political impact of the Internet."[147] Another study of the Chinese government's campaign against the use of the Internet by Chinese dissident groups reached a similar conclusion. The government combined low-tech solutions—the use of informers, human surveillance, and regulations—with high-tech ones—the use of software to block Web sites and e-mail messages, the hacking of foreign sites hosting dissident publications, and web patrol. As a result, "no credible challenges to the regime exist despite the introduction of massive amounts of modern telecommunications infrastructure," even though the regime's ability to subdue the information revolution remains doubtful in the long term.[148]

Reports in the Chinese media, as well as MPS publications, also provide useful revelations of the extensive efforts undertaken by the Chinese government to assert its control over the Internet—and over the activities of more than 80 million Chinese Internet users, as of 2003.[149] The Chinese government recognized early on the serious political threat posed by the introduction of the Internet. In an internal document issued in October 2000, the MPS bluntly warned:

Because the Internet can hold large amounts of information, transmit it quickly, and extend its coverage broadly, it has the characteristics of a high degree of openness and interconnectedness. The West is using the Internet as a means of political expansion, ideological penetration, and cultural aggression . . . Our enemies inside and outside our borders have set up forums, Web sites, and home pages on the Internet and spread a large quantity of reactionary articles. They conduct reactionary propaganda, instigation, and penetration activities . . . They use the Internet to establish illegal groups and parties, recruit members, maintain secret contacts, and instigate incidents . . . Our struggle against hostile forces and elements on the Internet will be long term and complicated. Strengthening the secure management of information networks . . . and maintaining the political stability of our society have become important and urgent tasks for the public security apparatus.[150]

The MPS established its Bureau for Supervising the Security of Public Information Networks (BSSPIN) (*gonggong xinxi wangluo anquan jiancha ju*) in 2000. The missions of this new division were to "monitor and control the net-based activities of hostile organizations and individuals in and outside Chinese borders; timely report various information and trends regarding social and political stability; strengthen Internet patrol; [and] closely watch developments on the Internet." The directive instructed:

[A]fter reactionary Web sites and harmful content are discovered, Internet monitors must work with other relevant authorities and take effective measures to block, filter, and clean up [such contents] . . . In order to strengthen our control of the net, [we] must establish secret forces and Internet liaison officers on some important Web sites and the networks of important institutions. They can supply the public security organs intelligence and technical support in the struggle on the Internet . . . Any public or media reporting of the means of detecting [subversive activities] and controlling the Internet is to be strictly prohibited.[151]

According to the directive, the Internet police must "step up the screening of domestic Web sites and home pages, conduct secure management of personal home pages, electronic bulletin boards, and free e-mail accounts, and collect information on important Web sites in and outside China."[152] The total size of the BSSPIN, or the "Internet Division," is not known, but one foreign press story quoted a figure of 30,000.[153] The division's own reports indicate that it has taken aggressive actions since it was established. From July to September 2000, the Internet Division of the Beijing Public Security Bureau conducted a sweep of the city's Internet cafés and closed down forty illegal ones. In

2002, the division checked 740,000 individual home pages, shut down or censored a hundred of them, and blocked the Web sites run by Falun Gong.[154]

The same office claimed that it conducted a census of Internet providers and users in 2002 and collected extensive data on them. More important, the office disclosed that it organized seventeen "training classes," which graduated 3,100 "Internet security personnel" (*xinxi wangluo anquanyuan*). Among the trainees, 189 came from Internet service providers, 410 were from Internet content providers, and 2,129 were sent by Internet café operators. The annual report of the Beijing Public Security Bureau also claimed that its Internet Division conducted a surprise spot-check of the nine largest news Web sites in Beijing on the sensitive date of June 4, 2002 (the Tiananmen anniversary). It found "harmful links" and "loopholes" on sina.com, Beijing-online, and netease.com and penalized the sites. Most intriguingly, the same annual report said that the Internet Division participated in a nationwide exercise "to deal with emergencies involving the Internet." This exercise was organized by the MPS, in collaboration with the Propaganda Department, telecom service providers, and regulators of major Web sites. The objective of this exercise was to see how various authorities could purge "harmful information" from major Web sites. According to the report, during the exercise, the police were able to locate the majority of "harmful information" within one hour and deal with it within two hours. In less than nineteen hours, the Beijing police successfully completed the exercise, twenty-nine hours ahead of the forty-eight-hour deadline. This disclosure indicates that the Chinese government has apparently developed an emergency plan and organizational capabilities to make sure that the Internet will not be used against the regime at times of national crisis.[155]

Besides using such labor-intensive methods, Chinese authorities adopted regulatory and technological tools as well. In 2000, the MPS ordered that all Chinese computing networks connected with the outside world must notify the ministry and file a record.[156] Another directive issued by the MPS in 2000 showed that the ministry was establishing a nationwide Internet surveillance system. It mandated that a network of control nodes at the provincial levels be built quickly so that an MPS-centered system of information surveillance and control could soon cover all provinces and municipalities.[157] In 2002, a government regulation required that all users of Internet cafés must register their government-issued IDs with café operators.

In its attempt to control the Internet, the MPS enlisted Chinese Internet firms to enforce its rules. According to a manager for sina.com, one of the most popular Web sites in China, the firm would "report illegal and unhealthy information to relevant authorities." In 2002, more than 130 Web sites signed a code of conduct, pledging to work against the dissemination of "information harmful to state security and social stability." To gain a technological upper hand, the MPS also issued detailed technical standards for Web software. Internet filter software developed in China must comply with these standards. In 2003 in Liaoning province, the local Internet police developed and installed surveillance software on the computers in all six hundred Internet cafés in Jingzhou city. To access the Internet from the computers equipped with this special surveillance software, users must show their official ID card to purchase a prepaid card. The software has a filter function that blocks access to banned sites and automatically alerts police when the user visits banned sites. In the city's Internet police station, one computer monitors more than 20,000 terminals in the city's Internet cafés. Liaoning's provincial Internet police chief revealed that all 7,000 Internet cafés in the province had this surveillance software installed. Since more than 40 percent of Internet users in the province accessed the Web from Internet cafés, this technology allows the authorities to monitor many users. According to press reports, this system was to be installed in the Internet cafés throughout China in 2004.[158]

Co-optation

The co-optation of social elites by the CCP, a logical complement to selective repression, has proved to be highly successful in shoring up the CCP's base of support, particularly after the suppression of the pro-democracy movement in 1989.[159] Some observers even characterized the CCP's strategy of co-optation as one of building a state-corporatist regime.[160] The implementation of this strategy was facilitated by the party's continual control of critical economic resources, as a result of partial economic reforms, and instruments of patronage, such as appointments, promotions, and professional and financial rewards, and by the increasing quantities of such resources available to the party as a result of economic growth.

The Co-optation of the Intelligentsia

The CCP had a contentious relationship with the intelligentsia in the 1980s. Dominated by the liberals, the Chinese intelligentsia in the 1980s constantly challenged the CCP's authority and demanded political reforms. The CCP responded with periodic crackdowns, such as the antispiritual pollution campaign in 1983–1984 and the campaign against bourgeois liberalization following the student demonstrations at the end of 1986 and beginning of 1987. In the aftermath of the Tiananmen crackdown, the regime gradually adjusted its policy toward the intelligentsia. This strategic modification became more evident in the 1990s as the CCP accelerated economic liberalization. Fortuitously, the CCP's strategic adjustment occurred at a time when the majority of Chinese intellectuals were moderating their demands. The tragic setback of Tiananmen and the turmoil following the collapse of communism in the former Soviet bloc undermined the rationale for the continuation of a confrontational approach. With the purge of liberal leaders such as Zhao Ziyang and Hu Qili at the top of the CCP hierarchy, the incarceration of many student leaders and activists, and the exile of the leaders of the Tiananmen movement, the intelligentsia had lost their strongest advocates, allies, and leaders. At the same time, the dramatic economic liberalization the regime took after Deng's southern tour in 1992 seemed to kindle the hope that economic reform would create more favorable conditions for political reform.

Taking advantage of these adverse circumstances for the Chinese intelligentsia, the CCP launched a systematic campaign of co-optation to recruit loyalists from among the intellectuals and professionals. This campaign mixed the traditional (and most likely ineffective) tools, such as ideological indoctrination, and the more sophisticated ones, such as salary increases, recruitment, cultivation, promotion, and special rewards. Published official documents indicate that the party began a concerted campaign to expand recruitment and give the party more patronage power on college campuses in the early 1990s. A joint directive issued in August 1993 by the CCP's Central Organization Department (COD), the Central Propaganda Department, and the State Education Commission delineated two specific tasks for party organizations in universities.

First, they were to recruit a group of outstanding cadres under the age of 45 into college administrations. The directive mandated that each college and university must have at least one to two such cadres. The implicit goal of this recruitment and promotion drive was to create avenues of political advancement for the intellectuals on college campuses, which were a hotbed of liberal ferment in the 1980s. To give the party more patronage power, the directive instructed that the party committees in universities would have decision-making power on the university's annual work plan, appointment and dismissal of cadres in departments, the promotion of academics, budgeting, and major capital projects. To make administrative and political appointments more attractive, the directive granted new perks to these appointees. For example, party and administrative cadres on college campuses would get opportunities to study abroad, teach, and conduct research.

Second, the directive urged that special efforts be made to recruit outstanding undergraduates and graduate students for filling administrative and political positions at the universities where they study after graduation. The students were to be mentored to become full-time party and administrative officials and awarded full academic ranks. Their housing allocation, pay, subsidies, and other benefits were to be kept in line with their academic peers. This call was repeated in 1995.[161] Official reports from the Beijing Higher Education Bureau provided evidence that this campaign was fully implemented. For example, in 1994, Beijing's colleges and universities recruited six hundred "red and expert" young "reserve cadres" who would be groomed for positions of responsibility. This was accompanied by a simultaneous drive to recruit new CCP members from college students. In 1994, the CCP admitted 6,665 new members on Beijing's college campuses, about 87 percent of them college students.[162]

The drive to expand the CCP's support among the intelligentsia was not restricted to college campuses. The CCP's innovative scheme of identifying "reserve cadres" (*houbei ganbu*) boosted the hopes of career advancement for tens of thousands of aspiring young professionals and well-educated individuals. It tied their prospects with their support for the party—even though what the party did was merely to designate them as the most promising candidates for future promotions. The campaign to recruit more reserve cadres intensified in the mid-1990s. In 1995, the CCP Central Committee issued a special circular, "Zhonggong zhongyang guanyu zhuajin peiyang xuanba youxiu nianqing ganbu de tongzhi" (CCP Central Committee Announcement on Intensifying the

Training and Selection of Outstanding Young Cadres), to expand the program. As a result, a large number of individuals were designated as reserve cadres. In Sichuan, fifty individuals were picked as reserve cadres for provincial-level positions and an additional five hundred were selected for the various provincial departments.[163] In Hubei, the number of reserve cadres was set at twice the number of available official positions. For those selected as reserve cadres for provincial-level positions, the age limit was fifty. Those groomed for prefect-level positions had to be younger than forty-five. And the age-limit for county-level positions was forty. Without actually expanding the size of the bureaucracy, the CCP managed to double the coverage of its patronage with this scheme.[164]

Although it is impossible to assess the durability of the party's success in enticing the intelligentsia's younger generation into its ranks, the drive apparently delivered some short-term success. According to a magazine survey of 1,532 college students in Beijing in May 2003, 62 percent said that they wished to join the CCP. But the same survey also showed that about 60 percent said that they would work for a private or foreign firm after graduation, and only 20 percent would work for a government agency or SOE. This mixed evidence suggests that what motivates younger professionals and aspiring college graduates to join the party is not ideological devotion, but promises of good careers and material benefits.[165] Judged by official figures, nevertheless, it is hard to deny that the party's efforts to recruit highly educated members appeared to have had a significant impact on the composition of the party. By 1999, nearly 20 percent of the CCP members claimed to have received college or college-equivalent education, almost six times the national average.[166]

Another successful instrument of co-optation was the granting of professional honors, recognitions, and perks by the government to a select group of senior scholars and professionals. The party controlled the selection and determination of the winners of these honors and perks. The criteria for the awardees were often explicitly political. A typical example was a program to pick outstanding social scientists. In April 1997, the State Education Commission issued a circular on "training outstanding social science talents for the new century." Under this program, the government would award such titles to thirty academics each year for five years. Among the listed qualifications were "high political caliber, support for the CCP, love of the socialist mother-land, outstanding academic achievements, and under 45." Most awardees were scholars in higher education institutions. The heads of the government's bureau of higher education would be the judges for the selection process. The winners would receive 100,000 yuan each in research support.[167] There were other similar administratively granted awards and perks for the intelligentsia. For example, as of 2004, 5,206 individuals were recognized as "middle-aged and young experts who have made outstanding contributions" (an honor that came with unspecified material benefits). Nationwide, 145,000 experts, or about 8 percent of the senior professionals, were receiving special government stipends in 2004.[168]

Besides recruiting and co-opting individual social elites, the party also tried to co-opt new social organizations. In 1998, the COD and the Ministry of Civil Affairs issued a joint document, "Guanyu zai shehui tuanti zhong jianli dang zuzhi youguan wenti de tongzhi" (A Circular on the Issue of Establishing Party Organizations Inside Civic Groups). To implement this program, Shanghai's party organization established party cells in NGOs and increased the party's penetration and influence in NGOs. The party also set up liaison offices in neighborhood committees. These offices received money from local governments and became the framework upon which civic groups could be built. The party placed 11,000 members in the three nominally private business groups, Shanghai Geti Laodongzhe Xiehui (Individual Entrepreneurs Association) and Shanghai Siying Qiye Xiehui (Association of Private Firms).[169]

The Co-optation of Private Entrepreneurs

The emergence of private entrepreneurs was initially viewed by the CCP with ambivalence, if not suspicion. In 1995, for example, a deputy minister of the COD publicly affirmed the party's official policy of not admitting private entrepreneurs into the party, even though some of them had been recruited by local officials.[170] Until Jiang Zemin promulgated his theory of the "Three Represents" and made the ideological case for recruiting private entrepreneurs into the party in 2001, the political status of private entrepreneurs remained in limbo.[171] But it would be a mistake to conclude, from an apparently inconsistent official policy, that the party had done nothing to turn the emerging private entrepreneurs into their supporters. The party tried to control this group of new social elites both through organizational penetration and individual recruitment.

The party's efforts to establish CCP cells in private firms were largely unsuccessful.[172] But the party's other efforts yielded, by comparison, more results. For example, Bruce Dickson's research on the party's attempts to reach out to business groups formed by private entrepreneurs showed that the CCP had established extensive links with business groups, such as Gongshanglian (The Industrial and Commercial Federation) to which nearly 80 percent of the owners of private firms belonged in 2002.[173] Although the official ban against admitting private entrepreneurs into the party was not formally lifted until 2001, the party not only made no attempt to expel those CCP members who had become private entrepreneurs, but also appeared to have carried out a systematic plan to recruit private entrepreneurs into the People's Congress and the Chinese People's Political Consultative Conference (CPPCC).

From 1997 to 2002, more than 9,000 private businessmen were selected to be delegates to local people's congresses at and above the county level. More than 32,000 were appointed to CPPCCs above the county level.[174] A survey of 3,635 private entrepreneurs in 2002 showed that 35 percent were members of the CPPCC at various levels. Surprisingly, 30 percent were party members, about six times the percentage in the general population. This represented more than a doubling of the percentage of private entrepreneurs who were CCP members in 1993. The rapid increase in the number of private entrepreneurs who were also CCP members, however, was not the result of a massive recruitment campaign.

Indeed, the survey revealed that only a tiny minority—5.6 percent—of private entrepreneurs joined the CCP after they had set up their businesses. Jiang's famous speech on July 1, 2001, in which he implicitly called for the recruitment of private entrepreneurs, appeared to have had no immediate impact on admitting private businessmen into the party. Only 0.5 percent of the private entrepreneurs in the sample had joined the CCP after the speech. This showed that nearly all the private entrepreneurs were already CCP members before they became owners of private firms. The privatization of SOEs appeared to be more responsible for the growth of private entrepreneurs inside the CCP than the party's organizational recruitment. Indeed, of the 3,635 firms surveyed, 837 were former SOEs and collectively owned enterprises.

Of these privatized firms, about half (422) were now owned by CCP members who were either party officials or well-connected CCP members who were able to gain control of these firms during the privatization process. The result of the survey implies that roughly half the privatized firms may have ended up in the control of CCP members.[175]

Given the CCP's dominant influence over the economy, it is rational for China's private entrepreneurs to maintain friendly ties with the regime. Many private entrepreneurs continue to depend on the government for favors, and close ties with the government can open up access to new business opportunities and capital. For example, the richest private entrepreneur in Xinjiang, Sun Guangxin, the president of Guanghui Enterprises, has received government support in marketing natural gas and developing real estate. His firm hired local party officials, one of whom happened to be the head of a government office that issued permits to demolish old buildings. Guanghui was exempted from paying local taxes on the land it used.[176] Another private entrepreneur in Henan, Zhou Wenchang, who gained control of a former state-owned bus assembly plant through insider privatization, had excellent connections with the local government. He used local police and courts to jail a business rival and kidnap debtors to enforce payment.[177]

To be sure, Chinese private entrepreneurs have not embraced the party wholeheartedly. Even though their policy preferences and political beliefs appear to be conservative and resemble those of the party elites, as Dickson's research shows, it may be premature to declare the party's strategy of co-opting China's new capitalists an unqualified success.[178] In all likelihood, China's new capitalists' support for the CCP is contingent upon the party's ability to provide favors and protect their privileges and property. The limitations of private entrepreneurs' support for the party are apparent in how they respond to the CCP's efforts of individual co-optation and organizational penetration. As a group, Chinese private entrepreneurs were more willing to be co-opted as individuals, as shown by their increasing membership in the people's congresses and the CPPCC. They apparently do not object to tight links between the party and the business groups they belong to. But they are more ambivalent on taking the initiative to join the party. Although party members who have become private entrepreneurs choose to maintain their party membership, only a small number of non-CCP private entrepreneurs appeared to have joined the party on their own.

Politically, such ambivalence makes sense. For those who were CCP members before they were private entrepreneurs, quitting the CCP would be unnecessarily risky because that step would signal disloyalty and could have negative political repercussions. Private entrepreneurs who are not CCP members, however, may see no additional advantages in entering the party because membership would come with burdensome chores and responsibilities. But private entrepreneurs, CCP members or not, seem to have drawn a firm line on the issue of allowing the party to establish its cells inside their private firms. The party's inability to extend its organizational presence into private firms shows that private entrepreneurs remain wary about having such a presence because it may not only interfere with their business operations, but also threaten the security of their property rights.

The history of post-Mao political reform can be better explained by a choice-based, and not structure-based, perspective on democratization. Documentary evidence suggests that senior Chinese leaders such as Deng were irreconcilably opposed to the idea of withdrawing from power and allowing genuine political contestation and participation. Their conception of political reform was narrowly and instrumentally defined—the only political reform that will be permitted should serve the needs of helping the CCP remain in power and further the party's goal of economic modernization. In contrast, political reform as understood by the liberals within the CCP comes much closer to a plan of democratization and institutional pluralism. However, the liberals' fall from power after the tragedy in June 1989 meant that such a plan would not be implemented. Consequently, the major institutional reforms of the political system that began in the 1980s stagnated in the 1990s. Despite their promise and potential, the strengthening of the legislative branch, legal reform, and grassroots self-government have produced only negligible effects on democratizing the Chinese political system. Most important, this chapter demonstrates that an authoritarian ruling party like the CCP, if determined to defend its political monopoly, does have the means and adaptive skills to confront its new challenges and contain the threats posed by rapid economic modernization and social change. Under these circumstances, democratic changes can occur only at a much slower pace than economic development and depend more on the initiatives of societal forces than on elite initiatives.

THREE

◆　◆　◆

Rent Protection and Dissipation:
The Dark Side of Gradualism

AS DISCUSSED in Chapter 1, gradualist economic reform is dictated by its political logic, the essence of which is the political survival of the ruling elites. Constrained by this logic, economic reform cannot infringe upon the ruling elites' ability to protect and allocate rents in critical economic sectors. This means that reform measures taken to improve the efficiency of these sectors are bound to be partial, compromised, and ultimately ineffective. Another insight from our theoretical discussion on the pitfalls of gradualism is that the rents protected through partial reforms are liable to be appropriated by the agents of the regime who, acting rationally, have the incentive to maximize their own gains at the expense of the economic health of the regime as a whole. This destructive dynamic of rent dissipation implies that gradualism is ultimately unsustainable.

In this chapter, I first apply these insights to case studies of three key sectors—the grain procurement system, telecom services, and banking—where the Chinese government has implemented gradualist reforms. These case studies are designed to test the hypothesis advanced in Chapter 1 about the underlying connection between regime survival, gradual reform, accumulated hidden costs, and persistent inefficiency, and demonstrate in greater detail why gradualist economic reform has not succeeded in subjecting some of China's most important sectors to market competition. The lessons drawn from these studies are meant to underscore the unsustainability of gradualist reform due to rent protection and rent dissipation. In addition, to reach a more comprehensive assessment of the overall achievements of China's gradualist reform strategy, I will review various measures of the degree of marketization and compare China's progress against that of its peers among both transition economies and developing countries.

The Grain Procurement System

The decollectivization of agriculture between 1979 and 1982 was the most radical economic reform implemented by the Communist Party. It laid the foundation for China's transition to a market economy. Following decollectivization, individual rural households regained their autonomy in agricultural production. But this reform did not end the government's use of administrative power to intervene in the agrarian sector. Through its continued monopoly of the procurement and sale of the most critical agricultural products (grain and cotton) and inputs (diesel fuel and chemical fertilizers), the state has retained its ability to extract rents from the rural sector despite having relinquished direct control over the farmers' day-to-day economic decision making.[1]

The grain procurement system provides a clue to the interlocking relationship among rent protection, regime survival, and economic inefficiency. From an economic perspective, the unreformed procurement system appears to have simultaneously achieved the worst of all worlds: high supply and price volatility, huge financial losses (both through subsidies and operating losses of SOEs in the system), and extraction of rural income (through purchase of grain from peasants at below-market prices).[2] Between 1990 and 1996, the total extraction of rural income through an implicit tax on grain collected through the procurement system totaled 259.2 billion yuan, averaging 37 billion yuan a year (roughly 18 percent of rural GDP).[3] Such a system, according to a wide-ranging assessment by the OECD in 2002, "has had adverse consequences for macroeconomic performance in recent years: grain surpluses and falling market prices have depressed agricultural incomes and contributed to a marked slowdown in rural consumption growth."[4] A case study of grain production and trade in Fujian province between 1986 and 1996 also concluded that the procurement system was too unpredictable to enable farmers to have confidence in the government's policies.[5]

Yet, from a regime survival perspective, the monopoly of grain procurement is critical. The grain procurement system has intrinsic political strategic importance. Like telecommunication services and banking, the monopoly of this system gives the government the control of a vital resource (food supplies). Allowing market forces to dictate the activities in such a strategic sector poses high risks for an autocracy because shocks to the sector can threaten the regime's hold on power. In addition, monopoly and government intervention in these sectors create high rents and plenty of opportunities for officials to profiteer, thus securing the loyalty of the regime's supporters.

The Evolution of the Grain Procurement System

Until 1985, the Chinese government had maintained a unified procurement system (*tonggou*) of grain procurement that required peasants to sell all their grain to the government at fixed prices. This system was replaced, in 1985, by the "contract procurement" system (*hetong dinggou*). Like China's dual-track prices for everything from steel to chemical fertilizers, the new system also had two prices. Grain-growing farmers signed contracts with the state for delivering a fixed quantity at a fixed price (quota price) to government-run grain purchasing stations (*liangzhan*).[6] Prior to the increase in the quota prices in 1995, the government intentionally kept such prices at artificially low levels to extract an implicit tax from grain growers. This hidden tax on grain disappeared only after 1995 as market prices, caused by a glut, fell below the quota prices.[7]

In addition, the government purchased grain from peasants at higher negotiated prices (or extra-quota prices) for the quantity that exceeded the quota. This dual-track system operated relatively smoothly from 1985 to 1991 and enabled the government to procure 73–88 percent of total marketed grain. Between a third to a half of the grain purchased by the state was transacted using negotiated prices.[8] Research by Chinese scholars shows that peasants did not like the arrangement because of its obvious economic disadvantages.[9]

Grain procurement remained basically unchanged until the early 1990s.[10] Under the pressure of rising fiscal outlays in grain subsidies, however, the government decided, in April 1992, to unify the purchase and sale prices for grain; prior to this change, the purchase prices were higher than sale prices, causing policy losses in the SOEs in the procurement system. The unification of grain prices eventually evolved into a brief but abortive attempt to fully liberalize prices in October 1993. Price liberalization unexpectedly gave monopoly SOEs in the system an opportunity to engage in hoarding and price gouging, which precipitated an artificial shortage of grain supplies. Provincial governments reacted by imposing restrictions on exports of grain, further exacerbating the shortage.[11] The ensuing panic buying in the cities forced the government to halt the reform abruptly.

In the wake of the failed liberalization of the grain procurement system, the state restored the previous administrative controls, reinstated the quota system, set price limits, and reimposed its monopoly. The government decided that it must control 70–80 percent of the grain on the market. In 1995, it set the target of 50 million tons to be purchased at quota prices (contracts signed with farmers directly) and an additional 40 million tons at negotiated prices (county governments were responsible for procuring this amount). The 1995 restoration of state control was also known as the Grain-Bag Policy, or the Governors' Grain-Bag Responsibility System (GGBRS), with provincial governors assuming primary responsibility over food production. The price for mandatory grain sales to the government was immediately increased by 40 percent at the end of 1994 to encourage more grain production.[12] In essence, the pre-1992 system was thus restored. The same old problems—such as regional barriers to grain trade, closed markets, SOEs' monopoly, and high operating costs—returned as well. Even though the government controlled 70–80 percent of the grain available on the market, the government did not set the sale prices, allowing the SOEs in the system to pocket the rent at the expense of the farmers.[13]

But the large price increases at the end of 1994 led to abundant harvests in the following years and caused a glut; China, a net importer of grain in the mid-1990s, became a net exporter at the end of the 1990s. With purchase prices substantially higher than sale prices, the state-controlled grain procurement system ran up huge losses. In 1998, losses totaled 40 billion yuan. Surplus grain was filling up the granaries as well. The costs of storage fees and loan interests on the grain reserves in 1998 were 50 billion yuan. Additionally, 8 million tons, or 20 percent of the grain in the granaries, was deemed unfit for consumption due to low quality and long storage.[14]

Faced with ever-rising grain subsidies, the government was forced to cut its quota and protection prices in 1998. Under the guise of a new

round of reforms, the government banned private firms from partici-
pating in the market and deployed the police, tax authorities, and other
regulatory agencies to crack down on private grain purchasers and ven-
dors. The core feature of the 1998 reform was the government's use of
administrative measures, instead of market mechanisms, in managing
supply and demand in the grain market. The government removed
certain grains (classified as low quality) from price protection and thus
forced peasants to reduce production. It also banned peasants from directly selling their grains on the market.[15] The reassertion of government control in the grain market marked a major reversal of reform in
this sector as it allowed SOEs to monopolize the grain procurement
market again.[16] In 2001, the government began to implement pilot reforms to open the grain market, with renewed emphasis on price liberalization, reduction of the quantities of grain purchased under the
quota system, and permission for more firms to enter the market. But
these reforms were restricted to grain-consuming provinces, while grain-
producing provinces remained under the old system.[17]

Analysis

In many ways, the experience of reforming the grain procurement system is a typical example of the gradualist approach to reform. The government experimented with various forms of price liberalization, only
to reassert control when such experiments led to unsustainable increases
in fiscal subsidies or market turmoil. Abortive reforms eventually made
little dent on the inefficient old system. However, the costs of failure to
reform continued to mount, as seen in the accumulated huge losses in
the grain procurement system (214 billion yuan from 1992 to 1998
alone) and high market volatility.[18] Throughout the reform period, two
different and sometimes conflicting impulses drove policy considerations. The government was determined to retain its ability to control
the vital market for grain because of its political importance. Yet at the
same time, the government was also averse to paying too high a price,
in the form of mounting fiscal subsidies, for such control. As a result,
whenever supply conditions improved or a glut emerged, the government behaved opportunistically by cutting the prices it set for grain
purchases and reduced the amount of grain it had committed to buying from the growers at the preset prices.

Indeed, the primary motivations for changing the procurement policy, mainly through reducing prices paid to grain growers, appeared to be the reduction of rising grain subsidies, as in 1985, 1992, and 1998.[19] But farmers responded to the state's opportunistic behavior by withholding grain. This quickly led to shortages, forcing the government to raise prices. In this game, the underlying market structure gave the growers a slight edge. Of all the grain produced in China, farmers themselves normally consume two-thirds and sell the remaining one-third—about 150 million tons in the mid-1990s—on the market.[20] To maximize their income, peasants sold the bulk of their surplus grain (about two-thirds and usually of poorer quality) to the state-owned grain bureaus and firms, which typically held down the prices. They sold the remaining one-third (higher quality grain) to private purchasing agents who offered higher prices.[21] As peasants could respond to market conditions either by withholding sales when prices were too low or reducing their own consumption when prices were attractive, the aggregate impact of their response to the government's behavior on the supply side was considerable.

This structural feature of the Chinese grain market, coupled with the flaws inherent in the state-run grain procurement and reserve systems, made the market more susceptible to supply and demand shocks. A small fluctuation in supply, either a shortage or excess supply of 10 million to 15 million tons, or 8 to 10 percent of the marketable grain supplies, could destabilize the market.[22] Also notable in the case of the failure to reform the grain procurement system is the striking fact that the government had never intended to alter the underlying organizational structure of the grain market. In 1985, 1992–1993, and 1998, the government adjusted prices, but did not set out to abolish the monopoly granted to the SOEs in the system. As the case of failed full liberalization of prices in 1994 demonstrated, removing price controls without ending the SOEs' monopoly was bound to encourage price gouging and market manipulation by these firms.

An intriguing question is: who has benefited from this inefficient and volatile marketing arrangement? The state, which has suffered huge fiscal losses, does not appear to be a winner, nor do grain-producing farmers, who had to accept below-market prices until the late 1990s. The only beneficiary of the system seems to be the SOEs. The interests of these monopolistic firms are at odds with those of the state and the peasantry. Their overriding objective is to maximize monopoly rents, not to ensure market stability (the state's goal) or increase income for the grain growers. Consequently, their behavior has been almost counter-cyclical: when there is a glut, SOEs will do everything to reduce purchases; when there is a shortage, SOEs will hoard.[23] In addition, government monopolies in charge of exports and imports of grain displayed the same rent-seeking behavior, which worked at the expense of market stability. For example, during the 1994 shortage, state-owned grain exporting companies exported, at low prices, 20 million tons of grain. The same firms imported 10 million tons at high prices during the glut in 1995.[24] The government's restrictions on private competition in this sector have benefited monopoly SOEs as well. Even though, in reality, private grain wholesale purchasers controlled a large share of the market, most private participants in this market were forced to work with SOEs in an opaque business environment rife with opportunities for corruption and irregularities.[25]

The story of the halting—and failing—reforms in China's grain procurement system is a cautionary tale of the limits of gradualist reform. The political imperative of maintaining direct influence in a vital economic sector led the government to restrict the entry of market forces and preserve its monopoly in this sector. When the costs of maintaining its direct control became excessive, the government behaved opportunistically by reneging on its commitments to the grain growers, an act to which farmers responded with lower production and the withholding of sales. This tit-for-tat game of opportunism and withholding of cooperation made the Chinese grain market unusually volatile during the reform period. In the meantime, the underlying infrastructure of an alternative, market-oriented grain procurement system remains to be built.[26]

The Telecom Service Sector

China's telecom service sector has been one of the fastest-growing industries in the reform era, measured both by the expansion of capacity and growth in revenues. From 1980 to 2002, the number of fixed line subscribers grew from 4.1 million to 213 million. Revenues of China's telecom service firms totaled 411.6 billion yuan in 2002. In 1980 the combined revenues of post and telecommunications were only 1.3 billion yuan.[27] At the end of 2003, China claimed to have 30.9 million computers connected to the Internet and almost 80 million people with access to the Internet.[28] Based on capacity and revenues, China's telecom service sector is among the largest in the world. Yet, despite such impressive growth, the telecom service sector remains one of the most closed industries in China, with the state-owned firms dominating the market through monopolies or duopolies. Private firms have been banned from providing fixed-line and mobile services. Before China joined the World Trade Organization (WTO) and was forced to open up the telecom service sector under the pressure of its trading partners, foreign telecom firms were kept out of this industry as well.

Monopoly and State Control

Until 1994, the Ministry of Post and Telecommunications (MPT) had maintained a national monopoly over the telecom sector, which included fixed-line long-distance, local, and mobile services, data transmission, and satellite transmission. MPT was also a dominant provider of paging services, with almost 70 percent of the market share.[29] Under MPT's monopoly, telecom services were both expensive and low quality.[30] The lucrative rents in the telecom service sector attracted other powerful players to the market. As early as in 1988, the Ministry of Electronic Industry (MEI), the Ministry of Electric Power (MEP), and the Ministry of Railways (MR) joined forces in seeking the State Council's authorization to establish a rival telecom concern to compete against MPT. However, the MPT's strong resistance delayed the State Council's action for six years. In December 1993, the State Council finally issued a directive allowing MEI, MEP, and MR to form China United Telecommunications Corporation, or China Unicom, along with thirteen other domestic partners. The State Council also authorized the formation of Jitong Communications Corp., a new SOE, to provide Internet services. In July 1994, China Unicom was born. Its registered capital was 1 billion yuan, and it received a generous allocation of radio frequency for a wireless network. With its specialized networks owned by MEP and MR, China Unicom had ambitious goals: it wanted to gain 10 percent of both domestic and long-distance service in China, and 30 percent of the mobile market.[31]

Despite the State Council's approval, however, the existing monopoly, MPT's China Telecom, tried everything in its power to prevent China Unicom from becoming a true competitor. Wu Jichuan, the minister of MPT, reportedly said, "I want not only to strangle Unicom, but also to bury it deep."[32] Because MPT was both an operator of the existing telecom monopoly and *the* regulator of the telecom sector, it had ample means to undermine its fledgling rival. Minister Wu insisted, "Unicom's entry into any market must be approved by MPT" because MPT had the power to interpret the State Council's December 1993 directive authorizing the formation of China Unicom. Consequently, MPT ruled that Unicom did not have permission to operate long-distance and local fixed-line services. MPT abused its regulatory power to delay Unicom's entry into certain markets. In some cases, Unicom had to wait as long as two years before MPT approved its applications. One was Unicom's application for its own GSM cell phone network. Initially, MPT was not interested in building a GSM network for itself. However, it changed its mind after Unicom had built its own GSM network. To prevent Unicom from gaining a competitive advantage, MPT effectively rendered useless Unicom's GSM by denying it access to the MPT's vast fixed-line network. Only after MPT's own GSM became operational did the ministry grant access to Unicom's GSM network. In addition, MPT's China Telecom used predatory pricing and cross-subsidization to undercut Unicom and charged Unicom excessive fees for access to its fixed-line networks.[33]

Such anticompetitive practices stunted Unicom's initial growth. Three years after Unicom was formed, it could not get into long-distance or local markets, in spite of its existing networks. Even its business in the cell phone market was severely curtailed. Although it had built its own wireless networks in twenty cities, it was able to operate its networks in only four (Shanghai, Beijing, Tianjin, and Guangzhou) because MPT prevented Unicom from gaining access to its local networks. At the end of 1995, Unicom had fewer than 50,000 wireless customers, though its networks had a capacity to serve 700,000. Its market share of the mobile telephone market was a paltry 1.38 percent.[34] At the end of 1997, Unicom's wireless service still had only 200,000 subscribers, about 2 percent of China Telecom's customer base.[35] And in 1999, China Unicom's share in the wireless market was only 6 percent, compared with China Mobile's 94 percent. In the paging market, China Telecom controlled 67 percent of the market share, and China Unicom had only 3 percent.[36]

The experience of China Unicom epitomizes the Chinese government's halting efforts to open the telecom service sector. On the surface, it appears that the government tried to break up China Telecom's monopoly through a series of reorganizational reforms of the industry. But in reality, the sector continued to be dominated by the monopoly firms formerly affiliated with MPT, which itself became the Ministry of Information Industry, or MII, in 1998. In 1999, China Telecom, which nominally was separated from MII in 1998 and became an independent SOE, reorganized itself into four entities: China Telecom (fixed-line service), China Mobile (wireless), China Paging, and China Satellite-com. During the reorganization, some of China Telecom's assets were transferred to China Unicom. In 2000, the government authorized a new telecom firm, China Network Communication Group, or China Netcom, to become an Internet service provider (ISP) and compete against China Telecom. China Netcom had four state-owned share-holders that managed to receive $325 million in equity investment from Goldman Sachs and News Corp. through a private placement. In 2001, a new fixed-line provider, China Railcom, was founded.

The largest restructuring of the sector occurred in 2002 when the government broke up China Telecom into two entities. The part that controlled fixed-line networks in the more prosperous twenty-one provinces, including the coastal regions, retained the China Telecom name. The networks in the other and less prosperous ten provinces were combined with China Netcom and Jitong Communications to form China Networks Communications Group. This restructuring effectively transformed a national monopoly in fixed-line services into a geographically based duopoly. In terms of market share, China Telecom remained the dominant fixed-line service provider in 2002, with 133 million users or 62.1 percent of the market; the newly combined China Netcom had 77 million users or 36 percent of the market. China Railcom had only 1.4 percent of the market. In the judgment of a government think tank, access to the fixed-line market was as closed as ever. Despite the breakup of China Telecom into two entities, there was no competition in this sector. The situation was hardly better in the wireless market. China Mobile, which was split from China Telecom in 1999, had revenues of 151 billion yuan in 2002, or 77.3 percent of the market; China Unicom, the upstart, claimed 22.7 percent.[37]

Throughout the reform era, the state not only successfully kept domestic private firms out of the telecom service sector, but also managed to prevent foreign investors from penetrating the sector. Despite their efforts, foreign telecom firms failed to crack the Chinese market. Even ingenious schemes—such as the Chinese-Chinese-Foreign equity investment model, under which a Chinese firm formed a telecom joint venture with a Chinese-foreign joint venture to bypass regulatory hurdles—eventually proved unsuccessful. Such a model was tried in the case of China Unicom, when twenty-one foreign investors—including the biggest multinational telecom firms such as Sprint, Nippon Telephone and Telegraph, Cable and Wireless, and France Telecom—poured $1.3 billion into China Unicom through their joint ventures in China. But in late 1999, under government pressure, China Unicom unilaterally forced these investors to withdraw their equities at a very low rate of return on their investments.[38] During its WTO accession negotiations, China's major trading partners, the United States and the European Union, forced China to make key concessions on the opening of the telecom service sector.

According to China's WTO accession agreements, the country would open the telecom service sector to foreign competition in stages. Foreign companies can get up to 50 percent of ownership in value-added services in 2005, and 49 percent ownership in both mobile and fixed-line services by 2007. China's tough stance on refusing to cede foreign telecom operators majority control almost caused its WTO negotiations to collapse. But this position reflects the Chinese government's determination to maintain its control of the telecom sector despite international pressure.[39] Indeed, foreign telecom operators appeared to get the message and did not take advantage of China's WTO concessions. In the two years following China's WTO accession, only the U.S. firm AT&T acquired a 25 percent stake for $25 million in a joint ISP venture with the Shanghai city government.

While strenuously trying to keep foreign competition from its telecom service sector, the Chinese government was eager to attract foreign portfolio investment in its state-owned telecom firms through overseas stock listings. The initial public offering (IPO) of China Telecom (HK) in Hong Kong and New York in 1997 netted $4.2 billion.[40] China Netcom was floated on the U.S. Nasdaq market in 2000. China Unicom received a staggering $5.7 billion at its IPO during the tech bubble of 2000. Following its reorganization in 2002, China Telecom, the fixed-line operator, sold 20 percent of its shares in an IPO in Hong Kong but raised only $1.66 billion due to a lack of interest from investors.[41]

China Network Communications Group, which was formed in 2002 after the breakup of China Telecom, planned to launch its own IPO in Hong Kong and New York in 2004 to raise $2 billion.

Thus, almost a decade after China began to liberalize its telecom service sector, the underlying dominance and exclusive control by the state over the vital industry has hardly changed. In 2002, six telecom service firms, all state-owned or controlled, divided the telecom service market among themselves. With revenues of 150.9 billion yuan, China Mobile claimed 36.7 percent of the market; China Telecom had 136.3 billion yuan in revenues and took 33.1 percent of the market; China Netcom, with 67.6 billion yuan, had 16.4 percent of the market. These three former entities of MPT still retained 86 percent of the market share. The two new telecom firms, China Unicom and China Railcom, had 12.4 and 1.2 percent of the market, respectively.[42] The state's direct control over the telecom firms contributed to their poor performance. In the judgment of a State Council think tank, state ownership and control encouraged them to "expand investment, seek market power, and increase insiders' income . . . these firms have distorted competitive behavior, such as excess debt and price wars."[43]

The monopoly of the state in the telecom sector was also responsible for the failure of the National People's Congress to pass the competition laws required to liberalize the sector. Although reformers in 1998 proposed telecom legislation that would have established a regulatory commission modeled after the U.S. Federal Communications Commission (FCC), the proposal was not enacted by the national legislature due to strong opposition from the telecom bureaucracy. As of 2003, the proposed legislation was still in limbo. Because MII, the successor to MPT and patron of the telecom monopolies, was put in charge of drafting the telecom legislation, prospects for real reform appeared dim.

Analysis

The persistence of the state's monopoly and control in the telecom service sector has led to high inefficiency and poor service and impeded further technological development in the sector. Official data show that the government's massive investment in the sector has yielded low returns. In the late 1990s, the net income/expense ratio in China's telecom sector was 1.14:1, compared with the international average of 3.3:1 and the U.S. average of 7.7:1. This comparison suggests that China's telecom sector is half as efficient as that of an average country and almost six times less efficient than the telecom sector in the United States. The transmission capacity utilization rate in China was below 40 percent, as opposed to the international average of 74 percent.[44] The management of the telecom industry was poor by international standards as well, resulting in inefficient utilization of equipment and high prices for end-users.[45] China Telecom's anticompetitive practices were also blamed for the poor interconnection that stunted the growth of the Internet in China.[46] Crossnational comparison of the performance and competition in the telecom service industry indicates that China lagged behind most transition economies and other large developing countries. A World Economic Forum survey of telecom industries in eighty-two countries conducted in 2002 placed China among the bottom quarter or third of the group in terms of competition, infrastructure quality, and costs of service.[47]

The troubled history of reform in the telecom service sector provides another illustration of the limits of gradualism. State monopoly has persisted along side high growth, stifled competition, and undermined efficiency. But this outcome becomes more understandable if we make the connection between rent protection and regime survival. There are several compelling reasons for maintaining the telecom service sector as a state monopoly. First, like the grain procurement system, the telecom service sector has the characteristics of a prized commanding height that a developmental autocracy cannot afford to cede. It is in a vital industry (information) that directly affects the regime's capacity of social control. This strategic importance makes it more difficult to open the telecom sector for competition because opponents of reform can easily justify their opposition on grounds of national and regime security. Second, the telecom sector is itself a huge patronage machine and a source of rent generation because it employs a large number of employees, invests massive capital, and collects monopoly rents. Direct control of this sector provides the regime the ability to reward and keep its supporters (the low returns of China's telecom SOEs should be an indication that their monopoly rents may have been dissipated among the insiders). Of course, the introduction of new state-affiliated competitors may temporarily upset the balance, as the case of

China Unicom illustrates, principally because it threatens the bureaucratic clout and rents of the existing monopoly (MPT's China Telecom). The ostensible "corporatization" of the state-owned telecom assets and the transition from a monopoly (a single SOE) to a duopoly (two SOEs) have not altered the nature of the state monopoly. Entrenched interests have succeeded in protecting their rents.

One intriguing question emerges from this examination of the telecom sector. Why has the Chinese government locked out domestic private competition from the sector and even prevented domestic portfolio investment in its telecom SOEs (none are listed on the domestic stock markets), but allowed minority foreign ownership in these firms, both through overseas stock market listings and potential post-WTO direct investment? Several explanations are likely. Minority foreign ownership does not threaten the regime politically even though it may force some changes in corporate governance on the margins. Instead, such ownership can actually add a gloss to these state-owned assets. As a result of overseas listings, the monopoly value of the state's telecom assets is instantly reflected in the share prices of the state-owned telecom firms listed in Hong Kong and New York. Perversely, this explicit link between capital market valuation and state monopoly becomes another obstacle to reform. Under the pretense of protecting the state's investments, the government can justify its monopoly because stock markets value monopolies. Indeed, since the listing of Chinese telecom firms overseas, MII and China Telecom have tried on at least two occasions to use their power to boost the stock prices of listed telecom firms.[48]

The Banking Sector

Of China's major economic sectors, the banking system is arguably the least reformed and most troubled. In this sector, as in other sectors critical to the CCP's ability to retain rents, gradualist reforms have not only failed to reduce inefficiency and promote competition, but also contributed to the build-up of a massive amount of nonperforming loans (NPLs) that has become the most serious threat to the sustainability of China's economic growth in the twenty-first century.[49] In many ways, the lack of progress with regard to financial reform in China is an anomaly. On the one hand, the country has achieved unprecedented financial deepening—a measure of progress in financial liberalization—during the reform era. The key indicator of financial deepening, the ratio of financial assets to GDP, rose from 0.94 in 1978 to 2.78 in 1998—a level higher than that reached in the early 1990s by the most developed financial markets, such as the United States, Germany, and the United Kingdom. The level of China's financial deepening also has exceeded that of the newly industrializing countries (NICs).[50] On the other hand, China's financial sector, dominated by the state-controlled banking system, is the weakest among the world's major economies, with a very high level of NPLs, pervasive corruption, and low efficiency. Judging by standard accounting criteria, all the major state banks became technically insolvent in the mid-1990s.[51] The main function of the Chinese banking system is to funnel credit to value-destroying SOEs, not to the thriving private sector. In this section, I will review the history of gradualist reforms in the banking sector, assess the results of such reforms, and analyze the factors that have contributed to their failure.

Banking Reform since 1979

During the prereform era, China had a mono-bank system. The People's Bank of China (PBOC) combined the functions of both central and commercial banking under state planning. The reform of the banking sector began gradually and tentatively in 1979, as China began its economic transition. That year, the government set up three specialized state-owned banks, the Agricultural Bank of China (ABC), the Bank of China (BOC), and the China Construction Bank (CCB). In 1984, it established the Industrial and Commercial Bank of China (ICBC). These specialized state-owned banks then became the primary institutions of financial intermediation, with the PBOC assuming its role as the central bank. In the 1980s and early 1990s, the government took additional steps in diversifying the banking system. State-affiliated joint-holding banks (the Bank of Communications, Guangdong Development Bank, Shenzhen Development Bank, Shanghai Pudong Development Bank, China Merchants Bank, and Fujian Industrial Bank) entered the sector. The ownership of these banks was spread among local governments, government ministries, and SOEs. In addition, the government allowed the establishment of a large number of nonbank financial institutions, such as rural credit cooperatives (RCCs), urban credit co-operatives, and investment and trust companies. Foreign banks were permitted into the Chinese market to conduct limited banking opera-tions as well.[52] These measures had a negligible impact on the liberal-ization and development of the banking system, however. According to top Chinese economists who were drawing up plans for financial re-form in the early 1990s, China's central bank was considered dysfunc-tional and failing in its management of monetary policy. Specialized state banks were similarly unable to perform their assigned tasks of fi-nancial intermediation efficiently. China's financial markets were judged to be chaotic.[53]

By all accounts, serious banking reform did not begin until 1994 and was probably precipitated by the overheating of the economy and credit explosion in 1992–1993 that alerted the Chinese leadership of the dangers of an unreformed banking sector. The reform package in-cluded most of the recommendations provided by liberal economists.[54] On the whole, the reforms introduced in 1994 and 1995 created a legal framework for the financial sector through the promulgation of the People's Bank Law and the Commercial Banking Law, strengthened the PBOC's role as the central bank, established three policy banks, and transformed the four specialized state banks into state commercial banks (SCBs). Additional reform steps included the strengthening of banking regulations, the consolidation of poorly regulated investment and trust companies, the establishment of one private bank (China Minsheng Bank in 1996), and the transformation of urban credit co-operatives into city commercial banks.[55] The East Asian financial crisis in 1997–1998 jolted the government into taking additional steps to strengthen its banks, as weak financial institutions were blamed for caus-ing the crisis. It imposed tighter prudential supervision and pushed Chinese banks to adopt more stringent standards for classifying loans. The PBOC abolished loan quota control over the four SCBs in January 1998. The Ministry of Finance (MOF) also issued 270 billion yuan in special treasury bonds in 1998 to shore up the capital base of the four SCBs. Additionally, in 2000, the four SCBs set up four asset manage-ment companies (AMCs), which took 1.4 trillion yuan in impaired assets off the balance sheets of the SCBs.[56] To streamline operations, the four SCBs cut their staff by 130,000 and reduced the number of branches by 40,000 between 1997 and 2000.

Although these steps prevented a full-blown banking crisis, they did not succeed in improving the financial performance of the SCBs. The asset quality in the banking sector continued to deteriorate. The leadership transition in 2002–2003 provided fresh momentum for banking reform. A new regulatory agency, the Banking Regulatory Commission, was established in April 2003 to strengthen the prudential supervision of all deposit-taking institutions. In a shift of reform strategy, the new leadership in early 2003 decided to focus on turning the SCBs into joint-stock companies and listing their shares on overseas and domestic stock markets in the hope of improving their corporate governance. This strategy was implemented in late 2003, when the government selected BOC and CCB, two SCBs with lower NPL ratios, for new capital injection and corporatization.

As part of the strategy, $45 billion from China's foreign reserves was transferred as core capital to BOC and CCB. In addition, the MOF wrote off its equity in the two banks, worth 300 billion yuan.[57] In return, the government intended to hold the revitalized banks to tough corporate governance and financial performance criteria.[58] Like other monopoly SOEs listed on overseas markets, BOC and CCB opened their arms to foreign strategic investors. Two large Western banks, the Deutsche Bank and Citigroup, expressed interest in taking stakes in CCB.[59] Altogether, the cumulative costs in bailing out the SCBs alone were more than 2.3 trillion yuan, about 20 percent of GDP.[60] But the eventual costs of writing off the NPLs in the banking sector would definitely be much higher. In all likelihood, capital injection and stock market listing, without substantial changes in the environment in which they operate, may not alter the nature of the SCBs as the conduit of government-directed lending.[61]

The overall assessment of China's reform efforts in the banking sector has been negative mainly because these reforms have failed to increase competition, improve efficiency, and reduce NPLs.[62] The state-dominated banking sector has failed in its role of channeling savings to the most productive sectors and areas. Loans extended by the banking sector at the national level have been found to have a negative impact on provincial economic growth because such loans were used to support SOEs.[63] A study by the IMF has shown that the state bank–dominated financial intermediation is inefficient in converting financial resources into productive assets in China. The country's most efficient and fastest-growing private sector, or the faster-growing provinces, has not used the financial system in any substantial way for financing its growth. For these firms and provinces, nonstate financing has contributed to faster growth.[64] In provinces with more diversified banking sectors and where state banks have weaker influence, the growth rate has been higher.[65] Due to the government's control of interest rate policy, loan rates still do not reflect risks. This has been responsible for macroeconomic instability, as subsidized credit encouraged excess investment during boom years while administrative tightening of loans led to hard landings, especially in the 1980s.[66] Financial sector reforms have failed to increase the integration of China's capital markets.[67]

SCBs' Dominance and Performance

To evaluate the reform measures taken by the Chinese government in the banking sector, three tests need to be applied. The first is whether such reforms have reduced the state's control and intervention in this vital sector. The second is whether such reforms have increased competition in the sector. The final test is whether they have improved the performance of the sector. Unfortunately, China's banking reform has failed all three.

The reforms have failed to reduce the state's control and intervention in the sector. This can be seen by looking at the ownership structure of the banks. In addition to the four dominant SCBs, which are wholly state-owned banks, virtually all the other major joint-stock banks are owned by state-affiliated entities and local governments. The newly formed city commercial banks are owned and controlled by local governments and SOEs.[68] Even rural credit co-ops, nominally owned by farmers, are run by local governments. The effective state monopoly of the banking sector has remained intact.[69] The only truly private financial institution is Minsheng Bank. But with assets of $30 billion in 2003, this bank is a relatively small player.[70] In 2003, there were signs that the government might be ready for the entry of additional private banks. One possibility under discussion is the establishment of private rural commercial banks in which local government would have no control.[71]

Compared with indigenous private sector players, foreign banks have fared only marginally better. Although they were allowed to open branches and representative offices in 1990, the restrictions imposed by the Chinese government have largely kept foreign banks out of the market beyond financing trade and servicing foreign-invested firms. In 1997, of the 173 foreign banks with foreign currency operations in China, only 9 were allowed to conduct local currency operations. Foreign banks had $38 billion in assets (about 3 percent of the assets in the four SCBs) and $27 billion in loans.[72] The situation in 2002 remained basically unchanged. Foreign banks accounted for only 1 percent of total bank assets in China.[73] Getting into China's banking sector via joint ventures was restricted as well. Only a small number of foreign financial institutions were allowed to make equity investments in several select small joint-stock banks (including Minsheng Bank).[74] By the end of 2003, China had only seven Sino-foreign joint-venture banks.[75] While foreign banks will gain unimpeded access to the domestic market in 2007 as a result of China's WTO commitments, the prospects for domestic private entrants remain cloudy.

The most immediate and important impact of the state's dominance in the banking sector is the government's tight control of the most critical price in allocating credit—interest rates. During most of the reform era, the government imposed strict control on loan and deposit rates. The pace of liberalization was extremely slow. Starting in 2000, limited flexibility was allowed only in certain types of transactions that would not likely have a substantial impact on the credit market. For example, the government allowed the free floating of borrowing rates on the interbank market. Rates on foreign exchange deposits became fully liberalized. RCCs were able to float their loan rates within a narrower band, as were city commercial banks, which could raise their loan rates, or lower them, within a very narrow band. However, deposit rates for all banks were set by the PBOC. Loan rates in the SCBs and eleven joint-stock commercial banks that controlled more than 80 percent of the loan market were also determined by the PBOC.[76]

China's banking reform has failed the competition test because the measures taken since 1979 have not brought about a fundamental structural change in the credit market, leaving the dominant positions of the SCBs essentially untouched. In 1986, the four SCBs controlled 83 percent of the deposits and accounted for 90 percent of the outstanding loans.[77] By 2003, they had lost considerable market share due to the emergence of other financial institutions. The four SCBs accounted for 65 percent of the total deposits and 66 percent of the outstanding loans. Nevertheless, the dominance of the four SCBs remained unchallenged.[78] The SCBs were able to defend their market share mainly because their owner—the state—used regulatory tools to stifle competition. For example, in the market for bank deposits, the SCBs had implicit state guarantees. SOEs could deposit funds only in the banks that lent them loans, which meant the SCBs. The PBOC provided cheap funds to the SCBs because nearly all of the PBOC lending went to the four SCBs. The operations of the newly formed joint-stock banks were also subject to geographical restrictions. Finally, the fixed rates on loans and deposits prevented competitors from offering more attractive rates to challenge the SCBs.[79]

The suppression of competition in the banking sector makes little economic sense because all performance data showed that new entrants—joint-stock banks, Minsheng Bank (the only private bank), and foreign banks—were more efficient operators and delivered far superior financial results. Joint-stock banks were six times more profitable than the SCBs in terms of returns on assets and net profits.[80] From 1994 to 1998, their returns on assets and on equity were ten times higher than the SCBs.[81] Their asset quality was higher as well. In June 2003, the NPL ratio for the eleven joint-stock banks was only 9.3 percent (based on the five-category classification), compared with 21.4 percent for the four SCBs.[82] City commercial banks, the successor to urban credit cooperatives, had fewer NPLs than the SCBs. Only RCCs had a higher NPL ratio (30 percent) than the SCBs.[83] Minsheng Bank's NPL ratio in 2002 was only 1.74 percent.[84] The NPL ratio for foreign banks operating in China was 4.3 percent.[85]

The most important reason for the higher profitability and asset quality for Minsheng Bank, foreign banks, and, to a lesser extent, joint-stock banks is that these institutions, compared with the SCBs, made more loans to nonstate borrowers that were less likely to default. In 1998, for example, 45 percent of the loans issued by ICBC to small and medium-sized SOEs were nonperforming, compared with 29 percent for Sino-foreign joint ventures and private firms.[86] Although the percentage of loans issued by joint-stock banks to private firms was relatively low, it was on average about twice higher than that issued by the SCBs.[87] Sixty percent of the loans made by Minsheng Bank went to private firms, as well as to medium and small firms.[88] By comparison, the

SCBs and, to a lesser extent, joint-stock banks gave nearly all their loans to SOEs. In the mid-1990s, about 95 percent of the SCBs' loans and 92 percent of the loans from joint-stock banks went to SOEs.[89] This situation did not improve in 2000. For example, in Jiangsu and Zhejiang, the two provinces with the most dynamic private sector, only about 5 percent of the outstanding bank loans went to the private sector, including TVEs.[90]

Among developing countries, China's lending to the private sector has been considered the most discriminatory. In 1999, of the seventy-eight countries surveyed by the World Bank, China's lending to the private sector—calculated as the ratio of credit by deposit money banks and other financial institutions to the private sector—was ranked the bottom fifteenth, just ahead of countries such as Haiti, Ghana, Syria, Rwanda, Algeria, Niger, and Sudan.[91] Lack of access to credit forced China's private firms to turn to internal financing, hampering their growth. A study of small and medium-sized firms, mainly private enterprises or TVEs, in Zhejiang and Jiangsu in 2000 found that only 24 percent of their capital was bank loans. These firms relied on the curb market SCBs and raised money from employees for expansion and operation.[92] During most of the 1990s, about two-thirds of the loans made by the entire banking sector went to SOEs. Only about 10 percent were provided to TVEs, private firms, and foreign joint ventures; about 6 percent of the loans made by the SCBs went to private firms, TVEs, and foreign joint ventures.[93] Starting in 1998, however, with the rapid increase of residential mortgage loans, consumer credit, and the transfer of 1.4 trillion yuan in NPLs from the SCBs to the four AMCs in 2000–2001, the share of the outstanding loans made to SOEs began to decline. By 2001–2002, it was estimated that half the loans extended by the banking sector were for SOEs, and the other half for the nonstate sector.[94]

Another consequence of maintaining the state's dominance in the banking sector and of defending the SCBs' privileged market positions has been an unbalanced structure in China's capital markets. With the SCBs maintaining a near monopoly on financial intermediation during most of the reform era, bank loans—direct financing—have been the primary source of capital. Indirect financing, through the issuance of stocks and bonds on the capital markets, grew very slowly. Equity issuance started in China in 1987, but did not raise any significant amount of capital until 1993, when proceeds from IPOs reached 37 billion yuan, and peaked in 1997, with IPOs raising 129 billion yuan.[95] Between 1995 and 1998, bank loans contributed more than 80 percent of the increase in the capital stocks of firms, equity investment accounted for only 5 percent, and bonds less than 2 percent. The ratio of direct financing in China (less than 10 percent) was much lower than in Japan and other East Asian countries (about 30 percent).[96] A financial system dominated by bank lending has concentrated risks in the banking sector. But such a system has served the government well. As a study by the State Planning Commission stated, "Because of the government's direct control of the financial system, the country's capital is concentrated in the state-owned banking system. Such capital, through implementation of the government's credit plans, flows to key projects and SOEs that fit with the government's plan."[97]

Finally, China's banking reform has failed the third test—financial performance. The dominant SCBs, which are among the largest financial institutions in the world, have also been the worst performers by international standards, with returns on assets in the 1990s ranging from 0.3 to 0.9 percent.[98] Measured by capital and loan loss reserves, the SCBs had fragile balance sheets. During the 1990s, their capital adequacy ratio was significantly below the 8-percent level recommended by the Basel guidelines.[99] In 2001, the average capital adequacy ratio of the four SCBs was only 4.95 percent, about half the level recommended by the Basel guidelines for banks in emerging markets.[100]

However, the most serious weakness of the SCBs—and of the Chinese banking system—is the huge amount of NPLs. Although the Chinese government spent more than $200 billion to recapitalize the SCBs and reduce their NPLs from 1998 to 2001, the impaired asset ratio in the banking system has remained stubbornly high, mainly because the recapitalization of banks has not been accompanied by more systemic reforms, and new NPLs have been generated in large volumes. For example, the official NPL ratio in 1999 was 25 percent. But in 2002, after the transfer of 1.4 trillion yuan of NPLs was completed and the asset base of the four SCBs increased considerably, their NPL ratio was still 25 percent, implying a rise of NPLs in absolute terms.[101] Indeed, from 1998 to 2002, 1.7 trillion yuan in new bad loans were created in the four SCBs.[102] Official data released in 2003 showed that, as of September 2003, the NPL ratio was 21.38 percent for the four SCBs and 18.74 percent for all major financial institutions (based on the five-category classification). But Standard & Poor's estimated in 2003 that the real NPL ratio in China's banking system was about 45 percent, more than double the official Chinese figure. The rate of recovery on NPLs was estimated to be only 20 percent. The U.S. rating agency deemed the Chinese banking sector technically insolvent. It would take at least fifteen years to bring the NPL ratio in the banking sector to 5 percent.[103]

Poor Governance and Corruption

In addition to politically directed lending, poor governance and weak management have also contributed to the deteriorating performance of China's banks. By international standards, Chinese banks have woefully weak internal control. For example, in 2003, internal auditing staff in Chinese banks accounted for only 1 percent of the bank employees, compared with 5 percent in Western banks.[104] Accountability has rarely been enforced. In a survey of bank employees in 2002, 20 percent reported that absolutely no action was taken even when mistakes that resulted in bad loans were discovered; 46 percent said "no efforts are made to uncover bad loans, so people [responsible for making bad loans] are not held accountable."[105] Researchers have documented systematic looting and abuse by insiders in the banking sector in the 1980s and 1990s.[106] A large number of senior bank executives, including the presidents of BOC and CCB, have been jailed for corruption. In 2003 and 2004, four of the five most senior executives of BOC's Hong Kong subsidiary, including its president, Liu Jinbao, were arrested on corruption charges. Government investigators found that the funds Liu stole from the bank, as well as the bribes he had accepted, exceeded 41 million yuan.[107] In the worst case of insider looting, managers at a BOC branch in Kaiping, Guangdong, stole $483 million from 1997 to 2002.[108]

The amount of money involved in uncovered corruption cases in the banking system has often been staggering. Audits conducted by the National Audit Administration in 1999 uncovered 400 billion yuan in misused funds at 4,600 branches of the ICBC and 1,700 branches of the CCB.[109] A separate audit of the Agricultural Development Bank (ADB) in 2001 revealed that between 1995 and 2000, the head office of the ADB used illegal means to siphon off 57 million yuan to cover questionable administrative expenses. In addition, from 1996 to 1999, the ADB illegally appropriated 800 million yuan in stock speculation, with profits pocketed by the insiders. In its audit of the Guangzhou branch of the CCB in 2002, the National Audit Administration found pervasive corrupt practices and irregularities, such as the concealment of income, fraudulent accounting, hidden slush funds, and fraudulent issuance of loans.[110] Poor governance, corruption, and irregularities appear to have contributed to the issuance of a large number of risky loans, particularly to real estate developers. In its inspection of bank loans in 2002, PBOC found that, of the 146.8 billion yuan in real estate loans issued by banks from June 2001 to September 2002, two thousand loans worth 35 billion yuan (25 percent of the total amount reviewed) were made in violation of regulations.[111]

A landmark study by two of China's leading financial economists in 2002–2003 documented the magnitude of corruption in China's banking system. The director of research at the PBOC, Xie Ping, and his colleague, Lu Lei, surveyed 3,561 bank employees, enterprise managers, farmers, and private entrepreneurs in twenty-nine cities in 2002.[112] In response to their question on whether "financial institutions use their power of credit/capital allocation to engage in corrupt transactions," 37 percent of the respondents thought such a practice was "prevalent" and an additional 45.2 percent believe it was "quite often." Forty-five percent also said that they must "give some goodies" as "extra costs of obtaining credit."[113] On average, firms had to pay bribes equal to 3.9 percent of the loan amount to obtain bank credit and offer an additional 4.9 percent in maintaining relationships with the banks. For individual farmers, they must pay 5.9 percent of the loan amount to get credit and 2.9 percent to keep the relationship.

It is worth noting that the extra costs of borrowing (bribery) for firms were exactly identical to those paid by individual farmers—8.8 percent of the loan amount to get credit and maintain access to bank lending. Levied on top of the nominal official rates, this "bribery premium" of 8.8 percent brought real interest rates of loans from banks close to the rates on the private credit market (the curb market rate was about 10 percent above the official rate). This implies that the true cost of credit was high for Chinese firms and farmers, even though bank insiders captured the difference—tens of billions of yuan every year.[114] Indeed, the same survey of bank employees showed that "the authority to make loans" and the "relationship with clients," not performance, determined the level of income of bank employees. As a result, top bank managers and loan officers had the highest income. Respondents to the survey estimated that the hidden income of bank managers likely comprised 48 percent of their aggregate individual income; for loan officers, the figure was perhaps 31 percent.[115]

Analysis

In retrospect, the Chinese government's belated, costly, and largely unsuccessful attempt to reform the banking sector should not be surprising. Like grain procurement and telecom services, banking is one of the "commanding heights" that the government cannot afford to abandon. Indeed, given the crucial importance of the banking sector's role in allocating capital, which is one of the scarcest resources in developing countries, this sector is even more important to maintain the CCP's ability to protect its patronage system and base of support. With 1.7 million employees, 150,000 branches nationwide, and, most critically, assets totaling 13 trillion yuan, no other economic organization or network could rival the power of the four SCBs in allocating resources and securing political support.[116] Indeed, it would be politically risky, even unthinkable, for the CCP to willingly cede its control of this economic artery at the early phase of the economic transition through real liberalization and destatization.

Constrained by the overriding logic of political survival, the Chinese government's strategy for reforming the banking sector has been focused on ensuring the state's control even in an overall environment of economic liberalization. Such control has been maintained by keeping out competition from domestic private actors and foreign banks and by, even among state-affiliated financial institutions, giving the four SCBs a virtual monopoly over the banking sector during the reform era. There is in this regard a striking similarity between the government's effort to protect the virtual monopoly of the SCBs and the MPT's persistent—and successful—campaign to prevent other (new) state-affiliated competitors from grabbing a significant share of the telecom services market.

An obvious explanation is bureaucratic politics: established monopolies such as the MPT (and its spin-offs such as China Telecom and China Mobile) and the four SCBs enjoy more bureaucratic clout within the regime, and they are reluctant to see their privileged positions threatened by new entrants. But this explanation does not address another puzzle. The top leadership is the ultimate arbiter in deciding the winners and losers in such bureaucratic turf wars. To the extent that the top ruling elites are aware of the aggregate benefits of improved efficiency that would flow from liberalization and competition in these sectors, they should rise above the fray and favor more liberalization and competition. Why did the top leadership side with the existing monopolies?

A plausible answer is that the introduction of new entrants, even state-affiliated, would likely produce an organizational shock to the existing patronage system and threaten to disrupt the CCP's ability to allocate critical resources. It is worth noting that the CCP itself has a highly centralized structure of power. Ideally, a centralized political structure is best served by a centralized economic decision-making structure. In the Chinese context, even creating competition without real destatization would lead to more economic decentralization. Even though two of the hallmarks of China's gradual reform were fiscal and administrative decentralization, it is worth noting that Beijing conceded its control over fiscal policy gradually and reluctantly, and, starting in 1994, began to recentralize the fiscal system.

Ironically, the central authorities' concessions on fiscal decentralization guarantee that they will maintain centralized control over credit allocation as a vital means of regime survival. In the context of declining on-budget fiscal revenues and rapidly increasing household deposits in the banking system, controlling the banking sector makes much more sense for the central authorities. Decentralizing the banking system following fiscal decentralization, even among new state-affiliated actors, would definitely undermine the central control of credit allocation, with potentially severe political repercussions.

Yet, the paradox of rent protection at the sector level and rent dissipation by insiders means that it is also very costly to maintain an unreformed banking system. Eventually, the combined effects of sectoral inefficiency and rent dissipation would threaten the stability of the entire financial system and demand government action. In China's case, the government was forced to introduce gradual reforms to slow the deterioration in the banking sector. In the early 1990s, as the SOEs' financial performance worsened dramatically, action was urgently required. In addition, the overheating in 1992–1993, blamed mainly on the government's loss of control over bank credit, and the effective takeover of economic policy-making by a reformist leader, Vice Premier Zhu Rongji, precipitated the reform measures adopted in 1994–1995.

But these incremental reforms have made marginal improvements at best. With the exception of the strengthening of the central bank, these reforms have not improved competition or transformed the SCBs into real commercial banks. Indeed, none of the reforms adopted were intended to end the state's monopoly of credit allocation, and indirectly threaten the regime's ability to distribute rents. The results of such partial reforms have been all too predictable: the banking system has remained under the control of the state and retains its vital function as a conduit of politically directed credit, and the deterioration of assets has accelerated. Less than a decade after these partial reforms, the government was forced to dip into its last cash reserves—the country's foreign exchange reserve—to shore up the fragile banking system. Revealingly, the bank bail-out package unveiled in early 2004 gave no sign that the government would relinquish its control over the banking sector. Even after capital injection, corporatization, and stock market listing, the state will retain its majority ownership in the restructured former SCBs. Domestic private entrants still face high hurdles. Even China's entry into the WTO would have a modest impact on reducing barriers to the entry of foreign banks into the Chinese market.[117] In other words, despite the huge economic costs, the government seems as determined as ever to defend the sector to which the CCP's own security has been inextricably linked.

The Economic Costs of Gradualism

In evaluating gradualism, its proponents tend to overlook and downplay the accumulated costs of partial reforms and reversals and the impact of such reversals on the overall reform process. In the Chinese case, such partial reforms and reversals, two steps forward and one step back, have been the hallmarks of most top-down reforms. When looked at individually and within the political context at the time of adoption, these partial reforms might appear to be positive, albeit small, steps forward. Although their costs, both in terms of residual rents and opportunity costs, were recognized, they were judged to be outweighed by potential gains from the adoption of reform. And in fact, on balance, incremental reform has been better than no reform. However, economic reform is path-dependent: bad initial partial reforms lock decision makers into a certain path and constrain their future choices with the mounting costs of reversing mistakes. Flawed reform measures have high reversal costs not only in terms of opposition from vested interests, but also in terms of reputation loss for reformers. Indeed, reformers cannot afford to suffer such reputation losses too often if they wish to sustain political support.

In addition, the gains from such partial reforms frequently turned out to be considerably smaller than expected or even nonexistent altogether, while costs were huge or exceeded expectations. It is easy to assume that an incremental reform step would be "Pareto positive" or efficiency-enhancing. What is not sufficiently recognized, however, is that each incremental reform step is a carefully negotiated policy move and embodies compromises that permit continuation of economic inefficiency. Under the right circumstances, partial reforms may produce more efficiency gains. But because residual inefficiencies are politically protected, it is equally likely that the costs of maintaining such residual inefficiencies may be high or even exceed any efficiency gains from partial reforms.

The best example is perhaps China's introduction of the so-called contract system in the 1980s in reforming its SOEs. Based on the model of the rural household responsibility system, this measure was initially thought to be capable of giving SOE managers new incentives to improve the performance of their firms with specific targets and more managerial autonomy—without touching the sensitive ownership issue. But the net result of this measure was asset-stripping and long-term deterioration. Insiders in SOEs improved short-term performance to maximize their pay at the cost of deteriorating balance sheets and asset quality. The reform was unceremoniously abandoned in the early 1990s.[118]

How Marketized Is the Chinese Economy?

The degree to which market forces determine economic activities in a transition economy is an important measure of the success of reform, regardless of the mode of transition. In assessing the achievements of China's gradualist approach, a crucial yardstick is the degree of marketization of the economy. Unfortunately, marketization is, at most, a subjective measurement. Estimates reached by Chinese scholars show that, at an aggregate level, the marketization of China's economy in the late 1990s was about 50 percent, implying that the transition was perhaps only half-complete.[119] There are enormous variations across regions and sectors, however. According to an official report, the level of marketization is higher for commodities and lower for factor inputs. The financial sector is the least marketized. Coastal areas in the east are more marketized than the western regions.[120] In this section, we will use a variety of economic indicators to assess the degree of marketization in China twenty-five years after the introduction of gradualist economic reform.

SOEs' Share of Economic Output and Employment

To the extent that direct ownership of firms allows the state to control or influence economic activities, the share of economic output from SOEs should be an important measure of marketization. The higher this share, the lower the degree of marketization, and vice versa. By this measurement, the Chinese economy can be said to have been significantly marketized. Official figures indicate, for example, that SOEs (including firms controlled by the state through majority holding) accounted for 44 percent of the gross industrial output in 2001, a decline of 20 percent from 1985.[121] Employment in SOEs has experienced a drop of similar magnitude. In 1985, employees in SOEs accounted for 68 percent of the industrial labor force; by 2001, the figure was down to 48 percent.[122] Taken together, however, these aggregate data suggest that, despite dramatic progress in marketization, the state retains an important presence in China's most important economic sectors. In particular, the state has maintained its monopoly or near-monopoly in several key sectors, such as telecom, banking, energy, power generation, civil aviation, and rail transportation. The control over these important sectors allows the government to have an ability to influence economic activities—and distort the market—that is perhaps far greater than its share of total economic output would indicate.

The State's Influence in Commodities and Factor Markets

Most economists agree that China's commodities markets have been more fully liberalized than its factor markets. The percentage of prices for commodities set by the state has fallen significantly. At the beginning of reform, in terms of aggregate value, the state set the prices for 93 percent of agricultural products, 100 percent of industrial production materials, and 97 percent of retail commodities.[123] In the mid-1990s, according to Thomas Rawski, market forces determined the prices of 93 percent of retail commodities, 79 percent of agricultural products, and 81 percent of production materials.[124] An official Chinese government research report claimed that in 2000, the prices of 90 percent of agricultural products and 86 percent of production materials were set by the market.[125] But these numbers may have greatly understated the government's effective control in setting prices. One Chinese economist argued that the government's ability to set prices for coal, steel, railroad transportation, crude oil, electricity, and other goods and services gave it enormous influence. As a result, only about 60 percent of the prices in China in the mid-1990s were fully set by the market.[126]

In the factor markets, the state has maintained considerable control. By one estimate, the level of marketization in the labor market was below 30 percent in the mid-1990s because of the government-imposed restrictions on the labor market, especially on the flow of rural labor into the cities.[127] But two other estimates suggested a higher level of marketization (in the range of 65 to 70 percent).[128] The state continues to dominate the real estate market, mainly through its ownership of land and restrictions on land transfers. Similarly, the market for corporate control has not fully emerged in China as a result of government limits on transfers of ownership rights. China's progress in developing a market for technologies has been very slow due to the weak protection of intellectual property rights.[129]

Without doubt, the financial sector remains the least marketized. Even the State Planning Commission admitted in its own assessment in the mid-1990s that the level of marketization in the financial sector was only 28 percent.[130] Rawski's study also confirms that China's capital market is least liberalized. Such conclusions are not surprising, given the government's direct ownership of the largest banking and other financial institutions and its tight control over access to capital. The distorting effects of low marketization on economic activities seem to be very large. Rawski argues that the government's control over investment is responsible for a pattern of macroeconomic behavior indicative of a command economy, instead of a market economy. His study of the seasonable fluctuations of the Chinese economy shows that its quarterly performance is erratic and volatile, with huge growth registered in the fourth quarter and large declines occurring in the first. Because growth in China is largely investment driven and the government maintains control of most investment capital, Rawski believes that such fluctuation is evidence of the government's strong influence in the economy.[131]

The degree of marketization also varies significantly across regions. Estimates by Chinese economists suggest, for example, that the most marketized regions scored three to four times higher than the least marketized regions on a range of indexes approximating progress in moving toward a market economy.[132] A study led by Fan Gang shows that, in 2000, Guangdong was ranked as the most marketized province (scoring 8.41 on a 0–10 scale); it was followed by Zhejiang (8.32), Fujian (8.10), Jiangsu (7.90), and Shandong (7.15). By comparison, the least marketized five regions were Xinjiang (3.15), Qinghai (3.40), Ningxia (4.02), Shaanxi (4.15), and Shanxi (4.53).[133] The results of this study reconfirm conclusions reached by previous, albeit less rigorous, analyses that demonstrated that coastal provinces were more marketized than central agrarian provinces, which were, in turn, more marketized than the western region.[134]

Fragmentation of Domestic Markets

One of the most serious criticisms of China's progress in economic reform concerns the persistent fragmentation and distortion of the country's internal markets. Chinese and foreign observers alike attribute such fragmentation and distortion to so-called local protectionism—administrative barriers to trade and investment that are erected by local authorities. Among the various factors blamed for the emergence of local protectionism in the postreform period (some scholars argue that this phenomenon did not exist in the prereform era), analysts have singled out administrative decentralization and China's unique form of fiscal federalism, which allows local governments to profit directly from the earnings of the firms through taxation.[135] In many ways, local protectionism has been further exacerbated by a weak and balkanized legal system that permits local political authorities to pressure courts in their jurisdictions to favor local firms. Consequently, judgments against firms located in other jurisdictions can rarely be enforced and collected because of obstruction by the local authorities. An investigation of Heilongjiang province courts conducted by the Chinese People's Political Consultative Conference showed, for instance, that local authorities issued specific instructions to the courts to protect sixty-seven firms that appeared to be losing their cases. The authorities explicitly told the courts not to render or enforce unfavorable judgments against these firms.[136]

Empirical analysis by Alwyn Young also demonstrates that the devolution of economic power to local governments during China's economic transition is responsible for both the fragmentation of markets and the rising output growth. To the extent that localities are better suited to control the local economy than the central government, aggregate output will increase because of decentralization and not because of the abandonment of control. The fragmentation of markets in China is evident in massive industrial duplication, inefficient allocation of factor inputs, local trade wars, and the emergence of regional autarky.[137] Research by other economists provides additional evidence of inefficiencies attributable to the fragmentation of markets. One study shows that economic inefficiency caused by irrational allocation of resources on an interprovincial basis began to worsen in the mid-1980s and saw no improvement in the 1990s, largely as a result of the fragmentation of markets.[138]

Specifically, the fragmentation of markets affects both the product and factor markets. In the product market, local governments erect barriers to entry of products made in other localities and exports of raw materials. They typically employ a variety of legal and illegal methods, such as quantitative restrictions, regulatory hurdles (health and trademark inspections), and imposition of fees (equivalent to local tariffs). For example, eighteen provinces have regulations that bar or limit the sale of alcohol produced in other provinces.[139] Another striking example of the use of fees to protect local producers is in the automobile sector. Customers who purchase automobiles made in other areas are required to pay additional costs for vehicle registration and inspection. In 1998, the total amount of fees levied on vehicles was 160 billion yuan, about half of which was judged unauthorized or illegal. In the meantime, the automobile industry made only 4 billion yuan in profits in the same year.[140] There is evidence that links market fragmentation with slow growth in interregional trade. From 1985 to 1992, China's exports and imports grew, respectively, 17 and 10 percent annually, but interprovincial trade grew only 4.8 percent a year in the same period— despite annual retail sales growth of 9 percent per year in the same period.[141]

Fragmentation also affects the factor markets. An IMF study suggests that China's capital markets remain highly fragmented. Cross-regional capital mobility within China in the 1990s was comparable to the cross-national capital mobility in developed market economies.[142] In the labor market, local governments protect their local residents from competition posed by migrants by forcing firms to favor local residents in their hiring and by increasing the costs for migrants seeking employment through the imposition of fees, the requirement of residence permits, and the need for certifications of skills. China's internal capital markets are fragmented as well because local political interference has impeded the flow of domestic capital and transfer of corporate control. Local authorities habitually limit outflow of local capital and restrict investment by nonlocal firms and their acquisition of local firms.[143]

Chinese enterprise managers report widespread practices of local protectionism. A survey of 3,539 enterprise managers nationwide conducted by the official Development Research Center in 2002 showed that local protectionism was prevalent in all provinces. Respondents singled out Henan, Shanghai, and Beijing as jurisdictions with the most discriminatory policies against nonlocal firms, followed by Hubei, Shandong, Hebei, and Hunan. Local protectionism was found to have no relationship with the level of economic development—the poorer agrarian provinces in the central region were as guilty as the more industrialized coastal provinces. The survey also found that local protectionism was costly for Chinese firms. Thirty-four percent of the managers reported that such practices affected their operations "a great deal or quite significantly," and 35 percent reported a "fair impact." Only a third said such practices had small or negligible impact. Local protectionism appeared to hurt the firms in the poorer western and central provinces more than those in the more prosperous coastal regions, except for firms in Shanghai, Beijing, and Shandong. Among various industrial sectors, the most seriously affected were tobacco, pharmaceuticals, petroleum refining, printing, food processing, plastics, and electrical machinery. The least affected were textiles and garments, synthetic fibers, and electronic communications equipment. Ironically, SOEs, which relied on other provinces for markets and raw materials, were more negatively affected than private firms, which were small in size and did little business in other localities. The least affected were foreign-invested (including Hong Kong and Taiwan) firms, apparently because such firms relied more on the international market for exports and imports.[144]

The fragmentation of local markets creates large distortions and inefficiencies, especially when local governments engage in investment activities that duplicate manufacturing capacities and generate negative returns. An analysis of regional industrial structures shows that duplication of capacity remains a core feature of the fragmentation of internal markets in China. For example, in 1989, the industrial structure of twenty-two provinces was 90 percent identical to that of China as a whole. In 1994, the industrial structure was 90 percent identical in thirteen provinces and 80 percent identical in twenty-one. Such data suggest massive duplication of industrial capacities regardless of local comparative advantages. This characteristic persisted through the 1990s, as most provinces continued to build up their own capacities to chase new demands. In 2001, twenty-three provinces manufactured washing machines, twenty-nine made television sets, twenty-three produced refrigerators, and twenty-seven assembled automobiles. Without changing the underlying incentives for local governments, duplication of capacity will remain a structural feature of the Chinese economy. In envisioning their long-term industrial goals, twenty-two provinces listed automobile manufacturing as a pillar industry, twenty-four listed electronics as a pillar industry, sixteen listed machine-building and the chemical industry as a pillar industry, and fourteen listed metallurgy as a pillar industry.[145]

Duplication has led to low capacity utilization. In 1996, textile and oil refining industries operated only at 70 percent of capacity. The utilization rate was 60 percent in the machine-tool, copper processing, tobacco, and alcohol spirits sectors, and 30–50 percent in the home appliances sector (televisions, refrigerators, and washing machines). Of the ninety-four major categories of industrial products, there was excess capacity in sixty-one, and the capacity utilization rate was below 50 percent in thirty-five of them.[146]

Official data also show a close connection between duplication of capacity and loss of economies of scale. Take the most notorious example of full-assembly automobile plants: China had 116 such plants in 1996, with average annual output of 12,600 per plant. Only 18 were making more than 10,000 per year. There were about 6,000 paper mills in the late 1990s, with an average capacity of 4,000 tons per plant (less than a tenth of the international average). Of the country's 800 beer breweries, only one-tenth reached the minimum capacity of 50,000 tons.[147]

Another indicator of low economies of scale is China's low concentration ratio, that is, the market share claimed by the largest firms in a country. More fragmented markets typically have lower ratios, implying a lack of economies of scale. In the Chinese case, official figures indicate that this ratio has been unusually low, compared with both developed and developing economies.[148] In 1985, the concentration ratio for the largest one hundred industrial firms in various sectors averaged 14 percent; in 1990, the concentration ratio fell to 12 percent; in 1995, it rose slightly to 16 percent.[149] Among the thirty-nine major industrial sectors in the mid-1990s, the largest eight firms in each sector accounted for less than 10 percent of the market share (measured by sales) in eighteen of them (these included paper, timber, and beverages). Econometric analysis performed by Chinese researchers showed that low concentration was responsible for the slow technological progress in Chinese firms.[150]

International Comparisons

Although it was the first to launch reform among state-socialist economies, China's slow progress toward building a market economy is evident. A World Bank study published in 1996 showed that China's economic liberalization lagged behind that of former state-socialist economies in Eastern Europe that had adopted radical reforms (Poland, Slovenia, Hungary, Croatia, the Czech Republic, and the Slovak Republic). For this group, the average liberalization index was 6.9, compared to China's 5.5.[151] International comparative data in 2001 further showed that, if anything, the gap in economic liberalization between China and the same Eastern European countries had remained virtually unchanged. According to an index of economic freedom compiled by the Fraser Institute, China lags behind Croatia, the Czech

Republic, Estonia, Hungary, Latvia, Lithuania, Poland, and the Slovak Republic, but is comparable to other laggards in economic reform, such as Russia, Ukraine, Albania, Bulgaria, and Romania. China's economic liberalization also falls behind that of other large developing countries, such as India, Mexico, South Africa, the Philippines, and Brazil.[152]

The above case studies and analysis of China's progress in marketizing its economy indicate that, despite the enormous gains in output achieved under gradualist reforms since 1979, the hidden costs of this approach are huge and understated. Of course, politically it has been a brilliant success for the CCP because gradualism has delivered all the expected political dividends: it has given the party a new lease on life, helped maintain its patronage system, and even provided it with more means to hold on to its power. But economically, a quarter century of gradualist reform has only modestly raised the efficiency in some of China's most important economic sectors. Instead, important sectors such as grain procurement and banking have become weaker, not stronger. Consequently, two factors threaten the sustainability of gradualist reform. First, the massive build-up of financial deficits in these sectors (all remain under state control) has greatly raised the systemic risks in the economy as a whole. Second, as dependent as ever on its control of the patronage provided by these critical sectors (even as the financial conditions in these sectors progressively deteriorate), the ruling elites have likely become even more risk-averse, taking half-hearted short-term measures but shying away from decisive reforms. As it happened with other gradualist reform experiences in the former Soviet bloc countries, reform will ultimately lose momentum as it grows, both politically and economically, more difficult and risky.

FOUR

Transforming the State:
From Developmental to Predatory

IN THE THEORETICAL discussion on decentralized predatory states, I argued that the nature of the Chinese state has undergone a critical transformation during the reform era and, consequently, a decentralized predatory state has emerged. In this chapter, I apply the analytical framework developed in Chapter 1 to explain why such a state has emerged in China during its economic transition.[1] It concludes with a description of the rise of the most extreme form of decentralized predatory state: the local mafia states.

The Institutional Dynamics of Decentralized Predation

The underlying causes of the decentralization of state predation can be traced to four institutional factors: the decentralization of property rights, the declining monitoring capability, the availability of new exit options, and the erosion of ideological norms. I now discuss in detail how changes in these institutional variables have transformed the Chinese state into a decentralized predatory state since the late 1970s.

Corruption and Decentralization of Predation

The decentralized predatory state perspective provides a useful analytical tool for understanding corruption. In the centralized predatory state, corruption tends to be centralized as well, with the regime's top leaders being the most corrupt figures and gaining a large share of the looted wealth. In a decentralized predatory state, however, corruption is also decentralized. Viewed from this perspective, the emergence of a decentralized predatory state in China should be examined in the context of the decentralization of corruption that have occurred in China since 1978. The rising level and scope of corruption have been extensively studied and documented. Compared with the prereform era, post-1978 corruption is notable not only because of its rapid growth, but also because of its decentralized characteristics, as corrupt activities permeate nearly all public sectors and all levels of the state.[2] Results from public opinion polls, which consistently show that official corruption had become one of the top three issues regarded as "of great concern" by the Chinese public in the 1990s, appear to support this view.[3] There were few reliable estimates of the level and scope of corruption, however.

Out of fear of losing legitimacy or revealing its ineffectiveness in fighting corruption, the Chinese government does not provide systematic data on official corruption. Nevertheless, official reports on the growth of the number of corruption cases investigated and prosecuted by antigraft agencies and courts may provide some clues on the extent of corruption. The number of cases investigated by various anticorruption agencies grew at an annual rate of 9 percent from 1993 to 1999, and the number of individuals investigated by these agencies in the same period grew at an annual rate of 12 percent.[4] In addition, if the number of people accused of corruption is used as an indicator of the *scope* of corruption, and the amount of money involved in corrupt activities is regarded as a measurement of the *level* of corruption, then official data would indicate a consistent increase in both the scope and the level of corruption (Table 4.1). The share of corruption cases characterized as "large" (involving large sums of money) doubled from 1990 to 2002, suggesting that the level of corruption, as measured by the amount of money involved, rose at least twofold in twelve years (after adjusting for inflation).

Table 4.1 shows that the scope of corruption (the type of officials involved) has expanded greatly. Compared with the early 1990s, when high-ranking officials (at county level or above, according to the official definition) were implicated in about 2 percent of all cases, the share of prosecuted corruption cases involving high-ranking officials rose threefold in a twelve-year period. The number of high-ranking

Table 4.1. Increase in Major Corruption Cases, 1990–2002[a]

Year	Share of Large-sum Corruption Cases (percent)	Share of Cases Involving High-ranking Officials (percent)	Number of High-ranking Officials Prosecuted
1990	22.7	1.7	1,386
1992	40.6	1.0	652
1994	47.5	2.6	1,768
1996	57.1	3.6	2,461
1997	68.3	3.8	2,222
1998	31.7	4.9	1,674
1999	34.0	5.7	2,200
2002	42.8	6.1	2,925

Sources: ZGFLNJ, various years.

[a] Cases involving large sums of money, called da an, are defined as those in which the sums of embezzlement and bribes exceeded 10,000 yuan; this sum was raised to 50,000 yuan in 1998. Cases involving high-ranking officials, called yao an, are defined as those in which government officials at or above the county (xian) or department (chu) level are implicated.

officials prosecuted annually more than doubled during the same period. The effects of corruption perpetrated by high-ranking officials are far more insidious than that by junior officials. Obviously, because high-ranking officials serve as agents monitoring the behavior of junior agents, corrupt high-ranking officials can hardly be relied on to perform this function effectively. Worse still, their venal habits are likely to inspire their subordinates to engage in similar corrupt activities, thus multiplying the effects of corruption.

The phenomenon of a corrupt top local official, or yibashou (number-one leader), merits special attention. According to the decentralized predatory state perspective, predation becomes effectively decentralized when local strongmen choose to appropriate to themselves the power of higher public authorities and monopolize the extraction of revenues, even though such action is illegal. To be sure, few Chinese yibashous could formally appropriate the state's fiscal power, but their nearly unchallenged political authority inside their jurisdictions—and their abuse of such authority—grant them probably most of the prerogatives of an independent political monopolist. During the 1980s, domineering and corrupt *yibashous* were relatively rare. But since the early 1990s, the power of *yibashous* has expanded considerably, mainly because the CCP failed to implement reforms to make the party itself more democratic. In a survey of 11,586 party members in Sichuan province in 1999, one-third said that their local party bosses monopolized decision making.[5] The concentration of power in local strongmen has led to a rapid increase in the number of corrupt *yibashous*. From 1993 to 2003 in Henan province, for instance, the provincial procuratorate investigated and punished 4,123 *yibashous* for corruption, accounting for 12 percent of all the embezzlement and bribery cases prosecuted in the period. About 40 percent of these corrupt *yibashous* were chief executives of SOEs, and 30 percent were grassroots-level rural cadres. Such local and departmental independent monopolists appeared to have grown more rapacious as well. In Henan province, *yibashous* were implicated in 52 percent of the *daans* (major corruption cases measured in terms of money involved) in 1999; in 2003, they were involved in 75 percent of the *daans*.[6] In the infamous Shenyang case, 17 *yibashous*, including the mayor and the heads of the city's intermediate court, procuratorate, construction commission, finance bureau, state asset bureau, tax bureau, and price bureau, were convicted of corrupt activities, including protecting a local mafia boss.[7]

The Growing Size of the Chinese State

The size of the state is the primary determinant of the degree of state predation. Larger states require more revenue for self-sustenance. As a rule, larger states are expected to have higher levels of corruption because they employ more agents and thus have more serious agency problems (it is more difficult to monitor and police large numbers of agents). Estimating the size of the Chinese state, however, presents a difficult challenge for two reasons. First, the official data regarding the number of state employees are hardly reliable and tend to underreport their numbers. Second, the true costs of maintaining the Chinese state are almost impossible to measure.

One of the ways to measure the size of the state is to count the number of agents employed by the state. By this standard, the Chinese state is large in absolute terms and has been growing rapidly in the reform era despite the government's repeated downsizing efforts.[8] Official data show that the Chinese state, when measured by the number of officials and employees in government agencies (excluding teachers and those working in nonprofit government institutions such as hospitals), had an average annual growth rate of 1.8 percent from 1953 to 1978. But from 1979 to 1990, the rate was 6.7 percent—more than three times higher than the rate prior to reform.[9]

Because of the lack of a uniform standard of classifying state agents and the routine underreporting of personnel employed by the state at various levels, however, there are few authoritative estimates. At the high end of the estimated range, China appears to have had more than 40 million cadres in 2000.[10] Official figures report that, excluding doctors and teachers, the number of employees in government agencies, CCP organizations, and other state-affiliated social organizations was 10.75 million in 2002, more than double the figure in 1978.[11] The official data probably underreport the number of state agents. It is very likely that the true size of the Chinese state is much larger because local government officials routinely underreport the number of their employees to conceal the problem of overstaffing.

In 1990, for example, the data released by the most authoritative agency, the Office of the Central Government's Staffing Commission (*zhongyang bianzhi weiyuanhui*), indicated that the number of excess personnel at various levels of the state was 55 percent larger than that authorized by the government (Table 4.2).[12] If anything, overstaffing may have become worse during the 1990s because the government has not been able to streamline its operations. It is worth noting that the pattern of overstaffing is illustrative of the characteristics of a decentralized predatory state. In the Chinese case, overstaffing is most serious at the lowest level of the Chinese state—district and township governments. While the number of excess personnel at the higher levels of government (except for prefecture government) was, on average, 15 percent higher than the authorized limit, the number of excess personnel in district and township governments was 157 percent higher than the authorized limit in 1990. In fact, excess personnel in district and township governments accounted for about 80 percent of all the excess personnel in the Chinese state that year.

The actual size of the Chinese state, especially at the local level, may be even larger than the official figures indicate. For example, most local governments have used the practice of *yigong daigan* (substitute cadres) to keep excess personnel on the payroll. In 1991, 6 million

Table 4.2. Excess Personnel in Party and Government Agencies in 1990
(in 1,000)[a]

Levels of Government	Number of Officials and Employees Authorized	Actual Number of Officials and Employees	Excess Number of Officials and Employees	Excess Rate (%)
Provincial	269	315	46	17.3
Prefect	147	197	50	34.0
Municipal	1,380	1,610	230	16.7
County	1,710	1,940	230	13.4
Township and District	1,362	3,500	2,140	157.1
Total	4,868	7,562	2,694	55.3

Sources: Zhongyang jigou bianzhi weiyuanhui bangongshi (Office of the Central Government's Staffing Commission), Zhongguo xingzheng gaige da qushi (Major Trends in China's Administrative Reform) (Beijing: Jingji kexue chubanshe, 1993), 247, 411. Ren Xiao, *Zhongguo xingzheng gaige (Administrative Reform in China)* (Hangzhou: Zhejiang renmin chubanshe, 1998), 242.
[a] These figures do not include police and judicial personnel.

government officials were employed under this classification.[13] Unlike cadres employed in the official nomenclatural system, substitute cadres work as government officials but do not have formal official ranks. They are not included in the employment data for government officials. If these substitute cadres are included in the estimate of the size of the Chinese state in 1991, the number of people employed in provincial and local governments was about 13.5 million (excluding teachers, doctors, judges, and police officers). The actual size of the Chinese state, below the level of the central government, was thus about 180 percent larger than the authorized limit.

With rising overstaffing, the costs of maintaining the Chinese state have been growing in both absolute and relative terms since the late 1970s. As a share of the national budget, administrative costs jumped from 5.3 percent in 1978 to 18.6 percent in 2002.[14] In absolute terms, administrative outlays grew seventy-six times in twenty-four years, or averaging 318 percent a year (unadjusted for inflation). In the same period, by comparison, budget revenues rose 65 percent each year (unadjusted for inflation). Administrative expenditures outpaced overall budget revenues by 11 percent annually.[15] During the same period, personnel costs within the administrative budget also rose in relative terms. In 1978, salary costs for personnel working in various government agencies (including the Communist Party) accounted for about 55 percent of the total administrative budgets in 1978; they amounted to 64 percent in 1998.[16] In the meantime, rising administrative costs seemed to have squeezed out public expenditures on social investments and poverty-relief programs. For example, government spending on the agricultural sector in 1978 was 13.4 percent of the budget; in 2001, it fell to 7.7 percent. Research and development spending decreased from 4.7 to 3.7 percent of the budget from 1978 to 2002.[17]

Given the underreporting of the number of people employed in the various bureaucracies of the state, the actual costs of maintaining the Chinese state could be much larger than the official data would suggest. Based on the data collected from various sources, the real costs of the Chinese state should include both the budget's administrative costs and the off-budget administrative costs incurred by excess personnel.

Anecdotal evidence gathered from official sources shows that it is very costly to maintain a government official (salary, benefits, and office expenses). According to a Ministry of Finance analysis of administrative expenditures in 1990, the staffing costs for each government official employed in the state's administrative agencies were 5,000 yuan a year, about 2,900 yuan more than the salary for an average government employee in the same year.[18] Another estimate, made in the mid-1990s, raised such costs to a much higher level. An analyst at the Ministry of Finance wrote that by the end of 1996, each additional employee in the administrative apparatus of the state would increase annual administrative outlays by 10,000 yuan to 20,000 yuan in compensation, and 10,000 yuan in office expenses, housing, and benefits.[19] These outlays apparently did not include the costs of entertainment and various hidden perks for government officials. At the aggregate level, it is impossible to calculate the costs of entertainment and official junkets. Because government policy formally prohibits lavish spending on such activities, local governments normally pay for such expenses using funds allocated for other spending items (such as capital investment, education, health, and even poverty relief). In many instances, such expenses are not even reported when local government officials use their own slush funds accumulated through the collection of various—often illegal—levies and fees.[20]

Overstaffing drives local authorities to raise additional off-budget revenues through fees and hidden taxes, many of which are declared illegal by the central government. Disclosures by official Chinese sources indicate that local authorities control a significant amount of illegally collected revenues. One estimate showed such revenues totaled about 10 percent of GDP in the 1990s.[21] Such an extractive capacity has helped the Chinese local state to support its bloated staff. Indeed, the annual growth rate of administrative expenditures in the government's off-budget account was, on average, 122 percent per annum between 1982 and 1992 (a period during which a uniform accounting standard was applied to off-budget revenues). This rate was more than 30 percent higher than the rate of growth of administrative expenditures in the official budget during the same period. This evidence establishes the link between the growth of the size of the state and the increase in off-budget revenues.[22] Besides aggregate data, local reports also confirm the practice of using off-budget revenues to support excess state personnel.[23]

Decentralization of Property Rights

A salient feature of China's economic reform is the decentralization of control rights (over the cash flow from operations of state-owned assets) from the national authorities to provincial/local authorities. Intended as an incentive to improve the efficiency of these assets, the decentralization of control rights fundamentally changed the system of property rights in China. To be sure, the process of the decentralization of control rights was gradual. In 1984, the central government decided that the control rights of SOEs were to be delegated from the ministries and provincial authorities to major industrial cities where SOEs were located. Such control rights included, most critically, the rights to determine wages, benefits, and bonuses, as well as the use of capital, thus making local governments and SOE managers effective owners of these assets. The central government, however, retained its control rights over large SOEs in critical sectors, such as power generation, telecom, petrochemical industries, machine tools, and coal production.

Within a decade, the central government exercised effective control rights over only 5.4 percent of all the SOEs in terms of number (although these large SOEs generated 34.8 percent of China's industrial output).[24] Decentralization of control rights contributed to decentralized predation through several channels. It created more opportunities for local officials and SOE managers to appropriate the rents created by local monopolies and other political intervention. Indirectly, the presence of these assets with decentralized control rights would attract local predators, such as various government regulators and tax collectors, who used to be kept away by the political power of the central government. Because SOE managers now in control of these assets were politically less powerful than these local state agents, the latter could demand various illicit payments from SOEs without fear of political retribution, thus joining the looting of public wealth (the liabilities of SOEs were ultimately assumed by Chinese taxpayers).

The trend of decentralization of property rights accelerated in the 1990s as the Chinese state further delegated the power to manage the state's most important asset—land. In the short term, the power to sell long-term land leases allowed a large number of state agents, mostly at the local level, to profit from sweetheart deals made with their friends. These deals resulted in the one-time loss of an incalculable amount of revenues for the state because the initial lease terms were significantly undervalued to allow the awardees to quickly make an easy and large profit.

Fiscal decentralization and predation

During the reform era, the relationship between the central government and the local governments has been fundamentally reshaped by deliberate policies and socioeconomic changes that have transferred a substantial amount of decision-making power to local governments. Theoretically speaking, the decentralization of decision-making authority from higher to lower levels of the state can be considered as part of the decentralization of property rights. Among such changes, fiscal decentralization—the transfer of revenue-raising power from Beijing to the provinces—is a near-perfect example of the decentralization of the state's property rights, as it grants public authorities at lower levels a greater share of the revenue flows from the central state's income streams.[25]

The dramatic shift in the relative revenue-collecting capacities of the central and local governments is an important piece of evidence of the decentralization of predation in post-Mao China. However, fiscal decentralization is only half the story. It may be a necessary, but not a sufficient, condition for decentralized predation. In all likelihood, *administrative decentralization*—the devolution of decision-making power concerning countless routine administrative matters—is more conducive to the emergence of a decentralized predatory state. In China's case, moreover, fiscal decentralization and administrative decentralization have jointly created powerful incentives for local authorities to adopt predatory policies and practices.

As reflected in the official data, fiscal decentralization has resulted in three profound shifts in the Chinese state's fiscal activities, and the effects of such shifts have remained only moderately changed even after the recentralization of the fiscal system in 1994.[26] First, the overall level of revenue-generation as a share of GDP has declined dramatically (Table 4.3). On paper, total government revenues, including off-budget revenues, fell from 41 percent of GDP in 1978 to about 18 percent of

Table 4.3. Government Revenues, 1978–2002[a]

Year	Budget Revenue (billion yuan)	Percent of GDP	Off-Budget Revenue (billion yuan)	Percent of GDP	Total Revenue as Percent of GDP
1978	113.2	31.2	34.7	9.6	40.8
1985	200.4	22.4	153	17.0	39.4
1990	293.7	15.8	270	14.5	30.3
1992	348	13.1	385	14.4	27.5
1994	521.8	11.2	186	4.0	15.2
1997	865	11.8	282	3.9	15.7
2000	1,339.5	15	382	2.9	17.9
2002	1,890	18	N/A	N/A	N/A

Source: ZGTJNJ 2003, 281, 288.

[a] Since extra-budgetary revenues do not include the intra-budgetary government fund (fee), the figures are not comparable to previous years; figures were also adjusted for extra-budgetary revenue in 1993–95, not comparable to previous years. Post-1993 figures understate the amount of extra-budgetary revenues.

GDP in 2000 (after bottoming out in 1994). Even if we include the government revenues not counted as budget or off-budget revenues (such revenues were estimated to be about 7.5 percent of GDP in 1995), total government revenues at the end of the 1990s would be about 25 percent of GDP, representing a 40 percent decline.[27]

Second, there has also been a dramatic shift in the relative share of the total revenues collected by the Chinese state. Official data on expenditures are a more reliable measurement of the state's fiscal capacity because a large portion of the central government's revenues was counted as local revenues prior to 1994 when such revenues were first collected by local governments and turned over to Beijing. These data document a spectacular relative decline of the central government's fiscal capacity over the last two decades. The central government's share of total public outlays fell from 47.4 percent in 1978 to 34.7 percent in 2000, while local governments' share rose from about 52.6 percent to 65.3 percent in the same period.[28]

Third, Chinese public finance—from the center to the provinces—has been completely transformed by the rapid growth of off-budget revenues (Table 4.3). Historically, off-budget revenues accounted for a relatively small portion of total government revenues. In the 1950s, for example, they were about 10 percent of budgetary revenues. In the 1960s and 1970s, they varied between 20 to 30 percent of budgetary revenues.[29] Through the 1980s and before the central government reclassified off-budget revenues in 1993 (by counting off-budget revenues as budget revenues), off-budget revenues exploded. At their peak in the early 1990s, they practically equaled budget revenues.[30]

The explosive growth of off-budget revenues per se should not be treated as the defining characteristic of decentralized predation. Rather, it is a symptom of a dysfunctional fiscal system. What makes the Chinese situation unique and more relevant to understanding decentralized predation, however, is the local governments' large share of off-budget revenues, as well as their growing dependence on and discretionary use of these revenues. Data on off-budget revenue collection indicate that more than half of the off-budget revenues (55–66 percent) went to local governments prior to 1992, when reclassification of revenue categories occurred. Under the new classification scheme adopted in 1993, nearly all off-budget revenues (75–95 percent) went into the coffers of local governments during the period of 1994–2002.[31] According to the data released by the central government for 1996 and 1997, almost all (85 percent) off-budget revenues were "income collected by administrative agencies." The share of local administrative agencies was 83 percent in this period. Thus, in the late 1990s, off-budget revenues were primarily administrative fees and levies collected by local government agencies.[32]

Off-budget revenues have become a preferred form of predation for two important reasons: discretion and opacity. Generally, off-budget and off-off-budget revenues were collected and spent at the discretion of local authorities with no central supervision. The absence of political constraints contributed to the rapacity and abusiveness with which local authorities collected these revenues, despite explicit prohibitions from the central government. In aggregate terms, such illicit off-off-budget revenues were considerable. One estimate provided by China's State Administration of Taxation claimed that they nearly equaled the budgetary revenues of the central government in the late 1990s.[33] The use of off-budget revenues was also opaque and subject to abuse. Prior to 1998, half of the off-budget revenues were spent without first being entered into specially designated fiscal accounts—accounts that would facilitate monitoring.[34] Many reports of egregious cases of corruption involved the use of off-off-budget revenue.[35] Official data reveal that off-budget revenues had become an important source of finance for the state's routine maintenance, even though such funds are supposed to be earmarked for social services and public projects. For example, about 20 percent of all off-budget expenditures were on administrative costs in the 1980s, compared to about 10 percent of budget expenditures in the same period.[36]

The behavior of local revenue collectors confirms the observation, made by Shleifer and Vishny, that independent monopolists have incentives to maximize their short-term revenues, even at the cost of lower aggregate government revenues. Indeed, decentralized predation has squeezed predation by the central state, as shown by the steady decline of the revenues collected by Beijing. It is likely responsible for a 25 percent decline of aggregate government revenue.[37] Ironically, contrary to popular belief, rising local revenues at the expense of central revenues have not improved local public finance. In fact, because a considerable (though hard to measure) portion of such revenues has been wasted or stolen, local public finance has deteriorated markedly across China. A Ministry of Finance study of local public finance in seven provinces conducted in the mid-1990s indicated that between half to three-quarters of county governments surveyed reported large fiscal deficits and had difficulty meeting government payrolls and performing routine functions of administration.[38]

Administrative Decentralization and Predation

If fiscal decentralization has provided incentives for local governments to adopt predatory policies, administrative decentralization has supplied them with the political means to create, for all practical purposes, local predatory states. In theory, administrative decentralization without political accountability creates conditions most conducive to a decentralized predatory state. In such jurisdictions, local officials who wield enormous discretionary power are poorly monitored by bureaucratic superiors and immunized from popular scrutiny and sanctions. In the case of China, however, administrative decentralization and its effects have not been fully explored because it is difficult to link measures of administrative decentralization to observed changes in local government behavior. Unlike China's well-documented fiscal decentralization that can be analyzed thoroughly with quantitative research methods, administrative decentralization does not lend itself easily to similar analysis. Nevertheless, the connection between administrative decentralization and decentralization of predation may be established by an examination of changes in the supervision of cadres and the devolution of routine economic decision making.

Supervision of cadres

Few measures of administrative decentralization affect the state's ability to control its own agents as that of the supervision of cadres. In practice, cadre supervision in the Chinese context means the recruitment, promotion, and monitoring of government officials. Since the late 1970s, the administrative power to recruit, promote, and monitor cadres has both been decentralized to lower-level officials and concentrated in the hands of local officials to whom such power has been delegated. The delegation of such power has greatly exacerbated the classical problem of information asymmetry in the supervision of state agents by their superiors, as the vertical links between superiors and subordinates in the bureaucracy have become much narrower.

Key officials—usually municipal and county CCP secretaries, or *yibashous*—have become critical nodes of information regarding the conduct of subordinate agents. This situation effectively creates local political monopolies under the control of CCP officials who are poorly supervised by their superiors. Further compounding this principal-agent problem is the repression of the media and civil society and weak horizontal accountability; the local judiciary and legislatures provide little counterbalancing power. As a result, local officials face no resistance when they adopt predatory policies within their jurisdictions. However, given the diversity in local conditions across China, the decentralization of administration has not produced uniform public policies and government practices at the local level. In some areas, mostly along the coast, this development appears not to have led to unrestrained local predation and may have contributed to more flexible and experimental reform policies that such decentralization was initially designed to encourage. In many other, and mostly inland, areas, the decentralized supervision of cadres has been responsible for a variety of misconduct by local officials, especially the illicit sale of government offices, widespread nepotism, and collusion with criminal gangs.

The practice of "selling official appointments" (*maiguan*) deserves special attention. It normally involves an underling who gives a bribe to his superior in exchange for a promotion or an appointment to a more desirable government office. Such practice was rare in the 1980s, but became prevalent in the 1990s. The spread of *maiguan* fits the logic of a decentralized predatory state well. In such a system, local strongmen become independent monopolists who can subcontract the monopoly to those who are willing to pay for a share of the spoils. Press reports of corrupt officials, usually *yibashous*, confirm this observation. In early 2004, the CCP's COD issued a public circular on four such cases. One involved Li Tiecheng, a party secretary in a county in Jilin province who took 1.43 million yuan in bribes from 110 individuals in exchange for appointments and promotions in the late 1990s. The price of each appointment averaged 13,000 yuan. Another case featured a county party boss in Liaoning province who appointed and promoted thirty officials after receiving bribes totaling 600,000 yuan (averaging 20,000 yuan per position) in the late 1990s. In the third case, a county party boss in Anhui sold appointments to fifteen individuals for an average of 20,000 yuan each in the late 1990s. The last example was a county party secretary in Hainan who sold appointments to thirteen people for an average of 49,000 yuan each.[39]

What is notable about these cases, as well as other examples of *maiguan,* is that local officials seemed to have a sophisticated understanding of the economics of decentralized predation and apparently decided to take advantage of it. By making an upfront investment in the form of a bribe, which equals to about one-year salary for an average county-level official, they can expect to recoup the investment quickly through their appointments to government positions that will allow them to extract bribes as well. In most cases, such an investment was, indeed, lucrative to these individuals, but enormously costly to the state and public.

Everyday economic decision making

Another important feature of China's economic reform is the decentralization of decision making in everyday economic activities. Such decision-making power includes that of granting business licenses, project approvals, government contracts, and land leases; allocating scarce resources (especially capital); regulating commercial activities; as well as decision-making power over the discretionary use of public funds and price control. In truth, there is nothing routine about everyday economic decision making in an economy in which the state plays a dominant role. Such power determines the amounts of rents and recipients of such rents. In political systems where the determination and allocation of rents is centralized, the beneficiaries are likely to be powerful interest groups whose support the rulers must court, as was the case in the bureaucratic-authoritarian regimes in Latin America in the 1970s. In kleptocratic regimes, the beneficiaries are most likely family members or cronies of the top ruler (as in Suharto's Indonesia and Marcos's Philippines).

But in decentralized systems in which local political bosses control the power of rent-allocation, they tend to distribute rents to those who can offer bribes in return. In some instances, this may result in rent-diffusion, as local political bosses select buyers of rents only on the basis of the amount of bribes they are willing to offer. Yet, such "democratization of rent-seeking" may be the exception in China because of the nepotistic nature of tight-knit local ruling elites. Consequently, the reality may resemble miniature kleptocracies. The devolution of everyday economic decision making and the subsequent formation of local kleptocracies have a direct bearing on the growth and operation of a decentralized predatory state. The ability to determine and allocate rents adds to the predatory capacity of local officials, as they convert such ability into extra private income. The victims of such predation are consumers and local businesses excluded from the network of rent-seekers, as they are forced to pay higher prices, fees, and taxes for goods and services.

Declining Monitoring Capability

The erosion of the state's capability to monitor and discipline its agents is a key institutional variable in the rise of decentralized predation. The Chinese case confirms this theoretical insight. Specifically, several factors contributed to the decline of the state's monitoring capacity.

First, as discussed above, a deliberate policy of administrative decentralization implemented in the early 1980s moved a significant amount of appointive and monitoring power from the central government to local governments. One study showed that the central government directly monitored only seven thousand officials after this decentralization.[40] The spillover effects of the decentralization of administrative monitoring were profound. With new administrative powers by the central government but unchecked at the local level, regional political bosses were able to establish fiefdoms and gain monopolistic power. Published reports show that such power was routinely abused, ranging from the sale of government offices by local bosses to their collusion with organized crime.

Second, simultaneous with the declining monitoring capacity of the state was the end of mass revolutionary terror that was the hallmark of the Maoist era. In prereform China, state agents were subject to monitoring and policing by ordinary citizens who could exercise extraordinary power through open or secret denunciations. In addition, enamored of the power of mass terror, Mao Zedong launched periodic mass political campaigns during which citizens were encouraged to expose official corruption and mete out brutal treatment to corrupt officials. Mass monitoring of local officials in the Maoist era was also made easier by the lack of means to consume or hide the spoils of corruption. With China closed to the outside world, few officials could transfer ill-gotten wealth abroad. The lack of consumer goods and the underdevelopment of the service industry in a planned economy meant that conspicuous consumption was practically difficult and could attract unwanted attention. Consequently, officials were discouraged from engaging in the more serious forms of corrupt activities because it was hard to store or enjoy their loot without taking excessive risks.

In the post-Mao era, the end of mass terror and political campaigns meant the end of monitoring by the masses. With the opening to the outside world and the growing availability of consumer goods and services, it became much easier and less risky for corrupt officials to hoard and consume their spoils. Had the post-Mao regime replaced the high-cost and violent form of monitoring by mass terror and by political campaigns with monitoring by the media and civic groups, the state would have acquired a more effective tool to control corruption by its agents. Despite its market-friendly economic policies, however, the CCP has focused its repressive energy on the liberal intelligentsia and the media, curbing the media's role of policing the behavior of government agents. Similarly, fearful of the political challenge posed by the emerging civil society forces, the government has limited the growth and political influence of civic groups. Indeed, a study of China's civic groups in the early 1990s shows that few of them could be classified as public interest groups.[41] And in combating corruption, the role of the civil society is practically nonexistent.

Within the regime's bureaucratic hierarchy, the mechanisms of monitoring government officials are faulty and ineffective. For example, the most important internal anticorruption body of the CCP is the Central Discipline Inspection Commission (CDIC), which has a vertical organizational structure that parallels the party organization. But this agency is not independent, and the post of the secretary of the CDIC is subordinate to the party secretary, who is the *yibashou*. In many cases, other local officials also outrank the party official in charge of the CDIC. This institutional arrangement greatly undercuts the effectiveness of the CDIC. If monitoring and policing hundreds of thousands of local officials is an impossible task for the central authorities, it also appears that Beijing does not have a working institutional mechanism to monitor frontline provincial cadres. The CCP's CDIC and the COD rely only on ad hoc inspection teams dispatched to the provinces to evaluate the performance and conduct of provincial-level officials.

This practice, begun in 1996, has produced dubious results because these inspection teams are made up of retired senior leaders who have little local knowledge and operate in isolation. Their movements and information sources can be easily controlled by the same provincial leaders they are supposed to evaluate. Because it takes four to five months for a team to complete its inspection in one province, only a small number of provinces can be inspected each year. In 2003, only five inspection teams were sent to ten provinces.[42] The head of one inspection team publicly complained that it was common practice for provincial leaders to feed the inspection teams with false information.[43] This makes it almost impossible for these central inspection teams to uncover corruption by provincial officials. Of the sixteen to seventeen provincial leaders (about 2 percent of the frontline provincial officials) who were punished each year for corruption, few were exposed by the inspection teams.[44]

Even CCP insiders openly admit that the monitoring system functions poorly. A survey of party officials conducted by the CCP's provincial organization department in Shanxi province in 1999 reported that only about 10 percent of the respondents thought the effects of monitoring leaders were "good and quite good"; 64 percent thought they were "so-so"; and 23 percent said they were "poor."[45] A similar survey in Sichuan in 1999 found that 42 percent identified "loose supervision and monitoring" as the most important cause of local corruption.[46] For state agents, who enjoy the advantages of information asymmetry, ineffective monitoring simply removes another deterrent against the abuse of power and corruption. As indicated by the results of the government audits of various bureaucracies, the misuse of public resources was pervasive among party and government officials. In 2003, for example, the National Audit Administration audited 36,000 cadres and discovered that 67 billion yuan were misused.[47] In Hubei province alone, an audit of 1,151 officials in 2003 found that they were responsible for the misuse, waste, and loss of 4.7 billion yuan in government funds.[48]

Crime and Punishment

The breakdown of the monitoring system is accompanied by an increasingly dysfunctional system of punishing corrupt officials—despite the frequent use of the death penalty against high-profile offenders.

The combination of ineffective monitoring and punishment unavoidably creates an institutional environment conducive to decentralized predation. In China's case, official data on the punishment of corrupt officials indicate that the reported increase in official corruption may be attributed to the relative leniency with which corrupt officials are treated by Chinese anticorruption authorities. The low rate of criminal investigations targeting individuals accused of corrupt activities and the negligible probability of criminal penalties make corruption a low-risk and high-return activity that is extremely attractive to officials. More important, this evidence also points to collusion and mutual protection among corrupt agents.

Low rates of investigation

Official figures on the government's enforcement efforts against corruption report that about 80 percent of the corruption cases originated from tips provided by the public.[49] But a public survey conducted by the CDIC in 1996 showed that 58 percent of the respondents reported that the information on corrupt activities they provided to authorities resulted in no action. Two-thirds reported reprisals from accused officials.[50] Published data on the prosecution of corrupt officials reconfirm these assessments. From 1993 to 1997, the procurators' offices received 1,637,302 tips from the public on corrupt activities such as embezzlement, bribery, and abuse of power. About half these tips (841,233) received some attention from government prosecutors. The number of corruption leads that eventually resulted in formal criminal investigations totaled only 387,353, or about 46 percent of the cases officially accepted by the procuratorate. This means that about only one in four tips led to a formal filing, which does not necessarily result in a criminal investigation, let alone prosecution.

Results of initial dispositions of allegations of corruption similarly point to a relatively lenient approach to officials accused of corruption. Take, for example, the data released by the Ministry of Supervision (one of the anticorruption agencies) for 1991. For that year, the ministry accepted 168,124 corruption cases. Of these cases, 32,236 (19.2 percent) were closed after the accused offered "clarifications"; 14,900 (8.8 percent) were closed after the accused received "criticism and education"; 11,021 (6.6 percent) were transferred to other government agencies; and 57,678 (32.1 percent) were disposed of in unspecified

manners. Only 31.2 percent (52,389 cases) were filed for formal investigation.[51] A closer look at those who were most likely to receive a slap
on the wrist shows that more senior officials were among the best protected. Whereas 21.4 percent of the township officials accused of corruption were formally investigated, only 4.5 percent of the officials at
and above the rank of department or bureau (*ting* or *ju*) were. About
half of the department or bureau-level officials were able to see their
cases closed after offering "clarifications," compared to about 21 percent of township-level officials.[52]

Moreover, the overall enforcement efforts slackened over the 1990s.
Official data on corruption investigations in the decade revealed a
marked decline in both the number of corruption cases "accepted"
and the number of corruption cases "investigated" by the procuratorate. From 1990 to 1999, the number of corruption cases "accepted"
declined by 41 percent, and the rate of investigation (that is, the share
of the accepted cases that resulted in official criminal investigations)
fell from 50 to 37 percent. Although the rate rose to 50 percent in
2002, the number of corruption cases investigated in 2002 (43,258)
was less than half of that in 1990 (88,595).[53] Given that the number of
staff in the procuratorate increased by 28.5 percent during the same period (from 176,028 in 1990 to 226,157 in 1999), the significant decline
in the number of cases accepted cannot be explained as the result of
lack of capacity. Rather, it indicates lagging enforcement efforts.[54]

Low probability of punishment

Analysis of the data on corruption provided by the CDIC suggests that
in the 1990s, the probability of criminal penalties against corrupt officials was extremely low and, for all practical purposes, almost negligible.
The commission's work report given in 1997 revealed the extent to
which corrupt officials were lightly punished by the criminal justice system.[55] According to the report, the commission closed investigations
on an average of 141,000 alleged corruption cases every year, but the
majority of the CCP members (about 82 percent) found to have committed corrupt acts received no more than a symbolic reprimand car-
rying no substantive administrative or financial penalties. Only a small
number of corrupt CCP members—18 percent of those punished—
were expelled from the CCP in the six-year period covered by the report (1992–1997). The expulsion rate had been steadily declining

since the early 1980s. According to Yan Sun's research, the rate was 23.4 percent during 1982–1986 and 21 percent during 1987–1992.[56] The likelihood of criminal prosecution is low. The overall prosecution rate is extremely low—just 5.6 percent of all the CCP members found guilty of corruption (averaging about eight thousand a year in the late 1990s) were subject to prosecution. In 2004, the prosecution rate fell to 2.9 percent when only 4,915 out of 170,850 party officials and members disciplined were transferred to judicial authorities for prosecution. Official figures show that China prosecuted, on average, 95,000 individuals for bribery, embezzlement, and illegal use of public funds in the same period.[57] This suggests that only one in ten individuals prosecuted on corruption charges was a member of the CCP.

Another set of numbers, released by the COD, also shows the lenient treatment corrupt officials received at the hands of Chinese authorities. Overall, only 6.6 percent of all officials found guilty of corruption received sentences, a rate indicative of the extremely low risk of participation in corrupt activities by Chinese officials, even though higher-level officials face modestly higher risks of criminal penalties (Table 4.4). The lenient treatment of corrupt officials remained unchanged despite the advent of a new leadership in late 2002, which vowed to take tougher measures against official corruption. From December 2002 to November 2003, the CCP's own anticorruption agency concluded 172,571 corruption cases and punished 174,580 party officials and members, including 6,043 county-level, 411 bureau-level, and 21 provincial-level cadres. But of the more than 170,000 cadres punished by the CCP, only 8,691 (5 percent) were expelled from the party and transferred to judicial authorities for prosecution. Among those criminally prosecuted were 418 cadres with county-level or higher rankings—6.4 percent of all the similarly ranked officials punished in the period.[58]

New Exit Options

The availability of new exit options is a key variable in state agents' calculations regarding self-dealing. Everything else being equal, the availability of such options may likely reduce the time-horizon of agents, increase their discount rates on future income streams, and motivate them to intensify the level of predation. Evidence from China supports this hypothesis. Whereas the closed system in Maoist China left few exit

Table 4.4. Punishment of Corrupt Officials, 1993–1998

Rank of Cadres	Disciplined by the CCP	Investigated by Prosecutors	Sentenced by Courts	Sentenced as Percent of Disciplined
Provincial/ Ministerial	87	15	9	10.3
Prefect/ Department	2,205	616	201	9.1
County/ Division	26,609	11,712	1705	6.4
Total	28,901	12,343	1915	6.6

Source: Calculated from the CCP Central Organization Department's data quoted in Zhang Yangsheng, "Lun dangqian zhongqingnian lingdao ganbu fubai de tezheng jiqi yuanyin" (Characteristics and Causes of Corruption of Middle-Aged and Young Cadres Today), *Zhongguo dangzheng ganbu luntan* (*Chinese Party and Government Officials' Forum*) 1 (2000): 33.

options available for state agents, the post-Mao economic opening has multiplied exit options for them. In the Chinese case, moreover, there are two institutional features of the cadre management system that influence the time-horizon of government officials. The first is the mandatory retirement of almost all government officials (except ministers and provincial governors) at the age of sixty. Originally implemented to inject fresh blood into the Communist Party and the state bureaucracy, this term-limit system drastically reduces the period during which officials may hope to recoup their political investment (mainly because it takes many years for an individual to work his way up the hierarchy). The second is the practice of rotation of cadres that began in 1990. As a measure to prevent the entrenchment of local political bosses, the regime frequently rotates county, prefecture, and provincial officials. The unintended effect of this institutional practice is to turn these officials, literally, into roving bandits. As a result, such involuntary exit motivates Chinese officials to cash in their political investments more quickly.

China's economic reform and opening to the outside world have also made available to the insiders of the CCP and the government new exit options. They can acquire capital through the spontaneous privatization of state assets and the takeover of formerly state-owned businesses, set up proxy businesses by channeling government contracts and bank credits to firms controlled by family members, seek appointments to executive positions in government-controlled businesses, and transfer illicit wealth to offshore accounts and businesses. By all accounts, the pace of the exit accelerated in the 1990s. The accelerated liberalization of the economy following Deng's southern tour in 1992 created new opportunities for the insiders to exercise the exit option. In addition, one of the lessons many Chinese elites learned from the fall of the Soviet Union was that they should have an exit strategy and an insurance policy.[59] In practice, this meant a rush to privatize state assets and set up private businesses. A survey of owners of private firms showed that the majority (60 percent) of those who became entrepreneurs in the 1980s were peasants, workers, and ordinary people—in other words, ordinary risk takers. But a survey of private business owners in 2002 showed that almost two-thirds of the 6.2 million owners of private firms had been former officials and executives in the SOEs and government agencies. This indicates that a very large number of officials—almost 4 million—had exited to the private sector in the 1990s.[60]

A somehow different exit option was double-dipping: officials holding administrative government positions would simultaneously acquire executive appointments in commercial firms with close ties to the government. Official press reports show that a large number of insiders have opted for this route. One representative example occurred in Wuhu, a city in impoverished Anhui province. Many of the city's party officials became the so-called red-cap businessmen by holding simultaneously government appointments and corporate executive positions. The city's party chief was the chairman of the board of a local automobile company. The head of the local tax bureau was the deputy general manager of a local real estate investment firm in which the municipal government happened to be a large investor. All the firm's senior executives were local officials, including the deputy director of the local land management bureau, which had the power to allocate commercial land use.[61] Similar stories were reported in many other jurisdictions. In Nanjing, a deputy mayor held the chairmanship of the board of a local industrial park; a district party chief occupied the chairmanship of a real estate development firm; and the head of the city's urban development bureau was the chairman of a local real estate investment firm.[62] In Beijing, nearly four hundred officials at or above the division level (*chu*) were found to be holding executive positions in business firms in early 2004.[63] In Chongqing, 1,122 officials were forced to resign from their executive positions in businesses in early 2004.[64]

China's growing commercial ties with the outside world have opened new channels through which insiders can find easy exits. Liberalized investment laws and increased financial autonomy have allowed SOEs and local governments to make sizable investments in foreign countries, thus giving them ostensibly legitimate foreign entities to conduct private business deals and hide illicit funds. Relaxed travel and immigration restrictions have allowed spouses and children of officials to study and emigrate abroad. In many cases, government officials' relatives and children who go overseas form offshore companies or manage nominally state-owned foreign subsidiaries that become the depositories of their ill-gotten wealth. Typically, insiders employ a three-step process, according to an official publication for government leaders.[65] Officials use their power to obtain foreign residency permits or passports for their immediate family members, who later set up businesses in foreign countries. The same officials then transfer money or direct contracts to their foreign-based family businesses or offshore bank accounts. After such exits are safely in place, the officials themselves flee China, often on the eve of a pending arrest, to these foreign safe havens. This was the case of Lu Wanli, the former head of the provincial transportation department in Guizhou. Lu amassed 60 million yuan through bribes and shady deals during his tenure. Before he was exposed, he had moved his wife and children abroad and then fled to Fiji using a false passport in 2002.[66] Yang Xiuzhu, a vice director of the construction bureau of Zhejiang province and a former deputy mayor of Wenzhou city, amassed even more. Before the police could arrest her, she fled China—along with her 253 million yuan and her family members.[67]

The number of officials who have sought this route of exit is significant, as is the amount of ill-gotten wealth they have absconded with. The MPS announced publicly in May 2004 that more than five hundred corrupt officials had fled China, with more than 70 billion yuan in stolen assets (averaging 140 million yuan per person).[68] Another report by an official news agency in December 2004 claimed that four thousand "corrupt elements" had escaped abroad with more than $50 billion in stolen funds.[69] The most senior official who had become a fugitive abroad was Gao Yan, who had served as the CCP secretary of Yunnan province, the governor of Jilin province, and the president of the State Electric Power Corporation. He allegedly escaped to Australia in September 2002, when he was still president of State Electric Power. A subsequent government audit of the corporation showed that the financial losses the company suffered during Gao's tenure amounted to 7.8 billion yuan. Nearly half the losses had resulted from illegal and arbitrary decisions Gao had made. An official investigation concluded that Gao "had betrayed the party and the country, engaged in a corrupt and decadent lifestyle, looted a huge amount of the wealth of the state, and must be held directly responsible for the massive loss of the state's assets."[70]

The problem of corrupt officials and criminals fleeing China with their loot became such a serious issue that the MPS singled out the interception and repatriation of such individuals as a top priority for the Chinese police. From 1998 to 2003, the MPS reported that it had successfully extradited 230 officials and individuals who escaped abroad with looted wealth.[71] In aggregate terms, it is likely that the real magnitude of the transfer of stolen money to offshore safe havens by insiders of the Chinese government is much larger than the published figure. Studies by Chinese economists estimate that capital flight—a proxy for the transfer of illicit funds from China to offshore accounts—averaged $17.7 billion between 1997 and 1999, according to China's Foreign Exchange Administration.[72]

The implications of this analysis are troubling on two accounts. First, the run-for-the-exit dynamics have a self-accelerating characteristic because insiders tend to increasingly fear missing out on the opportunities to cash in on their investments. This means that the availability of new exit options will contribute to more voracious decentralized predation. Second, insiders with secure exit options are less motivated to defend the regime because their future risks have been greatly reduced by the insurance policy they have acquired through such exit options. As a result, the regime becomes more brittle and less capable of withstanding crises.

Declining Ideological and Institutional Norms

Many scholars have observed the declining appeal of the communist ideology in post-Mao China.[73] The fact that the ruling Communist

Party launched innumerable "rectification" campaigns to reinvigorate the CCP ideologically in the reform era is, in itself, telling evidence of the erosion of ideological values. The causes of the erosion of ideology are easy to identify. Post-Mao political demobilization and promarket economic reforms necessitated replacing the communist ideology with economic incentives as the main source of motivation. Experience in other communist societies suggests that official ideologies need to be personalized by charismatic leaders to have real appeal to the masses. The death of such leaders also ends their personalized ideologies. Erosion of ideological appeal then becomes inevitable in spite of the ruling parties' efforts to resurrect or reinvent it.

Results from opinion surveys indicate that the old-style communist ideology has lost its attractiveness to both the ruling elites and ordinary citizens. A survey of more than seven thousand mid-level Communist Party officials conducted in the late 1990s revealed that half the respondents thought "communism is too far from reality."[74] A poll of 7,330 prefect and county officials conducted in 1997 found that 11 percent were skeptical about the goal of communism, 23 percent thought communism was "too far from reality," and 26 percent thought that the majority of local officials were skeptical about upholding the party's basic policy for one hundred years.[75] In a 1999 survey of 11,586 party members conducted by the provincial CCP committee of Sichuan province, 61 percent reported that their local officials did not devote time to "ideological studies" because "there was too much work," even though the same officials would always find time to take overseas trips. About two-thirds thought that local officials lacked "political perception" and "political judgment." Only 16 percent said that local officials would place "national interest" first in their decision making; 44 percent thought "local leaderships lacked self discipline."[76]

A survey of nearly 14,000 party members in Sichuan in 1997 reported that "the most striking characteristic of prefect and county-level officials was their superficial theoretical grounding in Marxism and Leninism." In a test of political and ideological knowledge administered to 439 division-level (*chu*) officials under the age of forty-five, 128 of them failed to answer a single question correctly. Some of them did not even know what Deng's four cardinal principles were. About 30 percent of the respondents complained that the young officials were "indifferent to ideals and values"; 24 percent thought such officials "lacked the sense of discipline demanded by the party and the government"; and 34 percent believed that such officials "were deficient in their sense of integrity and self-discipline."[77]

The loss of faith in the official ideology is expressed in both polling data and telling anecdotes. Press stories of official corruption show that perpetrators of corruption had little faith in communism and had sought spiritual guidance in religion or superstition. Cong Fukui, the executive vice governor of Hebei who received a suspended death sentence for corruption, had regularly consulted fortune-tellers about his political future and had become a patron of a Buddhist temple, to which he gave a large portion of the bribe money he had received. The head of the industrial and commercial administration in a county in Hainan set up a Buddhist altar in his own residence. He allegedly never convened a party group meeting to discuss personnel issues. Instead, he would ask prospective appointees to perform religious rituals in front of the house altar before he publicly announced their appointments. Jia Yongxiang, the president of the Shenyang Intermediate Court who was sentenced for corruption, spent 30,000 yuan on a *fengshui* master for picking the right date for the court to move into its new building.

The chief of the public security bureau of Qingyuan county in Guangdong, who had accepted more than 400,000 yuan in bribes, fretted that the front entrance of the bureau was not built in accordance with good *fengshui*. He suspected that bad *fengshui* was responsible for the downfall of his predecessor, who was in jail for corruption. So he consulted a *fengshui* master and ordered a new front entrance be built according to the master's specifications (although this intervention apparently failed to protect the police chief from the graft busters).[78]

The practice of retaining fortune-tellers was widespread among ranking provincial leaders in Hunan. A deputy chief of the provincial government's secretariat who was in charge of approving key infrastructure projects used his power to allocate 2 million yuan to a local Buddhist temple because one of its monks was able to forecast his promotions correctly on several occasions. A deputy mayor of Changde city paid 350,000 yuan to a fortune-teller to predict his political future. Many local leaders even developed a habit of consulting fortune-tellers before they made major personal decisions, such as assuming new appointments, building houses, and purchasing vehicles.[79]

Collusion and the Emergence of Local Mafia States

The breakdown of the institutional mechanisms that police state agents and enforce political accountability has also facilitated collusion among government officials in corrupt activities. In its most extreme form, a decentralized predatory state can spawn numerous local mafia states.[80] The glue holding such local mafia states is collusion among state agents. The spreading of official collusion within Chinese officialdom, thus, directly contributes to the growth of local mafia states.

By most accounts, official collusion was uncommon in the 1980s. An examination of published reports of major corruption cases uncovered in the decade shows that almost all corruption cases were committed by individuals acting alone.[81] In the 1990s, however, official collusion in corruption and other types of criminal activities became increasingly common. According to Liu Liying, a deputy secretary of the CDIC who oversaw many high-profile corruption cases in the 1990s, the most worrisome aspect of corruption in the 1990s was collusion among officials. In Liu's view, officials colluded in corrupt or even criminal activities because they had formed "alliances of interests." As a result, the number of *wo an* and *chuan an* (corruption cases involving multiple individuals) has increased dramatically. In an interview, Liu disclosed that 104 senior municipal officials in Shenyang were prosecuted in a major corruption case that led to the downfall of its mayor and the execution of its executive vice mayor in 2001.[82] In another notorious case, five senior provincial officials in Heilongjiang (a deputy governor, a vice chairman of the provincial people's congress, the president of the provincial high court, the chief of the provincial procuratorate, and the head of the provincial CCP committee's secretariat) were removed from office on the same day in October 2004 after they were implicated in corruption. Prior to their downfall, a former governor of Heilongjiang, Tian Fengshan, and the head of the provincial CCP's organization department, Han Guizhi, had been arrested for selling party and government appointments for personal gains.[83]

In Hebei province, the investigation of Li Zhen, the chief of the state tax bureau in Hebei province, uncovered 160 other senior officials who were involved in the same corruption case. In the corruption case of a vice president of the provincial branch of the Agricultural Bank in Heilongjiang, more than seventy were implicated; the case of Ma De, the party secretary of Suihua City in Heilongjiang who had collected 5.2 million yuan in bribes for selling government positions, involved 260 officials, including 50 *yibashou*s in the ten counties and various county-level departments in Suihua.[84] Anhui's disgraced vice governor, Wang Huaizhong, admitted to investigators that more than 160 officials were complicit in his corrupt activities.[85] In the case of Li Tiecheng, who served as party secretary for almost seven years in a poverty-stricken county in Jilin, prosecutors found that 162 county officials gave bribes to Li to secure promotions. They included the head of the county's People's Congress, a deputy party secretary in charge of law enforcement, the executive deputy county magistrate, two deputy party secretaries, five deputy county magistrates, and the chiefs of the county finance bureau, labor bureau, personnel bureau, and law enforcement agencies. The Li case, though extreme, is a vivid illustration of how the machinery of the party-state can be captured by a network of collusive officials.[86]

Although China's anticorruption authorities do not disclose data on the share of *wo an* or *chuan an* in all corruption cases, the information released by Guangzhou, Hubei, Fujian, Shandong, and Jiangsu suggests that collusive corruption is widespread. In Guangzhou, 65 percent of embezzlement and bribe-taking cases prosecuted in 2001 were found to have involved collusive officials.[87] Forty percent of cases classified as "using public office to commit crimes" in Hubei, in 2001, were those involving multiple individuals.[88] In Fujian, 30 percent of corruption cases investigated in 2002 were classified as "group corruption."[89] The prosecutor's office in Xintai City in Shandong disclosed that *wo an* accounted for 30 percent of the corruption cases it prosecuted between 1998 and 2000.[90] Data collected by the prosecutor's office in Nantong City, in Jiangsu, showed that the number of *wo an* cases steadily increased in the late 1990s. The number of *wo an* cases the office prosecuted was nine in 1999, fifteen in 2000, and twenty-five in 2001. On average, each *wo an* involved four individuals employed in the same "unit." Two-thirds of the perpetrators were cadres. Cadres participated in every *wo an*.[91]

In the worst cases, official collusion creates local mafia states—jurisdictions in which criminal elements have formed a close alliance with officials in key government positions. The extent to which the Chinese state has been penetrated by organized crime is unknown. The head of the office in charge of fighting organized crime (*daheiban*) at the MPS admitted in July 2003 that this scourge was widespread:

In some areas, local government organizations were weak and in disarray, and society was out of control. This provided opportunities for evil forces to breed and spread in rural townships. The local governments in these townships were in a state of collapse. Some of them degenerated to such an extent that they had allowed evil forces to run amok within their jurisdictions, control the governments, illegally interfere in local administrative affairs, and take over law and order. These jurisdictions became lawless fortresses and uncontrollable villages that openly defied the government and law enforcement agencies.[92]

Apparently, the collusion between organized crime and corrupt officials has extended beyond rural areas. The Supreme People's Procuratorate reported that, from 2001 to 2002, it prosecuted 557 government officials for protecting organized crime.[93] One representative example of a local mafia state is Shenyang, where in the late 1990s practically all the key local officials, including the heads of seventeen agencies (ranging from the city's intermediate court, the procuratorate, the tax bureau, and the state asset bureau) took bribes from the city's mafia boss, Liu Yong, in return for protecting his criminal activities, which included extortion, murder, assault, and fraud. The provincial government of Heilongjiang also appeared to have degenerated into a mafia state. As described above, nine senior provincial leaders were found to have engaged in collective corruption. A third example of a local mafia state was Fuzhou, where a criminal group headed by Chen Kai colluded with ninety-one key local officials, including the city's deputy party secretary and police chief, in drug trafficking, gambling, prostitution, and other illegal activities.

Although violence and outright criminal activities are among the defining features of the hard local mafia states in China, many of the local mafia states may be considered soft because of the absence of violence and involvement of hardened criminal elements. The Yuanhua smuggling case, which implicated more than two hundred officials in Xiamen, belongs to this category.[94] Jilin's Jingyu county and Heilongjiang's Suihua prefecture, where the local party chiefs effectively sold hundreds of government posts for personal gains, are two additional examples. In such cases, shady businessmen and local officials were primarily interested in maximizing their private gains, not terrorizing the local population.

To better understand the workings of the local mafia states, the Appendix (page 219) offers a sample of fifty high-profile corruption cases in seventeen provinces that were published in the official media.[95] All of them fit the two core characteristics of local mafia states: the involvement of organized criminal elements and the collusion of key local officials. Roughly half of the cases belong in the hard category—local officials were found to have provided protection for organized criminal groups in twenty-four cases. Hunan was the province reporting the largest number of local mafia states (seven), followed by Guangdong (six) and Fujian (six). Like their Western counterparts, China's organized criminal groups controlled businesses, such as real estate, construction firms, mines, transportation companies, the local produce market, and department stores. They used their political protection to extract monopoly profits, terrorize competitors and consumers, and fight off rival criminal groups. From 2001 to 2002, according to data provided by the Supreme People's Procuratorate, the government prosecuted ninety-nine officials for protecting organized crime in engaging in illegal economic activities. Of the 265 major criminal cases involving "violation of the economic order of the market," criminals received official protection in about a quarter of them.[96] In eighteen of the twenty-four cases of hard local mafia states, party secretaries, county magistrates or mayors, police chiefs, or the party secretaries of the politics and law committees were involved.

There are two subtypes of soft local mafia states. The first includes jurisdictions staffed by venal officials who collude in committing economic crimes, such as smuggling and collective bribe-taking. In the sample of fifty tainted jurisdictions, there were six cases of organized large-scale smuggling sanctioned by local leaders and ten cases of collective bribe-taking. Because of the scope of collusion in such illegal activities (which usually encompasses most of the key government agencies), these local governments have been practically subverted into collective illegal economic enterprises. The Xiamen smuggling scandal is the most extreme case. It is worth noting that, based on this limited sample, this subtype of soft local mafia states appeared to be more prevalent in the more prosperous areas. A possible explanation is that the profits to be made from these illegal economic activities were much greater than those from a more risky alliance with organized crime.[97]

The second subtype consists of mafia states formed through the sale and purchase of government offices.[98] There were eight such cases, involving more than one thousand officials, in our sample of fifty cases.

The worst case was the provincial government of Heilongjiang. In 2004, the central government sacked eight senior provincial leaders in Heilongjiang for purchasing and selling government appointments. In these instances, a soft mafia state emerges when a large number of local officials are tied to one another through payments of bribes and other corrupt activities. Two factors are worth considering here. First, because officials who have paid bribes to get government positions regard such bribes as investments, they are motivated to recoup their investments, plus an above-market rate of return is generated. Such a calculation leads these officials to use more aggressive means to maximize their private gains, thus intensifying decentralized predation. Second, as a large number of these officials are tainted by the corrupt means through which they get their jobs, they also have an incentive to protect one another in their corrupt activities and collude to cover up their illegal activities.

Governance deteriorates rapidly in jurisdictions where such incipient local mafia states control power. In many instances, official protection allowed organized criminal groups to penetrate local commerce and politics. Their control of real estate, retail, mining, passenger transportation, produce markets, construction, and loan sharking enabled them to gain significant economic and political privileges. Official press reports show, for example, well-connected mafia bosses were favored in real estate deals. In one case, the Shenyang municipal government gave, for free, 24,000 square meters of prime real estate to crime boss Liu Yong after Liu paid a $100,000 bribe to the executive vice mayor Ma Xiangdong. This was not the only shady deal between a mafia boss and party officials. In 2000, the municipal governments of Shenyang and Dalian both sold leases on land of similar size, but the Dalian government was able to generate 1.7 billion yuan in revenue, compared with only 70 million yuan received by Shenyang.

In other words, assuming equal value of land in the two cities, 96 percent of the proceeds from sale of land leases in Shenyang appeared to have gone to local party bosses and their friends, including criminal elements.[99] Similar large giveaways were reported in other jurisdictions. Wang Huaizhong, a disgraced vice governor of Anhui, whose case implicated more than 160 officials, reportedly allowed his cronies to pocket more than 1 billion yuan in profits from sweetheart land deals.[100] In some cases, well-placed criminal elements even gained access to China's financial institutions. For example, in Hunan's Lianyuan City, a local crime boss, Tan Heping, was the deputy director of the city's rural credit cooperative. Among his supporters in the city government were the party secretary of the political and law committee, police chief, president of the local court, and the chief procurator—all deeply involved in his criminal activities. They were exposed in 2001.[101]

The alliance between criminal elements and local elites in some jurisdictions facilitated the entrenchment of the power of the local mafia state in two ways. Through their commercial enterprises and insider deals, organized crime bosses generated the funds with which they could bribe local officials and help their allies to purchase promotions inside the government. Once these officials accepted these bribes, they fell under the control of the local mafia.[102] Officials beholden to organized criminal groups often returned favors by helping the leaders of these groups to gain political respectability and power, typically through appointing them as local legislators or even placing them in government agencies. Liu Yong, Shenyang's notorious crime boss and chairman of a conglomerate in real estate and retail, was a deputy in the Shenyang Municipal People's Congress. In Helong City, Jilin province, local crime boss Gu Decheng was also a deputy in the municipal People's Congress. Sang Yuechun, another crime boss in Changchun, Jilin, owned a private conglomerate with a net worth of 120 million yuan. Relying on his wealth to bribe local party leaders, Sang managed to be elected a deputy to the NPC in 1998.[103] He was expelled in 2002 after he was arrested for a criminal offense in October 2002. Zhang Wei, a mafia boss in Wenling, Zhejiang, controlled a large conglomerate in the province; before he was executed, he had held four official titles, including vice chairman of the political consultative conference of Yidu city in Hubei province. A member of the crime family that controlled both the local coal mines and government in Qianshan county in Jiangxi was the party secretary and mayor of a township.

Writing in the official publication of the Ministry of Supervision, a government prosecutor observed:

> Organized criminal groups in several provinces and cities have penetrated into the governments of counties and municipalities. They selected their representatives inside the government and worked together to arrange the appointments of local government leaders and heads of the local people's congress and political consultative conferences.[104]

The extent of the entrenchment of this interwoven network of criminals and party officials is shown by how long it operated in these jurisdictions. In the fifty cases listed in the Appendix, a hard local mafia state lasted from four to twelve years before it was uprooted.[105]

To the extent that the central authorities retain the ability to destroy these local mafia states during periodic anticorruption and antimafia campaigns, the risks posed to the survival of the Communist Party by this collusive network of corrupt officials and criminals are controllable. The top-down approach to the eradication of China's local mafia states provides, at best, a temporary solution because it does not address the underlying conditions that foster the emergence of such local mafia states. Without empowering the public or giving the media more leeway in monitoring and enforcing accountability on local officials on an everyday basis, the central authorities will unlikely never acquire effective capacities to police their local agents. If anything, the emergence of local mafia states, a clear and dramatic indication of regime decay, reveals not only the deterioration of governance in certain parts of China, but also demonstrates that the regime's institutional mechanisms of monitoring and policing its agents are breaking down. In particular, the breakdown of these mechanisms, coupled with the absence of constraints imposed by public opinion and political participation, has allowed local Communist Party bosses to turn their jurisdictions into personal fiefdoms. In the sample of 50 cases of local mafia states, party secretaries and/or mayors were implicated in half of them.

The emergence of a decentralized predatory state in China raises several disturbing questions. In predatory states, economic development and market-oriented reform may create a unique situation where the authoritarian ruling elites can enjoy, for a considerable length of time, both the fruits of economic growth and the privileges of autocracy. This combination, instead of weakening the old regime's resolve to hold on to power, may only create conditions more conducive to predation as well as strengthen such a resolve. In practice, this could lead the regime to devote considerable resources and efforts to the repression of opponents and potential challengers deemed most threatening to its power, while allowing various forms of decentralized predation to sap its energy and erode its political foundations. This explains why, as detailed in Chapter 2, the CCP has been relatively successful in responding to societal challenges and co-opting new social elites but seems to be impotent in addressing its internal decay.

The degeneration of the Chinese state during the reform era also calls into question the main thesis of developmental neoauthoritarianism: an autocratic regime pursuing market-friendly policies can promote sustained economic growth. The proponents of neoauthoritarianism discount—if not overlook altogether—the risks posed by a predatory state to sustainable growth. Without effective political constraints to check the power of rulers, it is impossible to guarantee that a state capable of pursuing worthy development goals will not be tempted to adopt predatory policies and practices. China's experience provides a sobering example of how an autocratic state can lose control of its agents even in an otherwise progressive process of decentralization and market-oriented reforms. Although there is no evidence to suggest that accompanying democratic reforms would have restrained decentralized predation by such agents, the absence of institutional checks on the power of neoauthoritarian rulers, especially at the local level, greatly increases the risks of decentralization of state predation.

The transformation of the Chinese state into a decentralized predatory state will have profound implications for China's political system, economic development, state-society relations, and prospects for democratization. Doubtlessly, China's state capacity will continue to erode, as state agents undermine the interests of the state with a full range of predatory practices. Sustainable economic development will be put at risk, since a decentralized predatory state tends to deliver insufficient public services and provide inadequate protection for property rights. More important, thieving agents directly threaten the fiscal health of the state itself. State-society relations are likely to grow tense because the predatory behavior of state agents unavoidably impinges on the property and civil rights of ordinary Chinese citizens. Prospects for a peaceful and gradual transition to democracy may also grow dim because these negative effects will hinder the development of the social, economic, and political infrastructures conducive to a peaceful democratic transition. Regime transition may still be possible, but such a transition, when it comes, is more likely to be tumultuous and disruptive.

* * *

FIVE

China's Mounting Governance Deficits

THE COMBINATION of lagging political reforms, entrenchment of rent-seeking groups, and decentralization of state predation is a recipe for deteriorating governance. As long as China's ruling elites refuse to confront these deeply embedded structural and institutional problems, they are unlikely to sustain the momentum of economic development that has played a critical role in maintaining the political monopoly of the Communist Party. In developmental autocracies that eventually degenerated into predatory states (the best example being Suharto's Indonesia), high rates of growth can mask the weak political foundations of authoritarian regimes. Rising prosperity and inflows of foreign capital, which serve as a measure of international confidence in the regime, often give the ruling elites a sense of security and reduce incentives for reforms that might shore up their political foundations.

China is no exception. Its sustained high rates of growth since the late 1970s have strengthened the ruling elites' belief in the idea that economic growth can be a panacea for most social and political ills. Thus, economic growth has produced a perverse effect: instead of taking advantage of the economic boom to push through difficult political reforms that can help sustain long-term growth, Chinese leaders in the 1990s saw no need for such measures. The ruling Communist Party's inability to implement meaningful political reform is responsible, in retrospect, for a rapid and substantial accumulation of governance deficits.

Conceptually, governance deficits refer to a government's deficiencies in fulfilling the most important functions in ruling a society. Such deficits include both the erosion of state capacity and the ruling regime's ability to mobilize political support. Accumulation of governance deficits constitutes a long-term threat to a regime's survival because these deficits will inevitably be reflected in declining performance of the state and the regime in executing the basic functions of government. But as with fiscal deficits, the immediate adverse impact of rising governance deficits may be more difficult to measure. A regime's ability to tolerate rising governance deficits may be similar to a national treasury's ability to absorb the effects of mounting budgetary deficits. In theory, a political system's capacity to tolerate governance deficits should be much greater than a treasury's ability to tolerate budgetary deficits. After all, any nation's ministry of finance must go to the market to issue bonds to cover the budgetary deficits, or risk high inflation through printing paper money. Given the discipline imposed by the market, there is a finite limit to a state's ability to finance budgetary deficits.

In comparison, as poor, even dismal, governance is found in a large number of developing countries, a society's capacity to tolerate governance deficits may be highly elastic. In most cases, only the availability of a credible political alternative would limit a society's tolerance of bad governance. Nevertheless, governance deficits do matter. To the extent that accumulation of such deficits progressively weakens the capacities of the state and the ruling regime, growing governance deficits can contribute to the increase in systemic risks in a political system. Such risks may ordinarily have little visible effect on the stability of a given political regime. But the existence and constant increase of these risks will, in the long run, reduce the resilience of the regime and threaten its durability.

In this chapter, I first describe and analyze the two principal manifestations of China's rising governance deficits—the state's eroding capacity and the ruling party's declining capacity for political mobilization. Then I examine the political effects of rising governance deficits on state-society relations.

Governance Deficits and State Incapacitation

Among developing countries, China is thought to have a strong state. Compared with countries at comparable income levels, the Chinese government has demonstrated relatively good performance in providing basic services such as health, education, public safety, and environmental protection. Indeed, the reputed effectiveness of the Chinese state has made investment in China attractive for foreign investors. But comparing China with countries with very low state capacity does not address two key issues: has China's state capacity been declining or growing since it began the economic transition in the late 1970s, and how does it really compare with China's peers in the developing world? If evidence points to a trend of state incapacitation, it should raise concerns about the sustainability of the transition. Indeed, a closer look at many specific indexes of government performance would show that the capacity of the Chinese state has been deteriorating during the last two decades. In several important areas, China's performance actually compares unfavorably with that of some of its peers in the developing world, those countries with large populations such as India and Mexico, or its East Asian neighbors.

The incapacitation of the state is shown in the erosion of the government's ability to provide essential public services, such as public safety, education, health, environmental protection, and enforcement of laws and rules. In China, there are numerous telltale signs that these indexes of state capacity have been slipping. Such slippage should be especially alarming because it has occurred in a period during which China experienced unprecedented economic prosperity. The key indexes of government performance ought to have improved, rather than declined.

Public and Workplace Safety

Most of the evidence for deteriorating performance is mundane but telling. Take, for example, the number of road fatalities, a key measure of a state's capacity to regulate a routine, but vital, social activity—transportation. A study of the change in traffic fatality rates (measured at deaths per 10,000 vehicles) between 1975 and 1998 shows that the growth rate in China—243 percent during the period—was the second highest in the world. Although rising traffic fatality rates are closely associated with a rising rate of motorization, weak states tend to have relatively higher death rates.[1] The incidence of traffic accident fatalities in China almost doubled between 1985 and 2000 (about fifty-eight road fatalities per 10,000 vehicles in 2000, compared to thirty-four in

1985).[2] In 2002, China reported 109,381 road fatalities.[3] An international comparison using the 1995 data shows that traffic fatality risks were much higher in China than in many of its neighbors. Road fatalities per 10,000 vehicles were twenty-six for China, twenty for India, and eight for Indonesia. China fared better only than Tonga (fifty-two), Bangladesh (forty-four), Myanmar (thirty-six), and Mongolia (thirty).[4] Road hazards are not the only example of the state's poor ability to protect the public. Due to weak regulatory enforcement, more than 100,000 people were made ill or killed by rat poison alone each year.[5]

Data on workplace safety in China reveal a similar state weakness. The Chinese workplace may be among the most hazardous in developing countries. A survey conducted by the official All-China Federation of Labor Unions in 1997 found that 10 percent of the workers polled reported having suffered injuries on the job.[6] Official figures record 13,960 industrial and mining accidents in 2002 that resulted in 14,924 fatalities.[7] Figures compiled by the International Labour Office for 1997 show that mining deaths in China (3,273) were more than thirteen times those in India (242).[8] The rate of fatalities in coal mining accidents in China is the highest in the world, with seven deaths per 1 million metric tons of coal produced in 2001; India's rate was 0.9.[9] Most of the mining fatalities occurred in unsafe small mines run by private entrepreneurs, many of whom were either connected with local government officials or had held important official positions before. In the first five months of 2002, for example, private coal mines accounted for 54 percent of the fatalities; coal mines operated by township governments reported 14 percent of the fatalities.[10] Unsafe private mines have powerful allies because many local officials are investors in these mines and use their power to protect them.[11] In one case, a local mafia group took over several coal mines in Jiangxi and bribed nearly all the local officials, including the police chief, in return for protection.[12]

Education

The Chinese government's ability to provide access to education does not compare well, either. China's education spending, around 2 percent of GDP in the late 1990s, was considerably below the average of 3.4 percent of GDP for low-income countries. According to UNESCO's data on public expenditures on education as a percentage of GDP,

China spent significantly less on education than did India, Mexico, Brazil, and the Philippines. During 1998–2000, public expenditure on education in China was 2–2.1 percent of GDP, compared with 3.2–4 percent in India, 4.2–4.4 percent in Mexico, 4.2 percent in the Philippines, and 4.2–5.2 percent in Brazil. China spent less on education than Bangladesh (2.4 percent of GDP), a much poorer country.[13] As a result, access to primary and middle-school education in 1998 was available to 85 percent of the school-age population nationwide and to only 40 percent of the children in the poor western regions. The middle school drop-out rate in rural areas was 42 percent in the late 1990s. In some parts of the south, the rate was 30–50 percent.[14]

According to a study by UNESCO in 2002, China will not achieve UNESCO's literacy goal for 2015. Another study, conducted by the UN Development Programme (UNDP), showed that China's underinvestment in education may have contributed to hundreds of thousands of preventable deaths of children. According to the UNDP, had China maintained the same rate of education as Vietnam, where per capita income was a third of China's, 264,500 fewer Chinese children would have died in 2002.[15] A study of China's investment in human capital by the Nobel laureate James Heckman in 2002 concludes that Chinese government policies during the reform era favored physical investment over schooling, resulting in underinvestment in human capital.[16]

The central government contributes only a small portion to China's educational expenditures; for example, it provided 13 percent of the 334.9 billion yuan spent on education in 1999. Spending on compulsory education, in particular, is borne almost exclusively by subnational governments: township governments are responsible for 78 percent, county governments pay 9 percent; and provincial governments contribute 11 percent. The central government pays only 2 percent. This structure of financing compulsory education makes China an outlier in education spending. For example, in Mexico in 1994, 79 percent of education spending came from the central government; in South Korea, 96 percent came from Seoul. Among OECD countries, the average contribution from the central government is 50 percent.[17] In addition, education spending by the central government was biased toward higher education: 94 percent of all the education spending by the central government in 1999 was for higher education; its combined contribution to secondary and primary education was 0.5 percent of its total education

budget. In other words, local governments are responsible for all secondary and primary education spending.[18]

As a whole, the state's contribution to education spending had been
declining in the 1990s. From 1991 to 1997, the share of the state's contribution to total education spending fell from 62.8 percent to 53.6 percent.
The shortfall was made up through increased tuition and fees, thus
reducing access to education, especially in poorer areas.[19] One scholarly
estimate suggests that government funding contributed to only 31 percent of the expenditures in middle-school education, 24 percent in
primary-school education, and 40 percent in kindergarten education.[20]

Public Health

China's public health delivery system has deteriorated considerably in
recent years and compares poorly with that of its neighbors.[21] In the
World Health Organization's (WHO) *World Health Report 2000,* China's
overall health system performance in 1997 ranked 144, placing China
among the bottom quartile of WHO member states, behind India
(112), Indonesia (92), and Bangladesh (88), countries often thought
to have less effective governments. On the score of "fairness in financial contribution," a proxy measure of equality in access to healthcare,
China was ranked 188, ahead of only Brazil (189), Myanmar (190), and
Sierra Leone (191). In terms of "overall goal attainment," according to
WHO, China was placed 132, again behind Indonesia (106), India
(121), and Bangladesh (131).[22] The decline in the state's ability to provide health services has hit especially hard China's rural population
and people living in less developed areas.[23] According to a study by the
Development Research Center of the State Council, only 14 percent of
the net increase in the government's healthcare spending in the 1990s
was channeled to the countryside; about 90 percent of this new spending was used on personnel and administration.[24]

In the 1970s, 90 percent of the rural areas were covered by a system
of basic cooperative healthcare. By the end of the 1980s, this system
survived in only 5 percent of the villages. Despite a halfhearted effort by
the government to rebuild the cooperative health system in the 1990s,
nearly all the 700,000 rural village and township clinics were privatized
after local governments sold these facilities to private entrepreneurs
and physicians in the 1980s.[25] The collapse of the rural cooperative

health system was further exacerbated by the antirural bias in the government's health spending. Only 15 percent of the government's health budget goes to rural areas, even though rural residents account for 70 percent of the Chinese population. On a per capita basis, rural residents receive only a third of the healthcare enjoyed by their urban counterparts.[26]

Replacing the prereform cooperative healthcare system is a patchwork of fee-for-service private clinics and hospitals, many of which provide substandard care. A study of four hundred village clinics published in 2001 reported that two-thirds did not keep patients' medical records and only half of the injection tubes and needles were sterilized.[27] Rural doctors and medics are poorly trained and many of them have no licenses. A reporter found that about 40 percent of the scores of clinics he visited did not have licenses.[28]

Consequently, both the access to and quality of healthcare in rural China have declined dramatically. Whereas 85 percent of the rural residents had health insurance in 1970, less than 20 percent of them were insured in 2003.[29] According to the 1998 National Health Service survey conducted by the Ministry of Health, 37 percent of farmers who got sick could not afford to seek medical treatment, and 65 percent of sick peasants who should have been hospitalized were not admitted because of inability to pay. Both figures were higher than in 1993, when a similar survey was carried out. In 1993, nearly 77 percent of rural women gave birth at home and only a third of rural children had physical checkups. The overall access to healthcare hardly improved ten years later. The 2003 National Health Service survey revealed that 49 percent of the Chinese population do not go to the hospital after they get sick and 30 percent of the patients who ought to be hospitalized are not, due to unaffordability of care.[30]

For rural residents who cannot afford health care, the consequences are often dire. Poor health has become the chief cause of poverty in rural China. In Henan province, 40 percent of the rural residents fell below the poverty line again after they were struck by disease and lost their ability to work; in Shaanxi province, the figure was 50 percent, and in Jilin province, the figure was 60 percent.[31]

Even in urban areas, considered privileged relative to the countryside, access to healthcare has been declining as the costs of healthcare rise rapidly. According to the Ministry of Health, 27 percent of the urban residents in 1993 were uninsured; by 2003, the percentage of unin-sured in the urban population had risen to more than 50 percent, and 44 percent of urban residents who got sick did not go to the hospital for treatment in 2003.[32]

Deterioration in the public health infrastructure and declining ac-cess to health services may be responsible for the persistently high levels of some communicable diseases. For example, at the end of the 1990s, 10 percent of the population had hepatitis A, and 5 million people were stricken with tuberculosis.[33] A Ministry of Health report disclosed that, in 2002, 810,000 people suffered from schistosomiasis, a debilitating disease.[34] China was also ill-prepared to deal with an emerging HIV/AIDS crisis. Estimates of the infected ranged from 850,000 to 2 million in 2002. The rate of infection was growing at 40 percent per annum in 2003–2004, according to the Ministry of Health.[35] At this rate, the num-ber of infected will most likely exceed 10 million by 2010.[36] Although the rate of infection was high, the government's spending on AIDS pre-vention and treatment averaged only 15 million yuan a year in the 1990s. Despite a modest increase in funding—when the amount was in-creased to 100 million yuan in 2001, in addition to a one-time appro-priation of 1.25 billion yuan—the total government resources available for AIDS prevention and treatment remained insufficient.[37] Alarmed by this trajectory and the Chinese government's inadequate efforts, the United Nations issued a report in 2002 titled "HIV/AIDS: China's Titanic Peril." It warned that China was on the verge of a public health and humanitarian catastrophe, and singled out, as factors contributing to the spread of the epidemic, "insufficient political commitment and leadership at many levels of government, insufficient openness when dealing with the epidemic, insufficient resources both human and fi-nancial, scarcity of effective policies, lack of an enabling policy envi-ronment, and poor governance."[38]

The insufficient supply of public goods may have contributed to a slowdown in poverty reduction since the mid-1980s.[39] One study shows that although the poverty rate fell 22 percent from 1978 to 1984, progress since then was virtually stagnant; between 1985 and 1995, de-spite strong economic growth, the poverty rate fell only 2.58 percent.[40] The pace of poverty reduction slowed even further during 2001–2002, with fewer than 2 million people lifted out of poverty each year. In 2003, for the first time since reform began, the number of people living in poverty actually rose by 800,000.[41] Based on the World Bank's definition of "extreme poverty" (per capita income of $1.08 a day, compared to the official Chinese standard of $0.21 a day), a Chinese researcher concluded that in the late 1990s China had 120 million people in the rural areas who lived below the poverty line; half of them were concentrated in the western region. In urban areas, about 20 million people were classified as poor in 2002.[42] This implies that China's real poverty rate is about 10 percent, about five times the official rate. Even this high figure may understate the poverty rate. In the World Bank's *World Development Indicators 2003*, the number of people living in "extreme poverty" was estimated to be 222 million, or about 18 percent of the Chinese population.[43]

Environmental Degradation

State incapacitation in China is reflected in the worsening environmental degradation that threatens the sustainability of economic development.[44] Official reports admit that a third of China's land suffers from severe soil erosion. As a result, about 67,000 hectares of farmland are lost each year. Major waterways have also become clogged with silt. About 1.5 billion tons of soil, sand, and gravel are washed into the upper reaches of the Yangtze, for example. The authorities blamed the buildup of such silt in the Yangtze on the devastating floods along the river in 1998. Soil erosion has endangered China's reservoirs, where more than 20 billion tons of silt have accumulated. Each year about 2,500 square kilometers of land are turned into desert, resulting in 54 billion yuan in direct economic losses. The expansion of the desert has also led to a large increase in the frequency and magnitude of sandstorms that hit the northern parts of the country. Acid rain has polluted 30 percent of the country.[45]

With 80 percent of wastewater discharged untreated, three quarters of the lakes and about half of the rivers (measured in length) have been polluted. The head of China's State Environmental Protection Administration admitted in early 2003 that checks conducted in 740 sections of the country's major rivers found water to be of drinkable quality in only 29 percent of them.[46] Sixty percent of the water in the Yangtze, China's most important river, was found to be polluted to varying degrees in 2003. Each year, 20 billion tons of polluted water, or 40 percent of China's total, are discharged into the Yangtze.[47] In addition, two-thirds of the underground water in the 118 major cities is rated as "severely polluted." Water pollution alone costs China 1.46–2.84 percent of GDP each year. By international standards, China's use of water is among the most inefficient. For each unit of GDP, China's water usage is 15 times higher than the average of developed countries—35 times higher than Japan and 25 times higher than France. It is also higher than India and Pakistan.[48]

Environmental degradation incurs huge direct economic losses. The World Bank estimated in the mid-1990s that major forms of pollution in China cost 7.7 percent of GDP.[49] More than 20 million tons of SO_2 (a product of burning coal) is released into the air each year (the largest in the world); this emission alone cost China about 2 percent of GDP.[50] China's State Environmental Protection Administration reported that tests of air quality conducted in 1999 in 338 cities found that air was considered "good" only in one-third of them. Of the ten cities with the worst air pollution in the world in 1999, seven were located in China.[51]

In addition, China's agricultural infrastructure built in the prereform era steadily deteriorated due to a lack of funding. Spending on agricultural infrastructure fell from 18 percent of total government spending on infrastructure in the 1970s to less than 6 percent by the mid-1980s. Particularly hard hit has been the rural irrigation system. Of the nation's 84,300 reservoirs, one-third were classified as "unsound and dangerous" in the mid-1990s. The total capacity of these reservoirs had been cut by 30 to 50 percent, dramatically reducing the country's ability to fight floods and drought.[52] The combined effects of environmental degradation and the severe deterioration of much of the agricultural infrastructure built before the 1980s may have exacerbated the devastation of natural disasters. Grain output losses resulting from natural disasters more than doubled from the 1950s to 1990s, from 2.1 percent to 5 percent of total grain output. Output losses accelerated mostly in the 1990s. Whereas average annual losses from natural disasters ranged 50 billion to 60 billion yuan (in constant prices) from the 1950s to the 1980s, they had doubled to 120 billion yuan by the mid-1990s.[53]

Crisis in Rural Public Finance

The erosion in the fiscal capacity of the Chinese state in general, and the crisis in rural public finance in particular, have severely undercut the government's ability to fund public services. In addition, the consequences of a dysfunctional fiscal system have been made much worse by a deeply flawed political incentive structure that motivates local officials to devote limited resources to projects that promise to maximize their individual political gains but yield low social returns. Thus, projects and services that can deliver high social returns, such as environmental protection, education, and public health, are neglected.

China's fiscal problems have been extensively studied.[54] The deterioration in the state's extractive capacity, if measured by official data on the performance of China's fiscal system, seems dramatic, if not precipitous, as the government's tax receipts fell from 31 percent of GDP in 1978 to 14 percent of GDP in 1999.[55] The truth, however, is quite different. Aggregate government revenue during the last two decades has remained at the same level of about 30 percent of GDP. Erosion of the state's fiscal capacity may be modest. As discussed extensively in Chapter 4, what has changed is the massive diversion of revenue from the government's official budget. The explosion of various forms of revenue collected by the government but not entered into the budget has squeezed the on-budget tax revenue streams. At its peak, such off-budget revenue exceeded budgeted tax revenue by a two-to-one ratio. For example, in 1995 and 1996, budgeted tax revenue was about 11 percent of GDP, but off-budget and other types of unrecorded government revenue was about 20 percent of GDP.[56]

Provincial and municipal governments are the primary beneficiaries of this dysfunctional fiscal system because it allows them to raise revenue outside the normal tax streams. Even after the implementation of the 1994 fiscal reform, which is generally regarded as a measure to strengthen the central government's fiscal capacity, provincial and municipal governments were able to increase their share of the revenue. One study of the changes in the effective share of government funds claims that the share of provincial governments rose 2 percent each year between 1994 and 2000, from 16.8 to 28.8 percent, while that of the central government actually fell slightly in the same period, from 55.7 to 52.2 percent.[57] The relative decline in the central government's revenue has significantly reduced Beijing's ability to invest in social services.

As a result, the central government increasingly relied on unfunded mandates—by ordering subnational governments to provide the social services Beijing no longer has the ability to finance. Local governments have few incentives to provide these services, however, because the political returns from doing so are lower than those derived from devoting the same resources to more showy projects demonstrative of their ability to maintain high rates of growth. A study of budgetary allocations in five provinces—Jilin, Hebei, Xinjiang, Qinghai, and Shandong—from 1980 to 1998 found that public expenditures for agricultural production fell from 7.54 to 2.15 percent of the budgets of these provinces, and spending on agriculture, forestry, and water management declined from 7.58 to 4.21 percent. In contrast, expenditures on urban maintenance, a category of spending usually associated with burnishing the image of the major urban centers, doubled.[58] Because local officials are more likely to get promoted for delivering short-term high growth rates or other forms of tangible results, off-budget revenue tends to be spent on building local industries and other projects that contribute little to improvements in education, health, or the environment.

There is another reason for government officials to favor off-budget revenue. Since normal budget rules do not apply to the collection and use of such revenue, officials enjoy near total discretion. Abuse and corruption is rife. A large portion of the off-budget funds has been found stashed away in secret slush funds controlled by government officials. According to the finance minister, investigations found that theft and corruption was detected in every slush fund.[59] In a report released in June 1999, the National Audit Administration claimed to have uncovered slush funds and illegal expenditures that amounted to 96 billion yuan, equal to 10 percent of the 1998 tax revenue.[60]

An important consequence of this dysfunctional fiscal system is the near-collapse of local public finance in many counties and townships, particularly in the interior agricultural provinces with large populations, such as Henan, Anhui, Hunan, Hubei, Jiangxi, and Hebei. Although China's 2,400 counties and 46,000 townships provide most of the daily government services, they rely on a slim tax base, collecting 20 percent of total government revenue.[61] Nationally, counties could generate revenue equal to only two-thirds of their expenditures in 1999. About 40 percent of the counties can generate revenue sufficient to cover only half of their expenditures.[62]

The fiscal conditions for rural township governments are even more dire. Though saddled with the mandate to pay for most local services, the most costly of which is public education, these townships have practically no tax base and must extract their revenue from farmers, mostly through an inefficient and coercive collection system. Most studies of the indebtedness of rural governments pinpoint the mid-1990s as the period when this problem began to emerge. In the 1980s and early 1990s, indebtedness was not a serious issue in rural public finance. Among the causes that contributed to the debt problem, the 1994 tax reform was singled out as the most important. Intended to strengthen the fiscal capacity of the central government, this reform placed the heaviest burdens on the politically weakest township and village governments. Unwilling to cede their share of the revenue, provincial and municipal governments increased the pressures on township and village governments to meet ever-rising revenue goals and even threatened local officials with dismissal should they fail to deliver. As a result, township and village governments were forced to cut services and increase taxes and fees on rural residents. This, in turn, fueled rural discontent and sparked tax resistance as peasants saw their taxes rise while local services deteriorated. According to one study, tax resistance was a major factor in the decline of local fiscal capacity. Unpaid taxes and fees accounted for one-third of village debts.[63]

The magnitude of the township and village fiscal crisis in the late 1990s was captured by a study of the Ministry of Agriculture. According to its findings, at the end of 1998, 90 percent of townships and 83 percent of villages were deeply in debt. The total amount of debts owed by these townships and villages totaled 325.9 billion yuan. Townships owed 177.6 billion yuan, averaging 4 million yuan per township; villages owed 148.3 billion yuan, averaging 210,000 yuan per village. The amount of debts grew 17.5 percent in 1999 and 11 percent in 2000. This means that township and village debts reached 423 billion yuan by 2000, equivalent to almost 30 percent of agricultural GDP in 1999.[64] A senior researcher at the Ministry of Finance who led a team to study the issue of rural public indebtedness estimated that, by 2004, the total amount of public debts owed by townships and villages ranged between 600 billion to 1 trillion yuan, or close to 10 percent of GDP.[65] Agricultural regions were most heavily indebted. The debt-to-asset ratio was 26 percent in eastern coastal regions, 42 percent in central agricultural regions, and 24 percent in the poor western regions.[66] Media reports on rural indebtedness in individual provinces provide further evidence of fiscal stress in large agrarian provinces. A survey of township governments in Hunan in 2000 found that 88 percent were in debt; they owed 8.5 billion yuan, about half the province's total fiscal revenue. In Henan, debts accumulated by township governments reached 9 billion yuan, or 40 percent of the total provincial fiscal revenue. Nearly all the township governments owed their employees back pay.[67] In Anhui province, debts owed by township and village governments amounted to three times their annual revenue in 1998.[68]

Several factors were responsible for the rapid accumulation of debts in rural China. A Ministry of Agriculture survey found that the most important cause of the indebtedness was failed investments in TVEs. Loans borrowed to finance these enterprises, many of which eventually failed, accounted for 38 percent of the debts owed by township and village governments. Borrowing to provide basic services and finance local roads, bridges, and other infrastructure accounted for 18 percent of the accumulated debts. Some Chinese researchers criticized such spending as a wasteful use of resources that benefited the political careers of local officials. In particular, they singled out the building of image projects, especially paved highways and roads, as an example. Almost 8 percent of all debts were loans borrowed to build roads. Loans borrowed to finance everyday commercial and agricultural operations amounted to 8 percent of the debts; 4 percent of the debts was attributed to the loans used by township and village governments to pay taxes; and 5 percent of the debts was used to pay the salaries for local officials.[69]

The case of an unnamed county in Anhui was representative. In this county, bad loans borrowed to finance village and township industries accounted for 37 percent of the debt. In villages, 15 percent of the debt was owed as a result of building local public infrastructure such as schools and roads. In townships, the figure was 30 percent. The costs of the image projects launched by local officials to burnish their record accounted for 8 percent of the debts. The costs of supporting bloated local bureaucracies and their administrative expenses added an additional 20 percent to the debt load.[70] One study reported that about half the loans borrowed from banks by township governments were used to pay the salaries of township officials in 2001.[71]

According to Chen Xiwen, a leading expert on rural China, township and village governments relied on three sources for borrowing: local agricultural cooperative credit associations (*nongye hezuo jijin hui*), which provided loans for commercial projects; local entrepreneurs; and state-owned banks and rural credit unions.[72] A more detailed breakdown of these credits showed that banks and rural credit unions were the single largest source of loans, providing 42 percent, or 136 billion yuan, in loans. More than half of these loans (53 percent) were overdue, with half of these unpaid loans three years overdue.[73]

In addition to forcing rural governments to cut services, the distressed local public finance is viewed by many in China as directly responsible for the rural political decay and rising tensions between the state and the peasantry.[74] For example, village governments and party cells grow progressively weak as local elites become more reluctant to serve in these heavily indebted villages.[75] In township governments, high debts and unpaid wages demoralize officials.[76] In early 2001, for example, unpaid salaries for township officials and workers in Jilin totaled 46 million yuan, or about half the province's unpaid salaries. Similar situations were reported in Anhui. The rural public finance crisis is also a major contributor to rising tensions. In heavily indebted townships, tensions between cadres and rural residents are high. Local government officials often meet strong resistance in implementing government policy and collecting revenue.[77]

Erosion of the CCP's Mobilization Capacity

In measuring a state's governing capacity, a crucial variable is the mobilization capacity of its major political parties. As institutions to aggregate different social and political interests and build coalitions, political parties play a crucial role in generating support for the legitimacy and policies of the government. The political party's role in mass mobilization and governance is perhaps even more critical in authoritarian regimes than in democratic polities. As Samuel Huntington observed, "The one-party system is the principal modern form of authoritarian government." And the strength of an authoritarian regime depends on the strength of its party.[78] The key to the viability and durability of the ruling party in an authoritarian regime is its capacity to mobilize mass political support and maintain legitimacy. Despite the conventional wisdom that authoritarian regimes depend mainly on repression for survival, monopolistic ruling parties actually use a mixture of ideological appeal, redistributive economic policies, organizational penetration, and repression in governing their societies.

In the Mao era, the CCP had an unusually strong capacity of mass political mobilization. The combination of a charismatic leader, a sinicized communist ideology, a youthful revolutionary party tested by decades of war, a development strategy that maximized the control of the state, and the ruthless application of mass repression enabled the CCP to rally the Chinese nation behind its causes. Although weakened by the catastrophic failure of Mao's radical policies, the CCP retained a measure of mobilization capacity in the early years of the reform era thanks, in large part, to Deng's progressive policies. Post-Mao reforms launched by Deng managed, in the immediate aftermath of the Cultural Revolution, to repair the tarnished image of the CCP and build a broad proreform coalition. More important, the CCP's extensive organizational infrastructure in Chinese society and economy had yet to experience the impact of market-oriented reforms.

A quarter century of economic reform later, however, the extent of the atrophy of the CCP's mass mobilization capacity began to be visible, even as it had grown more adept in using selective repression and targeted co-optation to maintain its rule. Market-oriented reforms have undermined the economic infrastructure upon which the CCP's organizational system was built, leading to the party's decline, first in the countryside, and later in the cities. Within the party itself, the breakdown of discipline and institutional norms has caused widespread corruption and degraded the party's organizational integrity. The party's mass appeal practically disappeared, as well, mainly because of exclusivist and proelite policies pursued by the party and its subsequent transformation from a mass revolutionary party into a group of self-serving elites.

In practical terms, the erosion of the CCP's mass mobilization capacity means that the party no longer can build broad-based social coalitions to pursue its policies and defend itself. Instead, it has to rely more than ever on economic performance to maintain legitimacy and use the repressive power of the state to defend its power. The best example to illustrate the political consequences of the CCP's declining political mobilization capacity was the party's suppression of the quasi-spiritual movement, Falun Gong, in 1999. During the Maoist era, the CCP could have easily mobilized its loyal supporters, such as workers and peasants, to contain and even destroy a nationwide social network like Falun Gong without resorting to the use of police. But in 1999, the only effective instrument the CCP could mobilize was the police. Despite a massive official propaganda campaign against Falun Gong, the

CCP could not mobilize a single social group to support its crackdown. In the end, it was the application of brute force, not the mobilization of the masses, that enabled the CCP to destroy the movement inside China.

Economic Reform and the CCP's Organizational Decline

The organizational decline of the CCP, in retrospect, was almost predetermined. Leninist parties like the CCP have maintained their durability only in economies dominated by the state. Such economies provide the economic infrastructure (SOEs and collective farms) that form the organizational backbone for the ruling parties. By pursuing market reforms that gradually eliminated collective agriculture and privatized a large number of SOEs, the CCP may have become a victim of its own economic success. The new economic infrastructure, based on household farming, private ownership of capital, and individual labor mobility, proves inhospitable to the organizational presence of the CCP. The sign that market reforms were undermining the party's organizational health first emerged in the rural areas, which spearheaded China's economic reforms.

Economic reform weakened the party's hold in the countryside through two mechanisms. First, the dismantling of the people's communes and the return to household farming directly reduced the power of the CCP because the party's grassroots cells lost much of their relevance in the social and economic activities of rural residents. Economically, individual farmers, not local CCP officials, make most daily decisions. Competitive market forces have also compelled the majority of rural CCP members to devote their energy to the demands of their own household farms, instead of the political requirements of the party. To the extent that the CCP's rural cadres continue to inspire loyalty and support, it is mainly due to these cadres' ability to create economic opportunities and improve the standard of living of their villages—not to their political status as the representatives of the ruling party.[79] In addition, the amount of social services provided by local governments has steadily contracted. Prior to reform, the party had played an indispensable role in mobilizing rural resources in supplying social services, such as maintaining public health and building rural infrastructure. After the reform, most local rural governments either withdrew from providing these services or forced rural residents to pay for them.[80]

Second, the gradual opening of the labor markets to rural migrants in the urban areas has allowed the younger, more educated, and entrepreneurial rural peasants to move to the cities in search of better jobs, thus reducing the pool and the caliber of potential party recruits.[81] These new opportunities have also encouraged many rural CCP members to move into the cities.[82] A survey of party officials in five hundred poor townships in Sichuan in the late 1990s found that about 40 percent of them were unwilling to stay in the villages. Of the 300,000 rural CCP members in four impoverished prefects in Sichuan province, half of them had less than a primary school education as of 1998.[83]

Consequently, the CCP has suffered severe organizational degradation in the rural areas. A report by the Shanxi CCP POD in 2000 admitted that the party's rural cells had neglected party-building and seldom organized political activities or recruited new members. A survey of one prefect in Shanxi in 1998 found that seven hundred villages had not recruited a single member in three years. Another survey of 620 villages in 2000, in the same prefect, showed that none of them had recruited a party member in the previous three years.[84] The CCP's village cells, the party's most important grassroots organization, have deteriorated as well. From 1994 to 2000, the party was forced to fix 356,000 of the rural CCP cells that were characterized as weak or paralyzed. They represented half the CCP village cells.[85] A report by the Zhejiang CCP POD disclosed that about 56 percent of the party's village cells in the province were rated third-grade (ineffective and paralyzed). The party's rural members appear to have grown disillusioned and demoralized as well. One survey of party members in Sichuan showed that 26 percent of them did not support or trust the party and would like to drop out of the party.[86]

In urban areas, the CCP's organizational integrity has also suffered from the effects of market reforms. The mass bankruptcy of SOEs since the mid-1990s has led to tens of thousands of factory closures—and the effective dismantling of the CCP party organizations in these SOEs. In Liaoning, one of the provinces hardest hit by mass closures of SOEs in the 1990s, 80,000 CCP members were among the 680,000 workers employed in closed or semiclosed factories. Almost 50,000 CCP members were among the laid-off and furloughed workers. Most laid-off CCP members lost contact with their former CCP organizations; only

8 percent applied for activity passes that would allow them to maintain organizational contact with their former CCP cells.[87] In an internal assessment in 2000, the Shanxi CCP POD reported that "in nonoperating SOEs, the party organization is almost in a state of collapse. It does not conduct organizational activities or recruit new members. It cannot even collect party dues."[88]

At the same time, the CCP has been stymied in penetrating the private sector.[89] In 2000, the CCP did not have a single member in 86 percent of the 1.5 million private firms and was able to establish cell organizations in only 1 percent of the private firms.[90] China's newly established professional service firms—such as law and accounting firms and private medical clinics—and professional associations also have not been receptive to the party's attempts to attract new members.[91] The party's efforts to set up its organizational presence in foreign-invested business have fared no better.[92] The reality of a "party-unfriendly" marketplace has led even the members of the ruling elite to question the need for the CCP to have an organizational presence in nonstate firms. A survey of six hundred officials in 2000 found that almost 40 percent thought private firms do not need party cells.[93] The long-term political implications of the CCP's failure to penetrate the private sector spell trouble for the party because foreign-invested firms and domestic private firms have become the main source of employment while the payrolls in SOEs have been shrinking. The number of employees in private, foreign, and collective firms in 2002 almost equaled that in SOEs.[94]

Internal Corruption

Internally, the CCP has been weakened by pervasive corruption and loss of ideological beliefs.[95] Far from being a monolithic Leninist party with tight internal discipline, the CCP in reality suffers from a serious breakdown of organizational discipline and norms due to patronage and institutionalized inability to enforce its own rules. As described in Chapter 4, because of the concentration of power in the hands of lower-level party functionaries in the reform era, these officials have acquired the ability to build mini-patronage machines inside the party that serve their individual needs, rather than the CCP's collective interests. The widespread practice of selling government appointments is a typical manifestation of such patronage.

Surveys of the party's officials found that appointments and promotions within the party depend more on personal relations with superiors than on merits or qualifications. About two-thirds of officials being trained at a municipal party school revealed in a survey that their promotion depended solely on the favors of their superiors; only 5 percent thought that their individual efforts could help gain career advancement.[96] In a survey of 1,159 officials in the northeastern city of Ha'erbin in 1997, 52 percent identified "personal connections determine cadre appointments" as the main factor in the selection of cadres.[97] The results of a survey of 1,230 officials in Anhui in 1998 provided additional confirmation. When asked about the reasons for demotion of incumbent officials, 59 percent thought such unlucky officials "lacked patrons above," and 41 percent thought that they did not "entertain or give gifts."[98] Unavoidably, such patronage has generated widespread resentment within the party. Of the 13,821 party members in Sichuan surveyed in 1997, 40 percent complained that the CCP's system of selecting cadres "lacks democracy and popular support," and 18 percent thought that "it does not enable the emergence of outstanding talents."[99]

The CCP also suffers from a chronic inability to cleanse itself through the expulsion of unqualified members and removal of incompetent or corrupt officials. According to the deputy minister of the CCP's COD, the party's own sampling showed that about 5 percent of the party members—or 3 million—are unqualified, but the party expels only a small number of the members it considers unqualified.[100] Another figure, disclosed by the CCP's COD, indicated that the CCP removed 473,000 unqualified members from the party from 1989 to 2000, averaging almost 40,000 a year. Thus, only about 1 percent of the unqualified members are forced to quit the party each year.[101] Revealingly, unqualified members have the characteristics normally associated with careerists and opportunists: most of them are younger than thirty-five, have a college or college-equivalent education, hold official appointments in the government and SOEs, and fail to participate in the party's activities or pay party dues.

The party appears to be less able to remove such elements today than before, however. In 1950, for example, about 4 percent of CCP members "exited" the party through expulsions and forced resignations. In 1999, only 0.05 percent of the CCP members exited the party.[102] The mechanisms of removing incompetent CCP officials are equally dysfunctional. Official data show few incompetent officials are dismissed. From 1995 to 1997 in Ha'erbin, only 1.43 percent of the local cadres were demoted, fired, or forced to resign.[103] In Jilin province, from 1994 to 1997, only 199 officials (at the county-level and above) were demoted or fired, accounting for only 2 percent of the officials.[104] Zeng Qinghong, head of the CCP COD, publicly disclosed that, from 1995 to 2000, only 366 cadres at the department/bureau (*ting* and *ju*) level were "adjusted" (demoted or removed) and about 10,000 cadres at the level of division (*chu*) had their jobs "adjusted" due to incompetence. They accounted for less than 1 percent of the total number of officials at those ranks.[105]

The CCP's organizational decay has led to widespread cynicism within the party's ranks. A survey of nearly 12,500 party members in Sichuan in 1997 showed that 55 percent of them had insufficient or no confidence in the government's ability to improve its system of demoting and removing cadres.[106] Another survey of 1,100 government officials in Changsha city in 1997 yielded similar findings: 31 percent lacked confidence in a good system of promotion and demotion of officials; 14 percent thought many of the officials in power were incompetent and their replacements might be no better; and 58 percent said that all the noise about reforming the cadre system was just talk.[107] Even more disconcerting than a dysfunctional system of promotion and demotion of party officials is the CCP's evident inability to punish the corrupt elements inside the party. As shown in Chapter 4, the majority—more than 90 percent—of officials caught for corruption are spared criminal prosecution. Indeed, self-cleansing may be impossible for a ruling party accountable to no one.

Mass Disenchantment with the CCP

No ruling party can mobilize the population if its policies serve the interests of a small elite and if it is perceived as corrupt and indifferent to the interests of the public. Indeed, the CCP's strategy—maintaining an extensive patronage for its loyalists, co-opting new social elites, and excluding a large segment of Chinese society (mainly workers and peasants) from equally sharing the benefits of economic growth—has led to mass disenchantment with the party. Unavoidably, this strategy has tarnished the party's image. A survey of 818 migrant rural laborers in

Beijing in 1997–1998 found that 22 percent of the respondents thought the authority of local cadres in their homes was low and 41 percent said it was very low. About 60 percent also said that such authority had declined compared to a few years back. The prevailing image of the ruling party among the respondents was that of a self-serving elite. Only 5 percent of the interviewees thought their local cadres "work for the interests of the villagers and do not use their power for private gains," and 60 percent said that their local cadres "only use their power for private gains and do not work for the interests of the villagers." Eighty-five percent said that their village heads and CCP secretaries were corrupt.[108] Another survey of almost 15,000 rural residents in Zhengzhou, Henan province, in 2000 found that 39 percent thought the cadres were corrupt and phony, and 7 percent complained that local cadres were arbitrary and abusive.[109]

The party's own research also found an elite that is increasingly out of touch with the public. A survey of 11,586 CCP members in Sichuan in 1999 showed that only 16 percent selected "ordinary people" as those they "contact the most often and closely in their daily work and lives," while 36 percent selected "superiors and close colleagues."[110] Some members of the ruling elite also admitted the deterioration of the party's image. A poll conducted among 673 CCP officials in northeastern Jilin province in 1998 found that 35 percent thought the status, role, and authority of party and government officials had declined.[111] Obviously, the most persuasive evidence of mass disenchantment with the CCP is the growing conflict between the regime and Chinese society, as will be detailed in the following section.

Of all the factors responsible for the declining political vigor of the CCP, the most crucial one is, ironically, the absence of competition that would have forced the ruling party to redefine its missions, recruit members with genuine public appeal, and maintain its competitive edge through constant challenges. In understanding the root cause of the CCP's declining mobilization capacity, it may be useful to draw an analogy with the behavior of corporate monopolies. Few monopolistic corporations have voluntarily given up their lucrative monopolies. Instead, they devote all their energy to prevent the emergence of competition. The same behavioral logic applies to political monopolies like the CCP. And like corporate monopolies that eventually succumb to the ills of inefficiency, political monopolies like the CCP, in the absence of competitive pressures from rival parties, will inevitably develop a full range of pathologies such as cynicism, patronage, organizational dystrophy, and unresponsiveness. One-party regimes can rarely take on new competitors when the political environment changes suddenly. The fall of monopolistic parties in the former Soviet bloc and in the developing world (Mexico and Taiwan, for example) shows that declining political mobilization capacity imperils the CCP's long-term viability.

Rising Tensions Between the State and Society

An unavoidable consequence of declining state capacity and appeal of the ruling party is the rising tensions between the state and society. Both aggregate data and press reports indicate a sharp increase in incidents of collective protests, riots, and other forms of resistance against state authorities.[112] Such increases were especially pronounced in the 1990s. According to a report released by a research institute affiliated with the MPS, the number of such incidents grew almost fourfold over seven years, from 8,700 in 1993 to 32,000 in 1999. Additionally, the size and the level of violence of collective incidents have increased as well. In 1999, 125 incidents involved more than a thousand protesters. The government also admitted that protests with more than 10,000 participants have become quite common. In rural areas, many localities have reported mob attacks by peasants on officials and government buildings. In 2000, the number of collective protests in rural areas exceeded half of all reported instances of collective protest for the first time.[113]

The Chinese media occasionally carry stories of such confrontations, many of which are dramatic and violent. Some of the collective protests in rural areas were increasingly well-organized, as research by Yu Jianrong in a county in Hunan province in the late 1990s shows.[114] In an in-depth look at rural unrest published in January 2000, the internal edition of the official magazine *Banyuetan* described in graphic detail a series of rural riots that occurred in the late 1990s in Hunan province, which, ironically, was where Mao fomented peasant uprisings in the 1920s.

Around the New Year's Day in 1999, 46 peasant leaders in Daolin township in Hunan's Ningxiang county met and decided to hold a rally of 10,000 people in front of the township government to demand "reducing peasant burdens and fighting corruption." On January 8, 1999, the authorities mobilized a large police force and blocked the highway leading to the township government complex. But rural residents from all over the township kept coming. At one point, the crowd exceeded 5,000 people. A small number rushed the police line. The police were forced to fire tear gas canisters. This led to one of the most violent collective riots in Hunan's countryside . . . In 1996, about one thousand farmers from Shangjia township surrounded the municipal government building of Lianyuan city and called for reducing taxes. Several farmers ransacked the home of the party secretary of the municipality. In 1998, peasants in the same township forcibly took over a local public school, hired teachers, and stationed security guards in front of the school—in open defiance of the local government. In a neighboring township in the same year, rioting farmers took away the signs in front of the government building, assaulted the party secretary and stripped him naked. Cadres dispatched from the city to mediate the dispute were detained as well . . . In the wee hours on November 7, 1998, a team of more than 30 policemen, tax collectors, and township officials conducted a raid on Guangyinyan village in Huatan township in Taoyuan county. Their objective was to arrest a local resident who had led a tax resistance movement. But before the team could leave the village, they were surrounded by angry farmers. In a violent confrontation, fifteen police officers and cadres were injured, and ten were stripped naked. Only after the peasant leader was released did the farmers let the hungry and tired police officers and cadres go. Similar violent incidents were reported in practically all the other large agrarian provinces, such as Hebei, Henan, and Sichuan.[115]

To be sure, economic transitions inevitably produce rising social frustrations because of the socioeconomic dislocation created by the introduction of market forces. In urban areas, for example, rising unemployment has fueled rising social dissatisfaction. Behind the specific social and economic factors closely associated with societal discontent, however, is a set of political variables that both contribute to and exacerbate social frustrations during economic transition. These factors include specific government policies, especially its policies on taxes, family planning, education, the social safety net, and SOE restructuring; the lack of effective institutional mechanisms for resolving social conflicts and private grievances; and the breakdown of political accountability that makes local government authorities insensitive and unresponsive to public needs. The combination of socioeconomic dislocation, harmful policies, and flawed political institutions turns social frustration into political protest, not merely because of economic deprivation, but because of a growing sense of political injustice.

Rural Decay and Discontent

As discussed in the previous section, the institutional decay of the ruling party is more advanced in rural areas than in the cities. Such political decay, coupled with the relative economic decline of the rural sector, is the main source of rising tensions in the countryside.[116] Media reports and official disclosures indicate that such tensions reached dangerous levels in the 1990s. In a startling internal report, the MPS admitted that "in some (rural) areas, enforcement of family planning policy and collection of taxes would be impossible without the use of police force."[117] Of all the incidents officially classified as "incidents of instability" in the rural areas, 70 percent was caused by "tensions between the cadres and the masses."[118] On the surface, economic factors, especially stagnant income growth, appeared to be mainly responsible for declining governability in the countryside. But a closer look shows that three political causes—high taxes on the peasantry, the decay of the administrative institutions, and the forcible seizure of land by local authorities for commercial use—have perhaps played a more important role in fueling discontent.[119]

Rural income, a gauge of the well-being of the peasantry, fluctuated during the reform era. At the initial stage (1978–1985), per capita income in the countryside rose sharply, averaging a net increase of 15.2 percent per year. But per capita income growth began to stagnate afterward, rising only 2.8 percent a year during 1986–1991. It recovered somewhat during the early 1990s, averaging 5.7 percent annually during 1992–1996.[120] In the late 1990s, rural income growth entered another period of stagnation. Official data show that net income per rural resident grew 9 percent in 1996, 4.6 percent in 1997, 4.3 percent in 1998, 3.8 percent in 1999, and 2.1 percent in 2000. Per capita net income from agricultural activities, however, registered negative growth from 1998 to 2000. In 1998, rural per capita income from agriculture fell 30.25 yuan from 1997; in 1999, it declined by an additional 57.42 yuan; in 2000, it registered a further decline of 43.94 yuan. The absolute three-year decline totaled 131 yuan, implying a 6.3 percent reduction in net income from 1997 to 2000. Because close to 80 percent of rural residents derived most of their income from agricultural production, this meant that a majority of rural residents experienced negative growth in net income.[121]

There were several reasons for declining income from agriculture, such as an oversupply of major agricultural products (especially grain), rising costs of inputs, low labor productivity, high taxes, and under-development of rural finance.[122] For example, the costs of agricultural inputs, such as seeds, fertilizers, and fuel, increased while prices for agricultural products fell steadily. During 1997–1998, for example, prices for agricultural products fell 22 percent, resulting in income losses estimated in the range of 300 billion to 400 billion yuan.[123] The combination of low prices, high production costs, and high taxes made agricultural production unprofitable. In 1999, the average costs of pro-ducing the three main grains—rice, wheat, and corn—reached 43 per-cent of their sale price. The agricultural taxes and other *legal* levies added an additional 16 percent. Thus, after paying for inputs and taxes, the residual for peasants was only 40 percent of their crops. The costs and effective land rent made grain production unprofitable. Indeed, the example of Qipan township, in Jianli county in Hubei, was representa-tive. According to the township party secretary, farming was unprof-itable for 80 percent of the peasants in his jurisdiction in 1999.[124] A leading agricultural researcher at the State Council's Development Research Center warned that, without the subsidies from nonagricultural cash income, grain production might be on the verge of collapse.[125]

Declining rural income growth alone might not be sufficient to gen-erate mass discontent. The most important source of tensions between the peasantry and the state is the onerous taxes and fees China's most underprivileged social group is forced to pay.[126] Officially, such taxes and fees, commonly known as "peasant burdens," should not exceed 5 percent of the net income of farmers. In reality, local authorities have levied numerous illegal fees that greatly exceed the 5 percent limit im-posed by Beijing. Because of the imposition of these illegal levies, none of which was reported or recorded in official statistics, it was difficult to determine the exact magnitude of the peasant burdens. At the low end of the estimates, according to data from the three hundred villages tracked by the Ministry of Agriculture in the 1990s, taxes and fees increased by 24 percent in the decade and amounted to 6.46 percent of per capita net income.[127] According to one study by the State Administration of Taxation, taxes and authorized levies in 1996 were about 10 percent of rural GDP. If additional illegal fees and levies are added, the total effective tax rate, broadly defined, could be 20 percent of rural GDP that year, excluding the cash income from nonagricultural activities.[128] At the high end of the estimate, according to surveys conducted by the Ministry of Agriculture in one hundred counties in 1996, taxes and fees paid by each peasant were three times the official national limit, or 15 percent of their net income.[129]

In addition, such taxes and fees were highly regressive, both for individuals and regions, as poorer peasants and less developed regions paid a higher proportion of their incomes in such taxes and fees, mainly because such taxes and fees were levied on a per capita basis and became, effectively, poll taxes. The poorest peasants, with annual income of 400–500 yuan a year, had to pay almost 17 percent of their income in 1996 in assorted taxes and fees.[130] Those earning 1,500–1,700 yuan paid 6.7 percent; those with incomes of 2,500–3,000 yuan paid 4.9 percent. The rate for those earning 4,500–5,000 yuan was a mere 2.8 percent. In regional terms, peasants in the wealthy coastal areas in the east paid 3.94 percent; those in the agrarian central regions paid 8.01 percent; and the rate in the impoverished western regions was 5.64 percent.[131]

Institutional changes and economic reform in rural areas have made taxes and fees extremely unpopular for several reasons. The replacement of collective agricultural production by household farming has severed the economic links between local governments and peasants, who have gained autonomy in their economic and social lives. On a daily basis, the government plays practically no visible role in the economic activities of peasants. Politically, the prospects of political advancement through membership inside the Communist Party are dim, and rural residents do not rely on the ruling party for their political welfare. In other words, the government and the ruling party have become almost irrelevant to peasants engaged in household farming. Such irrelevance makes taxes and fees, especially those levied for projects outside local communities, illegitimate.

What has further irked the peasantry is that their high taxes appear to have brought in return few government services, such as public health, education, and agricultural infrastructure. The combination of high and regressive taxes, heavy-handed collection efforts, and inadequate provision of public goods has turned a large portion of the rural population against the state. In a survey of two thousand rural residents in late 2001, 65 percent of the respondents selected "excessive tax burdens" as the principal cause of local social instability.[132]

Such resentments have led to widespread tax resistance. In a survey conducted in Xinjiang in 2001, tax resistance was found prevalent among peasants in 40 percent of the villages surveyed.[133] In many areas, peasants simply abandoned land as a form of protest. In one Hubei township, where this problem was considered serious, 25 percent of the farmland was abandoned by peasants who could no longer afford to till the land because of taxes, high costs of seeds and fertilizers, and low prices of grains.[134] In another Hubei township, according to its party secretary, peasants abandoned almost two-thirds of the township's arable farmland in 2000.[135]

As a result, collecting taxes and fees has become increasingly difficult. In most areas, this has become practically the predominant administrative task performed by local officials in rural areas, consuming 60–70 percent of their time.[136] A report issued by the National Bureau of Statistics revealed that, in its survey of six counties in Xinjiang in 2001, about 70 percent of the village cadres thought collecting fees was the most difficult task.[137] In response, local authorities, which depend on such taxes and fees to support themselves, adopted various collection methods.[138] Officials in many areas recruited thugs as their collection agents. Such a practice has resulted in illegal imprisonment, torture, and the deaths of peasants who were unable to pay. In Guangxi province, local officials even forced middle-school teachers to collect taxes from peasants who had refused to pay. Because teachers are highly respected among peasants, they usually were able to collect back taxes. Such tactics were used in many areas where tax resistance was high.[139]

The persistent and rising tensions between local authorities and the peasantry accelerated rural political decay, which in turn added to bad governance in the countryside and became another source of social discontent. In its most extreme form, rural political decay has led to the emergence of local mafia states. In his study of forty Hunan villages that had been labeled "out of control" (*shikong*), Yu Jianrong, a researcher at the Chinese Academy of Social Sciences, reported that rural township officials deliberately allowed mafia-type criminal elements to penetrate village governments. These officials used such elements to counterbalance other organized criminal groups or intimidate local peasantry and facilitate tax collection. In some cases, township officials themselves had turned into criminals and effectively formed their own mafia groups. Of the forty villages that were considered controlled by local mafia groups, the chairmen of the villagers committees in half of them were connected with organized crime and won their elections with the support of the mafia.[140]

At the other end of the spectrum, peasant resistance had led to a virtual collapse of government authority in villages. The following two examples from Anhui province are illustrative. A party secretary in Wugou township in Anhui gave this description of the conditions in his jurisdiction in the late 1990s:

> The township was known for violating the family planning policy and for sending petitioners to higher authorities. Peasants there refused to pay the agricultural tax. When local officials and police tried to enforce government orders, they were surrounded by villagers and forced to write self-criticisms before they were released. In 1998, the three inspection teams dispatched by the provincial family planning commission were attacked by the villagers and forced to flee. Hoodlums ran amok. The township's party secretary and mayor were repeatedly assaulted; the attackers were never punished. In 1998, the township government was reelected. All six candidates sent down by the higher authorities lost. The leaders of the city and county led 13 work teams to try to restore order, but all failed. The township was completely out of control. The government could not do a thing. The party could not lead.[141]

The official magazine *Banyuetan* (internal edition) provides another vivid but disturbing account of conditions in Liuzhai village in Lingquan county, Anhui province.

> The tensions between the village residents and township cadres were so high in the mid-1990s that for three years township and village officials did not dare to enter the village. As a result, no taxes or fees were collected. The family planning policy was not enforced . . . Whoever came forward to be the village official or cooperated with the government would have his crops destroyed and farm animals poisoned. Even though the authorities had sent six different work teams to the village,

they could not form a village government. For five years, the village had no party cell, no village committee, and no leaders.[142]

Worried about growing rural unrest, the Chinese government has attempted several remedial measures, the most important of which was the substitution of fees with taxes (*feigaishui*). But the initial results from the areas where the reform was tested were mixed. In a pilot program in Jingshan county in Hubei, this reform resulted in reduction of peasant burdens by 40 percent.[143] However, the *feigaishui* reform alone did not address the most critical issue behind high peasant burdens—a bloated rural bureaucracy. Without a drastic reduction in the size of the township government, *feigaishui* could provide only temporary relief. For example, in a township in Jingshan county, after the reform was implemented, tax revenue from agriculture totaled 4.7 million yuan a year, but the township government had 730 people on its payroll at a cost of 4.6 million yuan a year. This meant that the township government would have to extract additional revenue from peasants if it wanted to perform the most basic administrative functions and deliver local services.[144] Indeed, Ray Yep's study of the *feigaishui* reform concludes that replacing fees with taxes alone is unlikely to reduce rural tensions.[145]

Yet, in 2003, the Chinese government decided to implement the *feigaishui* reform nationwide, without any accompanying political reforms designed to reduce the size of the rural government. But even if the reform is fully and successfully implemented, its impact on reducing peasant burdens might be modest. It is estimated that 40 billion yuan, about a third of the fees levied on peasants, would be reduced as a result of the reform. This would be an overall reduction of 20 percent of "overt" peasant burdens (legally imposed taxes and fees). On a per capita basis, each rural resident would get to keep an extra 50 yuan a year, roughly about 2 percent of per capita rural net income.[146]

The Unemployment Challenge

Urban residents are, by comparison, far more privileged than their rural counterparts. During the reform era, their standard of living has also increased dramatically. Generally, polling data indicate that a large majority of China's urban residents are relatively satisfied with their lives and think China is stable at the beginning of the twenty-first century.[147] Yet, behind the polls was a more complex, if not disquieting, picture.

According to tracking polls conducted by Horizon Research, a respected private market research firm based in Beijing, the proportion of urban residents expressing satisfaction with their lives has been steadily decreasing since the late 1990s, while that of those expressing discontent has been rising. A Horizon poll conducted in ten cities at the end of 1997 showed that 80 percent were satisfied and only 19 percent were dissatisfied. Another Horizon poll of 5,673 residents in eleven cities in November 1998 found 70 percent were satisfied and 27 percent dissatisfied.[148] Horizon's poll of 3,502 people in 2000 reported that 55 percent of the urban residents expressed satisfaction with their lives, and about 27 percent expressed dissatisfaction. The firm's poll of 4,728 urban residents in 2001 reported that about 63 percent were satisfied with their lives and 33.6 percent were dissatisfied.[149]

A different poll, conducted by a research institute of the State Planning Commission in September 2001, confirmed a similar trend of rising discontent. It concluded that "optimism was not warranted with respect to residents' level of satisfaction with the country's social and economic development." Specifically, the institute's report cited a decline in the percentage of the respondents who viewed China's social situation as stable. In the institute's poll in 2000, 63 percent thought the country's social situation was stable; in 2001, 56 percent did, while the percentage that believed the situation was unstable rose from 10 to 13 percent.[150]

Unemployment, corruption, deterioration of SOEs, environmental degradation, and rising inequality appeared to be driving the level of discontent at the end of the 1990s.[151] In the annual polls of urban residents conducted by Horizon Research from 1997 to 2001, unemployment was rated the top issue in three years and the number two issue in two years. Corruption was mentioned as the top issue in one year and identified as among the top three issues in another two years. The plight of SOEs was mentioned as the top issue in one year and the number three issue in one year.[152] A poll of 2,430 residents conducted by the State Economic System Reform Commission in fifty-three cities in 1998 showed inflation, corruption, and unemployment were the three top social problems the respondents were most concerned about.[153]

The results of a poll of 1999 people in September 2001 conducted by the State Planning Commission showed that urban residents identified corruption, unemployment, and rising inequality as the three top issues threatening local social stability. In the countryside, the top three issues were excessive taxes and fees, corruption, and rising inequality.[154]

Capturing a slice of the public mood in urban areas, a poll of 2,359 residents in fifty-five cities conducted by a research group affiliated with the State Council in 2001 revealed the specific causes of discontent. The results of this poll confirmed that socioeconomic frustrations were generating most of the urban discontent. More than 60 percent of respondents expressed dissatisfaction with unemployment, unaffordable healthcare, shrinking economic opportunities, and rising crime. Unemployment elicited the highest degree of discontent. Of all the major social groups, workers were the least satisfied, with 75 percent of workers polled expressing discontent, even higher than among those without long-term employment (71 percent). It is worth noting that a large proportion of workers (36 percent) blamed the loss of their jobs on lack of social justice and social connections. Almost 80 percent were dissatisfied with their incomes. Among the reasons cited for not earning a satisfactory income, the most frequently listed was bad luck, followed by lack of social connections and social justice. About 54 percent thought that the principal means of becoming wealthy was by using connections, power, and illegal methods.

Official corruption also appeared to galvanize public ire. An overwhelming majority expressed strong objection to the accumulation of wealth by government officials and SOE managers through power and corrupt means. And 55 percent said they lacked confidence in the government's anticorruption efforts; 54 percent thought half to a majority of government officials were corrupt. Close to 80 percent of the residents were dissatisfied with the work of government regulatory and watchdog agencies, such as stock market regulators.[155]

The rising level of discontent could threaten political stability. Though the percentage of those expressing discontent was relatively small, their absolute number could be very large. Three leading Chinese researchers estimated that, based on survey data, about 22–45 percent of urban residents, or 100 million to 200 million people, were dissatisfied with their conditions. Among them were 32 million to 36 million who were "extremely dissatisfied."[156]

To the extent that the Chinese government delayed the painful re-structuring of SOEs until 1995, rising urban discontent, mainly fueled by increasing unemployment in the cities, was only to be expected. Nevertheless, unemployment in the Chinese context was fraught with political risks because of the huge number of laid-off and unemployed workers who had lost their jobs in bankrupt SOEs, the flimsy social safety net provided by the Chinese state, the drastic fall in their standard of living, and their low reemployment rate. Government figures show that during 1996–2000, urban SOEs shed 31.59 million workers while collectively owned enterprises (COEs) dismissed 16.48 million workers.[157] This massive wave of layoffs helped drive up unemployment rates in the cities. According to a CASS estimate, the real unemployment rate in 2002 was 7 percent, twice the officially reported rate (official data on unemployment excludes laid-off workers and redundant workers in SOEs).[158] Unemployment hit workers in manufacturing particularly hard. Manufacturing workers accounted for 83 percent of all laid-off workers.[159] A large proportion of the laid-off workers were middle-aged and had low skill and education levels.[160]

For SOE employees, a social group considered relatively privileged because of the generous benefits and job security before the mid-1990s, the loss of social status resulting from unemployment was precipitous and widely recognized in the cities. A poll of more than two thousand residents in sixty cities conducted annually by a research group at CASS found that, starting in 1997, respondents began to identify workers in SOEs as the group that had benefited the least from reform; they were followed by peasants and migrant laborers, two low-status social groups in China. Similar polls conducted in 1998 and 1999 yielded the same results.[161]

More important, laid-off workers experienced an instant and drastic decline in their standards of living. In 2000, per capita income in the families of laid-off workers was about 55 percent of the average per capita income in urban areas.[162] In some areas, the loss of income was even more severe. In Changchun, a city in China's rustbelt in the northeast, per capita income in the households of the workers who had been laid off was only 26 percent of their pre–lay-off level.[163] For most of the laid-off workers, the government provided very limited support. In 1998, for example, only half of the laid-off workers regularly received minimum unemployment benefits from the government.[164] Unemployment benefits were inadequate even when they were paid. When asked how they make ends meet, only 2.3 percent of the laid-off workers in Tianjin surveyed said they relied on government support. In Changchun, only 5 percent would count on the government to solve their economic difficulties. In Liaoning, unemployment benefits accounted for less than 7 percent of the income for laid-off workers in the late 1990s.[165] To survive, most laid-off workers cut down their spending, depleted their meager savings, and borrowed from relatives and friends.[166]

The government's efforts to reemploy laid-off workers were largely unsuccessful. Most of the laid-off workers found government-run reemployment programs ineffective. In Tianjin, only 13 percent of the laid-off workers found work through these programs.[167] Nationwide, reemployment steadily declined. In 1998, half of the laid-off workers were reportedly reemployed. In 1999, the reemployment rate fell to 35 percent; it declined to 26 percent in 2000 and plunged to 11 percent by mid-2001.[168]

The combination of an inadequate social safety net and low reemployment rate directly contributed to the rising poverty rate among laid-off workers. A study of more than two hundred incidents involving industrial workers' collective protests in late 2003 found that about 80 percent of such incidents were prompted by restructuring of SOEs, unpaid wages, arrears in unemployment and health benefits, and postbankruptcy unemployment.[169] In Tianjin, 54 percent of the urban households below the minimum standard of living were those of laid-off workers; nearly 80 percent of them had trouble making ends meet.[170] A survey of 6,660 urban families with laid-off workers in Liaoning in 1998 found that families with two laid-off workers accounted for a third of all households below the minimum standard of living.[171] As expected, surveys also found, among laid-off workers, rising frustration and propensity to participate in collective protest. In 1999, 70 percent of the laid-off workers were dissatisfied with their lives. In 2000, 50 percent expressed dissatisfaction with their lives.[172] In a survey of 1,127 laid-off workers in Changchun in late 1998, a third said that they would "take to the streets" to protest against "serious corruption"; another third said that they would do so if they lacked food and clothing, and 18 percent said that they would resort to collective protest if they could not afford medical care. Three-quarters of them sympathized with workers staging collective demonstrations, but only 14 percent expressed willingness to take part in them.[173]

Nevertheless, the incidence of worker protests increased rapidly.[174] For example, the number of officially reported labor disputes rose 30 percent each year from 1997 to 2001.[175] Such protests were especially frequent and contentious in the rustbelt in the northeast. In March 2002, for example, more than 20,000 laid-off workers from more than twenty factories participated in a week-long protest in the northern city of Liaoyang.[176]

The Institutional Breakdown

In the context of a closed political system, rising social frustrations tend to be amplified by the absence of pressure valves within the Chinese system. Even though several post-Mao political reforms—such as village elections, the strengthening of the legislative branch, and legal reform—were steps in the right direction, they have proved too limited and inadequate as institutional mechanisms for managing, let alone resolving, state-society tensions. Under the current Chinese system of redressing social grievances, individuals have access to four channels: offices in various government bureaucracies that handle "letters and visits" (*xinfang*); administrative litigation; the local and national People's Congress system; and the media. None of these mechanisms works well in addressing social grievances.

Although the Chinese media have become more aggressive in exposing corruption and covering abuse of power by local government officials, they remain under the control of the CCP and fall far short of becoming an effective resource that ordinary citizens can depend on in airing their discontent or seeking to rally public support. Occasionally, coverage by muckraking publications such as *Nanfang zhoumo* (*Southern Weekend*), *Zhonguo qingnianbao* (*Chinese Youth Daily*), and *Nanfang dushibao* (*Southern Metropolitan News*) could cause a public outcry and force the central government to take remedial actions. But such occurrences are infrequent and rare. Of course, reporters and editors must walk a fine line between defending aggrieved individuals and groups and risking retaliation by local officials. The case of *Nanfang dushibao* is instructive. After exposing the beating death of a college graduate wrongfully detained as a vagrant in Guangzhou and the cover-up of the outbreak of severe acute respiratory syndrome (SARS) epidemic in the city in 2003, the paper's two top editors were accused and later convicted of taking bribes by local authorities.

The role of the local and national People's Congress in resolving social grievances remains limited as well. The deputies to these bodies are selected by the CCP and lack independence and power. Their intervention on behalf of aggrieved citizens is often ineffective. Chinese courts have not demonstrated their capacity to resolve state-social conflict, either. The only legal recourse for citizens victimized by local authorities is administrative litigation, which allows ordinary citizens and economic entities to sue local government agencies for illegal administrative actions. Although the implementation of the Administrative Litigation Law following its passage in 1989 was considered an important breakthrough in China's legal reform, the institution of administrative litigation so far has produced no appreciable effects on reducing state-society conflicts.

Chinese courts adjudicate an average of only 100,000 administrative cases a year and only 20 percent of the plaintiffs (or 20,000 individuals or corporations) get some judicial relief through such litigation.[177] In most cases, therefore, ordinary citizens cannot count on the courts for solutions to their grievances. Indeed, a survey of 632 rural residents who went to Beijing in 2004 to petition the central government showed that 401 of them had sued their local governments in courts. But of the 401 peasant petitioners, 172 said that local courts refused to accept their lawsuits, and 220 said that local courts ruled against them. Nine said that even though they won their cases, the courts had failed to enforce the judgments.[178] Evidently, a legal system with such a limited capacity for adjudicating state-society conflict is woefully inadequate for a large country with a huge population.

The *xinfang* system, the principal channel through which ordinary citizens can petition government authorities to redress their grievances, has completely broken down. Official data show that the government's various *xinfang* offices received more than 10 million letters and visits in 2003, but few petitioners could expect results through such efforts. A study done by a research team headed by Yu Jianrong at CASS in 2004 found that only two in a thousand petitioners could have their problems resolved through *xinfang*.[179] Because the image of the central government was much better than that of local governments, most petitioners originally had high expectations about their success in seeking the central government's intervention. But their hopes were soon dashed as they met indifferent and irresponsive officials at the central government level. After visiting the State Letters and Complaints Bureau, the NPC Standing Committee, the SPC, the CDIC, the MPS, the Ministry of Land Resources, and other state agencies (a petitioner visits an average of six government agencies), most rural petitioners concluded that the central government did not look upon their visits favorably.[180] For many petitioners, failed attempts to seek the intervention by the central government could lead to dire consequences. Of the 632 petitioners interviewed by Yu's team, 55 percent reported that local authorities had retaliated by ransacking their houses and seizing valuables; 50 percent said they had been beaten by local officials; 50 percent said that had been illegal incarcerated; 72 percent said that they had been falsely charged with crimes; and 54 percent said that local officials used the mafia to retaliate against them.[181]

The CCP's failure to open up the political system and expand institutionalized channels of conflict resolution helped create an environment in which groups, unable to defend their interests, were forced to take high-risk options of collective protest to express frustrations and seek redress.

However, it is difficult to gauge the immediate and direct impact of rapidly rising incidents of social protest on political stability in general, and the survivability of the CCP in particular. Although some collective protests have become more organized, most incidents remain isolated and poorly organized events. Except for Falun Gong, no protesting group has managed to organize social movements across county boundaries or sustain their protests for more than a few days. In addition, the causes of protests are specific—unpaid wages, illegal seizure of land, higher taxes, and abuse of power by local officials. Few protestors have elevated their demands beyond redressing individual grievances or called for the overthrow of the CCP. Polling data suggest that local governments may have lost their legitimacy, but the central government has maintained a surprisingly high level of authority in the eyes of ordinary citizens. This suggests a relatively low probability for social protest movements, however numerous, frequent, and violent, to explode into large-scale, highly organized, and cross-regional groups intent upon the overthrow of the CCP. The CCP may also draw some comfort from survey findings that suggest that, on the whole, the majority of Chinese citizens were unlikely to participate in violent antiregime activities. In two tracking polls conducted in 2000 and 2001, a large majority of the respondents were willing to allow the government, the news media, and the courts to resolve their problems. A large minority (around 30 percent) would only complain privately. Only a small minority (although a sizable one in the countryside) would resort to protest or even violence. In 2001, about 6 percent said that they would participate in collective petitions and demonstrations, and 1 percent would participate in strikes. In 2000, more people were leaning toward the protest/violence options, with almost 12 percent in the cities and 20 percent in the countryside choosing the collective petitions and demonstrations option. About 3 percent would take part in strikes. Significantly, 4 percent of the urban respondents and 6 percent of the rural respondents would seek private revenge.[182]

It would be wrong to dismiss deteriorating governance and its effects on social unrest as inconsequential. Left ignored, deteriorating governance will lead to a vicious cycle. In the Chinese case, the massive accumulation of governance deficits—and systemic risks—threatens the sustainability of China's neoauthoritarian development strategy. As the analysis of this study shows, the build-up of governance deficits is an inevitable product of the transition strategy and policies adopted by the CCP. The party's resistance to substantive and meaningful democratic reforms has led to the breakdown of accountability, deterioration of internal norms, and exclusion of large segments of Chinese society from political participation. Unaccountable to the public, the ruling elites have pursued policies that are more likely to advance their personal political careers than increase social returns. The strategy of gradualist economic reform has created large pockets of rents and left untouched the party's extensive patronage system within the economy. The costs of protecting the rents and the patronage network are eventually borne by the public at large, in the form of the diversion of resources, which could be used to deliver more public goods, to a relatively small group of loyalists in the party. The emergence of a decentralized predatory state, with pervasive corruption and collusion, has caused local governance to deteriorate even further.

The accumulation of governance deficits places potential reformers in a difficult dilemma. As a rule, regimes enfeebled by misrule lack the political capital and confidence to undertake bold reforms to stop the rot inside the system. Inaction and procrastination, not risk-taking, tend to prevail. Even for forward-looking reformers, opening up the political systems with a large buildup of governance deficits presents an insurmountable challenge. Resistance from regime insiders who benefit from bad governance will likely be fierce while a mass popular political mobilization, similar to *glasnost* under Gorbachev in the former Soviet Union, will most probably precipitate a quick regime collapse because the political system is simply too brittle to pass the stress test of real political reforms.

Conclusion

BY FOCUSING on the critical weaknesses of the Chinese political system in general, and on many of the hidden costs of China's transition from communism in particular, this book attempts to show the limits of a developmental autocracy. Despite its awe-inspiring economic growth and progress, a set of self-destructive dynamics is weakening China's most vital political institutions—the state and the ruling party. Lagging behind the country's rapid economic modernization, China's closed political system is increasingly becoming an anachronism. At present, it is incapable of facilitating the representation of China's complex and diverse social interests or mediating the conflict between an authoritarian state and a liberalizing society.

The breakdown of the mechanisms of political accountability has led to pervasive corruption and collusion among the ruling elites, while the loss of confidence in the regime's own future has motivated its insiders to engage in unrestrained predation. The inevitable deterioration of governance that has resulted from these institutional failings has undermined the state's capacity, heightened social tensions, and cast into doubt the sustainability of the progress that China has achieved since the late 1970s. Even China's gradualist economic reform strategy, which has received almost universal endorsement for its flexibility and efficacy, is centered on the CCP's goal of political survival, and not the development of a true market economy. The economic costs of ensuring the CCP's political monopoly through policies of rent protection, though hidden, are real, substantial, and growing.

By critically examining the understated social and political costs of China's neoauthoritarian development strategy, this book also tries to question three ideas that have retained their allure despite mounting skepticism about their validity.

The first idea is that economic progress is the key determinant of political liberalization. While it is true that economic growth and modernization can create favorable conditions for the emergence of liberal political regimes, China's slow movement toward political openness in spite of twenty-five years of rapid economic growth suggests that the choices of its ruling elites are the real determinants of democratization. In fact, if anything, rapid short-term economic growth may have a perversely negative impact on democratization because it provides all the incentives for the ruling elites *not* to seek political liberalization.

The second idea is that the gradualist reform strategy works better than the so-called big-bang approach. Of course, the big-bang approach has failed miserably in Russia and several other former Soviet bloc countries, but the achievement of China's gradualist strategy has been greatly overstated. More important, as Chapter 3 shows, the gradualist strategy is ultimately unsustainable because of the dynamics of rent dissipation and the mounting costs of inefficiency incurred by path-dependent partial reforms.

The third idea is that of the efficacious neoauthoritarian developmental state. Despite the examples of successful neoauthoritarian developmental states in East Asia, the political logic and institutional determinants of autocracy—patronage dictated by regime survival, the political monopoly of the authoritarian regime, and ineffective monitoring and policing of the state's agents in the absence of the rule of law, civil liberties, and political opposition—are more likely to create a predatory state than a developmental one.

This book also underscores the centrality of politics in general, and the control of political power in particular, in setting the course of economic and regime transitions. As the analysis of the political considerations behind the Chinese leaders' policies on political and economic reforms shows, the most critical determinant of their strategies is whether they will strengthen or endanger their political survival. To the extent that the overall effects of the chosen strategies increase the chances of their political survival, the ruling elites can be flexible in tactical terms, allowing partial reforms to boost the short-term vigor of the political and economic systems. But such tactical flexibility and adjustment have strict limits and must not blind us to the fundamental incompatibility between a monopolistic ruling party's determination to perpetuate its power and a society's collective desire for a more autonomous and rule-based economic and political order. Having seized political power through the barrel of a gun, a formerly revolutionary party, such as the CCP, will unlikely seek its own demise through voluntary reform.

However, a developmental autocracy's overriding goal of self-perpetuation is ultimately imperiled by the self-destructive dynamics found in nearly all autocracies: low political accountability, unresponsiveness, collusion, and corruption. In most cases, an autocratic regime's collective interests are grossly misaligned with the individual interests of its agents. Acting rationally, self-interested agents seek to maximize their own gains, especially during a transitional period when changes in the rules of the game create abundant opportunities for self-enrichment. The economic and political costs incurred by these agents in their self-dealing are inevitably borne by *both* the autocratic regime—which suffers, as a result, from low legitimacy, weak authority, and organizational corruption—and society—which pays in the form of deteriorating governance and economic performance. Thus, it is inconceivable that a developmental autocracy can retain its vigor for long. On the contrary, the self-destructive dynamics embedded in a developmental autocracy will most likely lead to a gradual buildup of systemic risks within the autocratic regime and progressively sap its strength. That is why, except in a very small number of cases, most self-styled developmental autocracies eventually fail.

Given China's impressive growth performance, one may question the pessimistic logic behind the main thesis of this study. If the Chinese political system is so dysfunctional, why has the country maintained such rapid economic growth since the late 1970s? There are several explanations for this apparent paradox of bad governance and good growth. First, the pathologies of a trapped transition became more serious and visible in the 1990s, after the neoauthoritarian development strategy had gained dominance within the CCP and the liberal forces, both within the party and in society, were marginalized after Tiananmen. To the extent that deterioration in governance has a lagging effect on economic performance (for example, the deleterious effects of underinvestment in human capital and public health usually do not become visible until one or two generations later), it is possible that the pathologies of a trapped transition will have a material impact on macroeconomic performance in future years.

Second, in the short term, the growth rate can be pumped up by high savings and, hence, investment rates and massive shifts of population from agriculture to industry, the two major factors behind China's rapid growth in recent years. In the Chinese case, with a national savings rate of 40 percent and an annual flow of $40 billion to $50 billion in foreign direct investment since the late 1990s (about 3–4 percent of GDP), high investment rates can propel growth even though the economic system remains relatively inefficient.

Third, it is important to look at the quality of growth because the focus on growth rate alone tends to ignore the hidden costs and the low quality of growth. In other words, growth rates may inaccurately reflect or, indeed, can seriously misrepresent a society's welfare gains. For example, if high growth is achieved at the expense of rising inequality, underinvestment in human capital, damage to the environment, and pervasive official corruption, such growth must be considered low quality. In China's case, high growth rates have been accompanied by all these symptoms of low-quality growth. The massive accumulation of bad loans in the Chinese banking system due to government-directed credit must also be considered another symptom of low-quality growth, or a cause of artificially high growth because such wasted investments have been counted as economic output.

Finally, the effects of bad governance on China's economic performance may already be visible. By international comparison, China is growing too slowly, as Martin Wolf argued. Given its size, its low starting base, and its high savings rate and high investments, China ought to have grown much faster than the 6.1 percent annual rate recorded between 1978 and 2003.[1] A most likely explanation for China's not living up to its economic potential is the institutional weakness of the political system. Of course, identifying weak institutions as causes of poor performance gives one reasons for both optimism and pessimism. Should China manage to reform these institutions, its economic performance will undoubtedly improve. But if it fails to do so, then its growth rate will probably stagnate or even decline, especially when macroeconomic conditions become less favorable. In fact, China experienced such an episode of slow growth in 1998–2000. Research by Thomas Rawski shows that, contrary to official Chinese data, the Chinese economy barely grew during this period.[2]

Getting Out of a Trapped Transition

This study raises another important question: how can a partial reform equilibrium end? Put metaphorically, how can a country such as China get out of the transition trap? To the extent that a trapped transition will eventually create conditions that force the ruling elites to make fundamental choices, there are three possible scenarios or ways out. By and large, these choices are similar to those faced by political leaders trapped in an unsatisfactory and unsustainable status quo—as was the case following the end of the Cultural Revolution.

First, given the self-destructive dynamics of a trapped transition, a neoauthoritarian regime will soon exhaust its economic and political vitality. With deteriorating economic performance and increasingly rising social tensions, China's ruling elites will be forced to choose between maintaining a deteriorating status quo and taking the risks of more radical reforms to restore political accountability and curb decentralized predation. If they opt for reform, they will most likely mobilize new political groups to overcome the resistance of the beneficiaries of a trapped transition and help break the old partial reform equilibrium. As the experience of the former Soviet Union demonstrates, however, mobilizing societal forces to pressure a discredited regime to change can inadvertently unleash an antiregime revolution. Such "run-away reform," or the "de Tocqueville paradox," poses great risks to potential reformers.[3] Once the previously excluded groups are fully mobilized, reformers will lose their ability to control the agenda and the goals of these newly empowered groups. Therefore, a country can get out of a trapped transition without experiencing social convulsion only if reformers can maintain full control of the renewed reform process. As Guillermo O'Donnell and Philippe Schmitter showed, such an outcome is most likely only when reformers gain the cooperation of the moderate members of the societal opposition.[4]

Second, one of the alternatives to getting out of a trapped transition through renewed reforms is a regime collapse. The logic of rent dissipation and decentralized predation means that the institutional degeneration of a developmental autocracy will progressively spread, resulting in deteriorating performance of the authoritarian regime, especially in terms of economic growth. Facing declining political legitimacy and prospects of social turmoil, ruling elites with available exit options will most likely take them, particularly during a crisis when the regime's own survival is imperiled. Under such circumstances, we can expect the political equivalent of a bank run—a panicked rush for the exit by the regime's insiders who no longer have the will or the incentive to defend the regime. Unfortunately, the collapse of a developmental autocracy under crisis conditions may break the partial reform equilibrium, but is no guarantee of a return to a stable liberal political order, as shown by the difficulties experienced by Russia after the Soviet collapse and by Indonesia after the demise of the Suharto regime.

Third, for a large and diverse country such as China, it is often difficult to build a strong enough new reform coalition at the national level. But regional and local reform coalitions can be formed with a combination of the initiatives of forward-looking local elites and pressure from societal forces. Although the devolution of power has led to the decentralization of predation, two developments can potentially generate more positive dynamics for reform. Devolution of power will, in some cases, result in greater political accountability for local elites. More important, devolution of power in China's context has encouraged interregional competition for capital, labor, and markets. Local accountability and interregional competition may jointly motivate local elites and civil society groups to experiment with new institutional reforms that can address the ills of a trapped transition at the local level. It is worth noting that, in the 1990s, the most innovative governance reform attempts, such as the township-level elections and refining village elections, were "middle-up" initiatives—risk-taking ideas implemented by progressive local officials to remedy local problems. If more jurisdictions take the middle-up route, at least some of the social and political ills caused by a trapped transition can be ameliorated at the local level. In the end, local initiatives will probably encourage governance divergence across China, as some areas manage to get out of a trapped transition through reform and others continue to stagnate or even deteriorate further.

Implications for the International Community

One must not rule out the possibility that a country such as China can be stuck in a trapped transition for an extended period. It is conceivable that a developmental autocracy can continue to use the same mix of repression, co-optation, and adaptation to maintain an elite-based ruling coalition for decades. Deteriorating governance and economic performance may be the necessary—but not sufficient—conditions for the emergence of a fatal crisis. A combination of tactical adaptation, improvisation, luck, and mass apathy may allow the ruling elites to stay in power even as the country is mired in misrule.

The likelihood that China's transition to a market economy and open society has stalled has serious implications for policy. For Chinese leaders, a transition process trapped in a partial reform equilibrium endangers their ambitious goal of becoming a full-fledged global power. The combination of flawed economic and political institutions creates market distortions, inefficient uses of resources, and opportunities for massive systemic corruption. The rapid economic development China was able to achieve in the first twenty-five years of its transition will unlikely be sustained. Instead of becoming a global economic power, China may enter a prolonged period of stagnation.

In addition, the risks of domestic instability will likely increase, both as a result of the social frustrations caused by poor economic performance and the political dissatisfaction against an authoritarian, exclusionary, corrupt, and ineffective regime. Given the difficulties and costs associated with forming viable coherent opposition groups capable of opposing and offering a credible alternative to the CCP, it is difficult to imagine that the CCP behemoth can be dethroned by an organized coalition from below. Absent a deep and wide fracture that shatters the CCP from within, the collapse of the CCP may be a low-probability event. Thus, the unavailability of a credible alternative and the slim possibility of a regime implosion suggest that political stagnation would accompany economic stagnation, with further erosion of state capacity, the decline of the CCP's legitimacy, and increases in lawlessness, corruption, and social disorder. Ultimately, such stagnation will progressively increase the risks of regime collapse or state failure, as the strains accumulate in the dysfunctional political and economic systems.

For the international community, a China trapped in prolonged economic and political stagnation poses a set of challenges few have contemplated seriously. Since the 1990s, China's rapid economic ascendance has changed the West's assessment of its capabilities and prospects. Projecting China's future growth on the basis of its stellar development record in the recent past, the Western business community views China as an unprecedented commercial opportunity and a strategic market. Although China may be a difficult place to do business, Western businesses have learned how to manage and live with the risks inherent in that nation's political and economic environments. But if the implications of this study are borne out, the lofty expectations of Western businesses are most likely to be disappointed. China may be one of the biggest economies of the world, but the high rates of growth and generation of wealth projected by Western businesses will unlikely materialize. At the very least, the conclusions drawn from this study should make these businesses reassess their China strategy and adjust the risk premium they demand in return for their investments.

At the geopolitical level, the prospect of a rising China that could challenge the existing world order in general, and the preeminence of the United States in particular, has dominated the debate on the West's policy toward China since the mid-1990s.[5] Security analysts are preoccupied with China's potential military capabilities and intentions. Even though the China debate has spawned two conflicting policy approaches, often labeled "containment" and "engagement," the fundamental premise underlying these two opposing approaches is similar. Advocates of engagement and containment both assume China's rise as a given, and their differing policy prescriptions focus on projected Chinese strength, rather than its weakness. To be sure, China's weaknesses sometimes cause concerns in the West. But on such occasions, relatively rare in the 1990s when the Chinese economy boomed, analysis of China's problems tends to be extremely pessimistic, often with predictions of an imminent collapse of the Chinese political order and economy.[6]

Should China's rise fizzle, as this book suggests is highly likely if no fundamental political reforms are implemented, both the containers and engagers will be disappointed. For the hard-nosed realists obsessed with the potential threat from a China with peer-competitor capabilities, a China stuck in its incomplete transition means a much weaker China incapable of mounting a real challenge for global preeminence. In practical terms, the careful construction of a strategic balance of power designed to counter China's rising influence, as pursued by the George W. Bush administration through its efforts to recruit Japan and India into a potential anti-China security alliance, may turn out to be unnecessary. Needless to say, the tens of billions of dollars in military spending justified as a response to China's rising military threat will be wasted. Without China as a peer competitor, Washington's strategic thinkers will have to look elsewhere for new threats.

But liberal engagers will also have a harder time reconciling their expectations that economic progress will bring democratization with the hard reality that the Chinese experience has consistently defied such expectations. With progress toward a genuine open society frustratingly slow in China, Western liberals may find it increasingly difficult to maintain their optimism about China's future as a candidate for democratization. In policy terms, the intellectual case for engagement with China that has been made will rest on even more shaky ground.

The international community should take another look at China and start preparing, at least intellectually, for the unpleasant prospect that China may not only fail to fully realize its potential, but also descend into long-term stagnation. Such a reassessment of China's future should produce a new and more realistic framework in analyzing China's ongoing transformation and addressing the real challenges it brings. Instead of viewing China as the new superpower of the twenty-first century, the international community may want to see it as an underperforming giant that has failed to seize a historic opportunity for making a fundamental break with its authoritarian past and paid a heavy price for it.

In all likelihood, a China trapped in partial reforms would resemble, in several crucial respects, an *incapacitated* state. Unlike a completely failed state, an incapacitated state retains nominal national sovereignty, territorial integrity, and central government authority. Its ruling elites, through the monopoly of political power, remain unchallenged. However, in an incapacitated state, the government's comprehensive capability of governing is feeble, even though it may retain a limited ability to enforce its will and rule selectively, mostly under circumstances where such demonstration of state power affirms, at the symbolic level, the existence of a centralized political authority. Thus, over a wide range of issues deemed of critical interest to the international community—such as environmental protection, nonproliferation, antinarcotics, migration, control of the spread of HIV/AIDS, and poverty alleviation—an incapacitated state would be unable to honor its commitments or perform its governing functions effectively. The international community would likely find threats and problems posed by incapacitated states ultimately more frustrating and difficult to address because traditional approaches to foreign policy contain few effective prescriptions to treat state incapacitation. Given China's huge size and its role in global security and the international economy, the challenge posed by an incapacitated state in China would simply overwhelm the international community's ability (even if we assume willingness) to provide meaningful assistance. The spillover effects from China's internal woes and weaknesses would not only affect the interests of many nations, but also would make China's problems those of the entire international community.

Few may have viewed China's prospects through such dark lenses. But one ignores the self-destructive logic of predatory authoritarianism at his own peril.

Appendix

Notes

Acknowledgments

Index

Appendix:
Reported Cases of Local Mafia States

Hunan Province (seven cases reported)—The chief of the party's politics and law committee in Zixin city and two other officials were prosecuted in 2002 for protecting a local criminal gang. In Lianyuan city, thirty-nine officials—including the police chief, the president of the local court, the chief prosecutor, and the chief of the party's politics and law committee—were prosecuted in 2002 for protecting an organized criminal group. In Hengdong county, twenty-five officials, including the mayor and deputy chairman of the county People's Congress, were prosecuted in 2002 for protecting an organized criminal group. In Dong'an county, sixteen officials, including the chief of the party's politics and law committee and deputy police chief, were prosecuted in 2002 for protecting an organized criminal group. In Changde city, an unspecified number of local officials were prosecuted for colluding in smuggling automobiles. In Shuining county, seven officials—including the police chief, the head of the People's Congress, and chief prosecutor—were arrested in 2001 for protecting organized crime. In Chaoyang city, forty-three officials, including the deputy police chief and other law enforcement officials, were prosecuted in 2002 for protecting organized crime.

Guangdong Province (six cases reported)—Seventeen officials in Puning city, including the party secretary, were prosecuted for selling government posts in 2002. In Yunfu city, twenty-three officials, including a deputy police chief, were prosecuted for smuggling automobiles in 2002. In Lufeng, four officials, including a prosecutor, were prosecuted in 2001 for producing counterfeit currency. In Shenzhen, five senior officials—including the deputy mayor, a deputy director of the land bureau, and the head of the metro—were prosecuted in 2001 for collectively taking bribes. In Qingyuan city, three senior officials, including the police chief and the chief of the party's politics and law committee, were prosecuted in 2002 for smuggling. In Lianzhou city, five local officials, including the police chief and the secretary of the party's politics and law committee, were prosecuted in 2002 for smuggling.

Fujian Province (six cases reported)—Six officials in Minhe county, including the heads of the land and construction bureaus, were prosecuted for protecting a local mafia group in 2002. Six officials in Shunchang county—including the chief of the party's politics and law committee, a deputy party secretary, and a deputy chief of police—were prosecuted in 2002 for protecting a local mafia group. An unspecified number of officials in Zhangzhou city, including cadres in law enforcement agencies, were prosecuted in 2001 for protecting a local mafia group. In Wuping county, three officials, including a deputy county magistrate and a deputy chairman of the county's People's Congress, were prosecuted in 2001 for collectively accepting bribes. In Xiamen city, the infamous Yuanhua case led to the arrest and convictions of 279 local officials in 2001, including the city's party secretary and deputy mayor. In Fuzhou, seventeen city officials—including the party secretary of the politics and law committee, a deputy mayor, the party boss of a local city, a local chief prosecutor, and a vice president of a local court—provided protection to a local crime boss, Chen Kai, in exchange for large bribes. The case was uncovered in 2003.

Guangxi (five cases reported)—The provincial government's chairman, deputy chairman, and a deputy chairman of the People's Congress were prosecuted in 2002 for taking bribes. In Liuzhou city, the party secretary, police chief, and deputy police chief were prosecuted for protecting illegal gambling. In Zhanjiang city, a large number of local officials, including the city's party chief, were convicted of smuggling in 1998. In Nandan county, seven officials—including the party secretary, the magistrate, and a deputy party secretary—were convicted of protecting mafia-operated mines in 2002. In Ningming county, two of the county's party chiefs and two county magistrates were arrested for corruption in the 1990s.

Heilongjiang (three cases reported)—The provincial government itself could qualify as a mafia state. In 2004, the following were removed from office or prosecuted for collective corruption: a former provincial governor; a sitting deputy governor; the head of the provincial people's political consultative conference, who had served as the provincial CCP organization chief and was an alternate member of the CCP's 15th Central Committee; the president and vice president of the provincial high court; the chief of the provincial procuratorate; the head of the provincial personnel department; and the head of the provincial CCP secretariat. In Suihua city, the party secretary, Ma De, was convicted of selling government positions to more than 260 people in

2002. About half the division-level cadres in the ten counties in Suihua were implicated in the scandal. In Qitai city, a deputy party secretary, who was also the secretary of the politics and law committee, and an unspecified number of officials were convicted in 2002 for protecting organized crime.

Shanxi Province (three cases reported)—The party secretary of Changzhi county was prosecuted in 1999 for selling government offices to 432 people. In Gaoping county, seven officials—including the deputy mayor, police chief, and the party's organization chief—were prosecuted in 2001 for protecting a violent criminal gang. In Fanci county, both the party secretary and the mayor were prosecuted in 2002 for protecting criminals who owned local mines.

Jilin Province (three cases reported)—In Jingyu county, the party secretary was prosecuted in 2003 for selling government positions to more than 160 people. In Helong city, an unspecified number of officials were prosecuted for protecting a local mafia group. In an unnamed city, thirty officials were prosecuted for protecting a mafia group headed by Liang Xudong, an infamous local crime boss.

Sichuan Province (three cases reported)—In Jianyang county, eleven senior officials—including the mayor, two deputy mayors, and a deputy party secretary—were prosecuted in 1994 for collectively taking bribes. In Pi county, four officials, including the head of the agriculture bureau, were prosecuted in 1994 for protecting a local mafia group. In Renshou county, the police chief and his principal deputy were prosecuted in 2002 for protecting a mafia group.

Shaanxi Province (three cases reported)—In Fuping county, six officials, including the police chief and two of his deputies, were prosecuted in 2002 for protecting a mafia group. In Yang county, five officials—including the party secretary, the magistrate, one deputy party secretary, and the party's organization chief—were prosecuted for selling government positions in the mid-1990s. In Huanglin county, four local enforcement officials, including the police chief, were prosecuted in 2001 for protecting mafia-run mines.

Jiangxi Province (two cases reported)—In Qianshan county, two successive party secretaries, the deputy police chief, and the party's organization chief, along with twenty-three other officials, were prosecuted in 2002 for protecting a local mafia group. In Geyang county, an unspecified number of officials were prosecuted in 2001 for protecting organized crime.

Hubei Province (two cases reported)—In Tianmen city, the party secretary, the executive vice mayor, and the secretary general of the city government were prosecuted for taking bribes and embezzlement in 2002. In Xishui city, four officials were prosecuted for protecting the local mafia in 2002.

Shandong Province (two cases reported)—In Tai'an city, the party secretary, deputy secretary, secretary general of the municipal government, and police chief were prosecuted in 1996 for collectively taking bribes. In Rizhao city, the party secretary and the police chief were prosecuted in 1996 for collectively taking bribes and other crimes.

Zhejiang Province (two cases reported)—In Wenling city, sixty-seven officials, including the mayor and the chief of the party's politics and law committee, were prosecuted in 2001 for protecting a local mafia group that defrauded a local credit union of 300 million yuan. In Rui'an city, the party secretary and the mayor, together with more than thirty officials, were prosecuted in 2001 for protecting a local mafia group, bribe-taking, and selling government positions.

Anhui Province (one case reported)—The party secretary, mayor, police chief, and about 160 other officials in Fuyan city were prosecuted in 2000 for taking bribes collectively.

Henan Province (one case reported)—In Lushi county, the party secretary was prosecuted in 2002 for selling government positions to eighty people and behaving like a "dirt emperor."

Liaoning (one case reported)—Nearly all the senior officials in Shenyang, including the mayor, president of the court, the chief prosecutor, and the executive vice mayor, were prosecuted in 2001 for protecting the local mafia.

Notes

Introduction

1. One of the best brief surveys of the economic transformation of China since the late 1970s is the World Bank, *China 2020: Development Challenges in the New Century* (Washington, D.C.: World Bank, 1997).
2. *ZGTJNJ 2003* (Beijing: Zhongguo tongji chubanshe, 2003), 58.
3. www.chinanews.com.cn, May 18, 2004.
4. *ZGTJNJ 2003*, 34.
5. http:www.unchina.org/html/report.html. According to the United Nations, China's urbanization rate for 1978 was 29 percent.
6. *ZGTJZY 2000*, 83, 131, 161; *ZGTJNJ 1991*, 269; *ZGTJNJ 2002*, 562; *ZGTJNJ 2003*, 30, 31, 342, 790; www.chinanews.com.cn, April 1, 2004.
7. *ZGTJZY 2000* (Beijing: Zhongguo tongji chubanshe, 2000), 122; *ZGFLNJ 2000* (Beijing: Zhongguo falü chubanshe, 2001), 1221; *ZGFLNJ 1991*, 36; *ZGTJNJ 2002*, 573, 691.
8. *ZGTJZY 2000*, 105; *ZGTJNJ 2003*, 459.
9. *ZGTJNJ 2003*, 123.
10. See Nicholas Lardy, *Integrating China into the Global Economy* (Washington, D.C.: Brookings Institution Press, 2002).
11. www.chinanews.com.cn, December 28, 2003.
12. *ZGTJZY 2000*, 139, 144; *ZGTJNJ 2003*, 653, 671, 691.
13. See Michel Oksenberg, "China's Political System: Challenges of the Twenty-first Century," *The China Journal* 45 (2001): 21–35.
14. On a scale of 1–5, with 3 denoting no change compared with the pre-reform era and 5 denoting "significant improvement," respondents gave a score of 3.21 on political efficacy, 3.45 on equal treatment, 3.46 on

judicial independence, and 3.67 on individual political rights. Xu Xinxin, "2002 nian Zhongguo chengxiang jumin shehui taidu zhiye pingjia yu zeye quxiang diaocha" (A Survey of the Social Sentiments, Evaluation of Occupations, and Employment Preferences of Chinese Urban and Rural Residents in 2002), in Ru Xin et al., eds., *SHLPS 2003* (Beijing: Zhongguo shehui kexue wenxian chubanshe, 2003), 122. A survey of urban residents in 1999 found that they felt their political efficacy had decreased significantly compared with the early 1990s. Wenfang Tang, "Political and Social Trends in the Post-Deng Urban China: Crisis or Stability?" *The China Quarterly* 168 (2001): 890–909.

15. Li Rui, "Guanyu woguo zhengzhi tizhi gaige de jianyi," (Proposals for Reforming China's Political System), www.sawin.com.cn/doc/FLY/Free/politics.htm.

16. Ibid.

17. The Polity IV Project's data can be accessed from www.bsos.umd.cidcm/polity.

18. See www.freedomhouse.org.

19. Transparency International's ratings assigned to China fluctuate within a relatively narrow range—from 4.73 to 2.16 for the 1990s on a 1–10 scale (10 being the least corrupt).

20. *International Country Risk Guide*—IRIS III Data Set, available from the PRS Group at www.prsgroup.com.

21. Jeff Huther and Anwar Shah, "Applying a Simple Measure of Good Governance to the Debate on Fiscal Decentralization," *World Bank Policy Research Working Paper No. 1894* (Washington, D.C.: World Bank, 1998).

22. Daniel Kaufmann, Aart Kraay, and Massimo Mastruzzi, "Governance Matters III: Governance Indicators for 1996–2002," *World Bank Policy Research Working Paper No. 3106* (Washington, D.C.: World Bank, 2003).

23. On "voice and accountability," China's score was −1.38, compared with Angola (−1.39), Belarus (−1.45), Vietnam (−1.36), Saudi Arabia (−1.40), Afghanistan (−1.31), Russia (−0.52), Ukraine (−0.59), India (0.38), and Mexico (0.33). In terms of "regulatory quality," China's score was (−0.41). Scores for other countries were: Nicaragua (−0.41), Cambodia (−0.43), Papua New Guinea (−0.44), Egypt (−0.45), Mali (−0.49), India (−0.34), Mexico (0.49), and Russia (−0.30). On "control of corruption," China got −0.41, compared with Colombia (−0.47), Ethiopia (−0.35), Iran (−0.38), Romania (−0.34), Russia (−0.90), India (−0.25), Brazil (−0.05), and Mexico (−0.19). On "government effectiveness," China received 0.18, compared with Namibia (0.18), Croatia (0.19), Kuwait (0.16), Mexico (0.15), Russia (−0.40), and India (−0.13). On "political stability," China got 0.22. On "rule of law," China

received −0.22, compared with Mexico (−0.22), Madagascar (−0.19), Lebanon (−0.27), Russia (−0.78), and India (0.07). Kaufmann, Kraay, and Mastruzzi, "Governance Matters III," 98–114.

24. See Merle Goldman and Roderick MacFarquhar, eds., *The Paradox of China's Post-Mao Reforms* (Cambridge, Mass.: Harvard University Press, 1999); Elizabeth Perry and Mark Selden, eds., *Chinese Society: Change, Conflict and Resistance* (London: Routledge, 2000); Gordon White, Jude Howell, and Xiaoyuan Shang, *In Search of Civil Society: Market Reform and Social Change in Contemporary China* (Oxford: Clarendon, 1996).

25. See Minxin Pei, "Is China Democratizing?" *Foreign Affairs* 77(1) (1998): 68–82; Richard Baum, *Burying Mao: Chinese Politics in the Age of Deng Xiaoping* (Princeton, N.J.: Princeton University Press, 1996); Melanie Manion, *Retirement of Revolutionaries in China: Public Policies, Social Norms, Private Interests* (Princeton, N.J.: Princeton University Press, 1993); Li Cheng and Lynn White, "Elite Transformation and Modern Change in Mainland China and Taiwan: Empirical Data and the Theory of Technocracy," *The China Quarterly* 121 (1990): 1–35.

26. See Stanley Lubman, *Bird in a Cage: Legal Reform in China After Mao* (Stanford, Calif.: Stanford University Press, 1999); Pitman Potter, ed., *Domestic Law Reforms in Post-Mao China* (Armonk, N.Y.: M. E. Sharpe, 1994); Stanley Lubman, ed., *China's Legal Reforms* (Oxford: Oxford University Press, 1996).

27. See Murray Scot Tanner, *The Politics of Lawmaking in Post-Mao China: Institutions, Processes, and Democratic Prospects* (Oxford: Oxford University Press, 1998); Michael Dowdle, "The Constitutional Development and Operations of the National People's Congress," *Columbia Journal of Asian Law* 1 (1997): 1–125.

28. See Kevin O'Brien, "Villagers, Elections, and Citizenship in Contemporary China," *Modern China* 27(4) (2001): 407–435; Tianjian Shi, "Village Committee Elections in China: Institutionalist Tactics for Democracy," *World Politics* 51(3) (1999): 385–412; Robert Pastor and Qingshan Tan, "The Meaning of China's Village Elections," *The China Quarterly* 162 (2000): 490–512.

29. See David Zweig, "Undemocratic Capitalism: China and the Limits of Economism," *National Interest* (Summer 1999): 63–72; Bruce Dickson, "China's Democratization and the Taiwan Experience," *Asian Survey* 38(4) (1998): 349–364.

30. Zhao reportedly said this in a conversation with a longtime friend in July 2004 while still under house arrest in Beijing. *Mingpao,* January 30, 2005, A4.

31. The "neoauthoritarian development model" was distilled from the

successful developmental experience of East Asia's newly industrializing countries, which grew rapidly after their authoritarian regimes adopted market-friendly policies without opening the political system.

32. For a discussion of a partial reform equilibrium, see Joel Hellman, "Winners Take All: The Politics of Partial Reform in Postcommunist Transitions," *World Politics* 50(2) (1998): 203–234.

33. According to the three polls conducted by the Chinese Academy of Social Sciences in 1998, 1999, and 2003, party and government officials, tax collectors, law enforcement personnel, SOE executives, and employers in financial institutions were viewed as having gained the most from economic reform, and SOE workers, peasants, migrant laborers, and workers in township and village enterprises were seen as having benefited the least. In a poll of 15,000 in late 2002, 60 percent said that party and government officials had benefited the most. Xu Xinxin, "Zhongguo chengshi jumin de guanzhu jiaodian yu weilai yuqi" (China Urban Residents' Main Concerns and Expectations of the Future), in Ru Xin et al., eds., *SHLPS 2000*, 87; Liang Dong, "Zhongguo dangzheng ganbu ji ganqun guanxi de diaocha fenxi" (An Investigative Analysis of Chinese Party and Government Officials and Relations Between the Cadres and the Masses," in Ru Xin et al., eds., *SHLPS 2004*, 35. In a poll of 109 leading academics in 2003, 73 percent said that party and government officials had benefited the most from reforms and 67 percent said workers had benefited the least. Lu Jianhua, "Zhuanjia yanli de shehui xingshi jiqi qianjing" "Social Situation and Prospects in the Eyes of Experts) in Ru Xin et al., eds., *SHLPS 2004*, 18.

34. Wu Guoguang wrote a provocative essay, "Gaige de zhongjie yu lishi de jiexu" (The End of Reform and the Continuation of History), *Er shi yi shiji* (*Twenty-first Century*) 71 (2002): 4–13.

35. For an analysis of Zhu Rongji's failed reforms in the late 1990s, see David Zweig, "China's Stalled 'Fifth Wave': Zhu Rongji's Reform Package of 1998–2000," *Asian Survey* 41(2) (2001): 231–247.

36. Of the respondents, 30 percent were SOE executives and 70 percent were non-SOE executives. Development Research Center of the State Council (DRC), "Qiye jingyingzhe dui jingji tizhi gaige redian wenti de panduan" (Corporate Executives' Assessment of the Key Issues in the Reform of the Economic System), *DRC diaocha yanjiu baogao* (*DRC Investigative and Research Report*) 186 (2002): 4.

37. See Nicholas Lardy, *China's Unfinished Economic Revolution* (Washington, D.C.: Brookings Institution Press, 1998).

38. Nicholas Lardy, "China's Worsening Debts," *The Financial Times*, June 22, 2001.

39. Li Rongrong, head of the State Asset Management Administration, which oversees SOEs, admitted in late 2003 that SOE reforms remained in a difficult stage. He cited the failures to establish a modern corporate system, improve the corporate governance structure, reform internal management of SOEs, and reduce their massive bad debts. www.chinanews.com.cn, October 3, 2003.

40. See Lin Yi-min and Tian Zhu, "Ownership Restructuring in Chinese State Industry: An Analysis of Evidence on Initial Organizational Changes," *The China Quarterly* 166 (2001): 305–341; Edward Steinfeld, "Free Lunch or Last Supper? China's Debt-Equity Swaps in Context," *The China Business Review* (July–August 2000): 22–27.

41. Nicholas Lardy, "When Will China's Financial System Meet China's Needs," Conference on Policy Reform in China, Stanford University (mimeo, November 1999).

42. OECD, *China in the World Economy: The Domestic Policy Challenges* (Paris: OECD, 2002), 9.

43. The OECD study notes that real growth fell between 1996 and 2000 and argues that such deteriorating performance is not cyclical. OECD, *China in the World Economy*, 22.

44. Wanda Tseng and Markus Rodlauer, eds., *China: Competing in the Global Economy* (Washington, D.C.: International Monetary Fund, 2003).

45. According to the World Bank, China's official growth rate from 1978 to 1995 was inflated by an average of 1.2 percent a year. World Bank, *China 2020*, 3. Alwyn Young argues that China's GDP growth from 1986 to 1998 was overstated by 3 percent. Young, "Gold into Base Metals: Productivity Growth in the People's Republic of China during the Reform Period," *NBER Working Paper No. 7856* (Cambridge, Mass.: National Bureau of Economic Research, 2000); Thomas Rawski argued in 2001 that China's growth statistics for the late 1990s were so inflated that real growth was probably close to zero. See Rawski, "China's GDP Statistics—A Case of Caveat Lector?" www.pitt.edu/~tgrawski/papers2001/caveat.web.pdf.

46. Morris Goldstein and Nicholas Lardy, *What Kind of Landing for the Chinese Economy?* (Washington, D.C.: Institute for International Economics, 2004).

47. www.chinanews.com.cn, February 18, 2004; *NFZM,* July 1, 2004.

48. In 1999, forty-two of the fifty leading academics interviewed by a Chinese Academy of Social Sciences research group said that the political system has lagged behind the economic system. Lu Jianhua, "Mianlin xinshiji tiaozhan de Zhongguo" (China: Facing Challenges of the New Century), in Ru Xin et al., eds., *SHLPS 2000,* 112–123; for the results of the 2003 study, see Lu Jianhua, "Zhuanjia yanli de shehui xingshi jiqi qianjing," 20.

49. The question posed to 116 senior and midlevel officials in 2003 was how they viewed "adjustment in the major relationships in recent years." On "the relationship between economic reform and political reform," 66.4 percent said "little change"; 21.6 percent said this relationship "has become more out of sync"; only 11.2 percent said the relationship had become "more in sync." Xie Zhiqiang, "Dangzheng ganbu dui 2003–2004 nian Zhongguo shehui xingshi de jiben panduan" (Party and Government Officials' Basic Assessment of China's Social Situation in 2003–2004), in Ru Xin et al., eds., *SHLPS 2004*, 27.

50. Each poll surveyed about 120 officials. Between 2000 and 2003, about 30–36 percent of the respondents identified "political reform" as the issue they were "most concerned with." Qing Lianbin and Xie Zhiqiang, "Dangzheng ganbu dui 2000–2001 nian shehui xingshi de jiben kanfa" (Party and Government Officials' Basic Views of the Social Situation in 2000–2001) in Ru Xin et al., eds., *SHLPS 2001*, 47–48; Qing Lianbin, "Zhongguo dangzheng lingdao ganbu dui 2002–2003 nian shehui xingshi de jiben kanfa" (Chinese Party and Government Officials' Basic Views of the Social Situation in 2002–2003), in Ru Xin et al., eds., *SHLPS 2003*, 130; Xie Zhiqiang, "Dangzheng ganbu dui 2003–2004 nian Zhongguo shehui xingshi de jiben panduan," 29.

51. Fifty-six percent of the officials selected economic reform as the most important factor. Qing Lianbin, "Zhongguo dangzheng lingdao ganbu dui 2002–2003 nian shehui xingshi de jiben kanfa," 136.

52. Yan Sun, *Corruption and Market in Contemporary China* (Ithaca, N.Y.: Cornell University Press, 2004).

53. The most systematic polling data were cited in the annual *SHLPS* compiled by the CASS.

54. Hu Angang included the amount of rents in various monopolized industries and provided a higher estimate of the costs of corruption (17 percent of GDP). Hu Angang, ed., *Zhongguo: Tiaozhan fubai* (China: Fighting Against Corruption) (Hangzhou: Zhejiang renmin chubanshe, 2001), 61; Minxin Pei used a more conservative estimate that showed the cost of corruption in the late 1990s was about 4–5 percent of GDP. See Minxin Pei, "Will China Become Another Indonesia?" *Foreign Policy* 116 (1999): 99.

55. He Qinglian, *Xiandaihua de xianjing: Dangdai Zhongguo de jingji shehui wenti* (*The Trap of Modernization: Economic and Social Problems in Contemporary China*) (Beijing: Jinri Zhongguo chubanshe, 1998).

56. Wang Shaoguang and Hu Angang sounded the alarm that China's state capacity, mainly its extractive capacity, was declining, in their influential *Zhongguo guojia nengli baogao* (*A Report on the Capacity of the Chinese State*)

(Shenyang: Liaoning renmin chubanshe, 1993). Although government revenues rose steadily after the tax reforms were implemented in 1994, they remain about 30 percent lower than the level in the early 1980s. Also see Minxin Pei, "China's Governance Crisis," *Foreign Affairs* 81(5) (2002): 96–109; Li Qiang analyzes the erosion of state capacity in his "Jingji zhuanxing yu jigou gaige" (Economic Transition and Institutional Reform), *Jingji shehui tizhi bijiao* (*Comparative Economic and Social Systems*) 4 (1998): 30–34.

57. *BYTNB* 1 (1997): 24–27.

58. See Kenneth Lieberthal, "Introduction: The 'Fragmented Authoritarianism' Model and Its Limitations," in Kenneth Lieberthal and David Lampton, eds., *Bureaucracy, Politics, and Decision Making in Post-Mao China* (Berkeley: University of California Press, 1992), 1–30.

59. In August 2002, the Hainan-based Institute for Reform and Development held a conference on "Transition and Imbalances," at which some of China's leading academics voiced their concerns about growing structural imbalances in Chinese society, economy, and polity. The transcripts of the conference are at www.chinareform.org/cn/cgi-bin/kxwk/Library_Read.asp?type_id=1&text_id=500.

60. For example, income inequality and urban-rural inequality worsened dramatically in the 1990s. A study by the Ministry of Finance shows that the Gini index for income had risen from 0.282 in 1991 to 0.458 in 2000. Research by the CASS shows that in 2002, the ratio of per capita income between urban and rural residents reached 3:1, the highest ever. www.chinanews.com.cn, June 16, 2003; www.chinanews.com.cn, February 25, 2004.

61. Wang Shaoguang, Hu Angang, and Ding Yuanzhu, "Jingji fanrong beihou de shehui buwending" (The Social Instability Behind Economic Prosperity), *Zhanlüe yu guanli* (*Strategy and Management*) 3 (2002): 26–33.

62. Sun Liping, "Women zai kaishi miandui yige duanlie de shehui?" (Are We Facing a Split Society?), *Zhanlüe yu guanli* 2 (2002): 9–15.

63. One press report cited an official figure of 30,000 collective protests in 2000, about 80 per day. *The Washington Post*, January 21, 2001, A1. Also see Lianjiang Li and Kevin J. O'Brien, "Villagers and Popular Resistance in Contemporary China," *Modern China* 22(1) (1996): 28–61; Thomas Bernstein, "Farmer Discontent and Regime Response," in Goldman and MacFarquhar, eds., *The Paradox of China's Post-Mao Reforms*, 196–219; Anita Chan and Robert Senser, "China's Troubled Workers," *Foreign Affairs* 76(2) (1997): 104–117.

64. See Xueguang Zhou, "Unorganized Interests and Collective Action in Communist China," *American Sociological Review* 58(1) (1993): 54–73.

1. Why Transitions Get Trapped

1. See Seymour Martin Lipset, "Some Social Requisites of Democracy: Economic Development and Political Legitimacy," *American Political Science Review* 53(1) (March 1959): 69–105; Barrington Moore, *Social Origins of Dictatorship and Democracy: Lord and Peasant in the Making of the Modern World* (Boston: Beacon Press, 1966); Dietrich Rueschemeyer, Evelyne Huber Stephens, and John Stephens, *Capitalist Development and Democracy* (Chicago: University of Chicago Press, 1992); Robert Dahl, *Polyarchy: Participation and Opposition* (New Haven, Conn.: Yale University Press, 1971).

2. Samuel Huntington, *The Third Wave: Democratization in the Late Twentieth Century* (Norman, Okla.: University of Oklahoma Press, 1991), 62–64.

3. According to the World Bank, Chinese per capita GDP in purchasing power parity terms reached $1,150 in 1987 and $3,617 in 1999.

4. Adam Przeworski et al. argue that the level of economic development is a poor predictor of democratic transition. See Adam Przeworski, Michael Alvarez, Jose Antonio Cheibub, and Fernando Limongi, *Democracy and Development: Political Institutions and Well-Being in the World, 1950–1990* (New York: Cambridge University Press, 2000).

5. Guillermo O'Donnell and Philippe Schmitter, *Transitions from Authoritarian Rule: Tentative Conclusions about Uncertain Democracies* (Baltimore, Md.: Johns Hopkins University Press, 1986).

6. Mikhail Gorbachev turned to *glasnost* in 1986 only after he encountered strong resistance for *perestroika*.

7. Economic growth in 1986 fell by almost 5 percent from 1985, *ZGTJNJ 2002,* 53.

8. Steven Solnick used this "bank run" metaphor to analyze the collapse of the political institutions in the former Soviet Union. See Solnick, *Stealing the State: Control and Collapse in Soviet Institutions* (Cambridge, Mass.: Harvard University Press, 1999).

9. Many high-ranking officials caught for corruption were superstitious. They typically hired fortune-tellers to forecast their chances of promotion. In a news story on Hunan, the official news agency, Xinhua, reported that all the provincial department heads prosecuted for corruption between 2001 and 2004 had retained fortune-tellers or "masters." www.xinhuanet.com, July 14, 2004. Shao Daosheng, "Gaoguan fubai yu xinyang weiji" (Corruption by Senior Officials and Crisis of Faith), www.cas.ac.cn/html/Dir/2003/11/11/4484.htm.

10. These confessions were quoted in www.chinareform.org/cn/cirdbbs/

dispbbs.asp?boardID=6&OD=2083; www.chinanews.com.cn, November 14, 2003.

11. According to the data provided by the CCP COD in 2004, 14 percent of the county-level officials were about thirty-five, 13 percent of the officials at the city/prefect level were about forty. www.chinanews.com.cn, May 19, 2004.

12. news.xinhuanet.com/legal/2004–02/17, February 17, 2004.

13. The most comprehensive review of this literature is Gérard Roland, *Transition and Economics: Politics, Markets, and Firms* (Cambridge, Mass.: MIT Press, 2000).

14. See Mathias Dewatripont and Gérard Roland, "The Virtues of Gradualism and Legitimacy in the Transition to a Market Economy," *The Economic Journal* 102 (1992): 291–300; Lawrence Lau, Yingyi Qian, and Gérard Roland, "Reform without Losers: An Interpretation of China's Dual-Track Approach to Transition," *Journal of Political Economy* 108(1) (2000): 120–143.

15. See Peter Murrell, "What Is Shock Therapy? What Did It Do in Poland and Russia?" *Post-Soviet Affairs* 9(2) (1993): 111–140; Gérard Roland, "The Political Economy of Transition" (Department of Economics, University of California, Berkeley, 2001), 7.

16. William Byrd, "The Impact of the Two-Tier Plan/Market System in Chinese Industry," *Journal of Comparative Economics* 11(3) (1987): 295–308.

17. Shang-jin Wei, "Gradualism Versus Big Bang: Speed and Sustainability of Reforms," *Canadian Journal of Economics* 30(4) (1997): 1234–1247; Mathias Dewatripont and Gérard Roland, "The Design of Reform Packages under Uncertainty," *American Economic Review* 85(5) (1995): 1207–1223.

18. See Thomas Wolf, "The Lessons of Limited Market-Oriented Reform," *Journal of Economic Perspectives* 5(4) (1991): 45–58; Richard Ericson, "The Classical Soviet-type Economy: Nature of the System and Implications for Reform," *Journal of Economic Perspectives* 5(4) (1991): 11–28.

19. János Kornai, *The Road to a Free Economy: Shifting from a Socialist System: the Example of Hungary* (New York: W. W. Norton, 1990).

20. See David Lipton and Jeffrey Sachs, "Creating a Market Economy in Eastern Europe: The Case of Poland," *Brookings Papers on Economic Activity* 1 (1990): 99–103.

21. See Kevin Murphy, Andrei Shleifer, and Robert Vishny, "The Transition to a Market Economy: Pitfalls of Partial Reform," *The Quarterly Journal of Economics* 57(3) (1992): 889–906; Alwyn Young, "The Razor's Edge: Distortions and Incremental Reform in the People's Republic of China," *The Quarterly Journal of Economics* 65(4) (2000): 1091–1135.

22. Wu Jinglian, "Zhongguo gaige de huigu yu qianzhan" (A Review of and Forward Look at China's Reform), *Jingji shehui tizhi bijiao* 2 (2000): 2.

23. See Lardy, "When Will China's Financial System Meet China's Needs?"

24. Bruce Dickson's study shows that the CCP has been successful in co-opting entrepreneurs. Bruce Dickson, *China's Red Capitalists: The Party, Private Entrepreneurs, and the Prospects for Political Change* (New York: Cambridge University Press, 2003).

25. Thomas Rawski, "Reforming China's Economy: What Have We Learned?" *The China Journal* 41 (1999): 153. Among the most influential studies endorsing China's approach, see Barry Naughton, *Growing Out of the Plan: Chinese Economic Reform, 1978–1993* (New York: Cambridge University Press, 1995); Nicholas Hope, Dennis Tao Yang, and Mu Yang Li, eds., *How Far Across the River: Chinese Policy Reform at the Millennium* (Stanford, Calif.: Stanford University Press, 2003); Lau, Qian, and Roland, "Reform Without Losers," 120–143; Alan Gelb, Gary Jefferson, and Inderjit Singh, "Can Communist Economies Transform Incrementally? The Experience of China," *NBER Macroeconomics Annual 1993* (Cambridge, Mass.: MIT Press, 1993), 86–133. For a sample review of the literature by Chinese economists, see Wu Jinglian, "Zhongguo gaige de huigu yu qianzhan"; Lin Yifu, Cai Fang, and Li Zhou, "Weishemme Zhongguo jingji gaige qudele chenggong?"(Why Is China's Economic Reform Successful?), *Jingji shehui tizhi bijiao* 4 (1995): 28–36; Zhao Renwei, "Dui woguo jingji gaige ershinian de ruogan sikao" (Several Thoughts on Twenty Years of Economic Reform in China), *Jingji shehui tizhi bijiao* 3 (1999): 9–16; Fan Gang, *Jianjin gaige de zhengzhi jingjixue fenxi* (*A Political Economy Analysis of Gradual Reform*) (Shanghai: Yuandong chubanshe, 1996).

26. Roland, *Transition and Economics.*

27. Byrd, "The Impact of the Two-Tier Plan/Market System," 295–308; Yingyi Qian, "How Reform Worked in China," in Dani Rodrik, ed., *In Search of Prosperity: Analytical Narratives on Economic Growth* (Princeton, N.J.: Princeton University Press, 2003), 297–333; Rawski, "Reforming China's Economy," 137–156.

28. Lau, Qian, and Roland, "Reform Without Losers."

29. William Byrd and Qingsong Lin, eds., *China's Rural Industry: Structure, Development, and Reform* (New York: Oxford University Press, 1990); Jianhua Che and Yingyi Qian, "Insecure Property Rights and Government Ownership of Firms," *Quarterly Journal of Economics* 113(2) (1998): 467–496; Jianhua Che and Yingyi Qian, "Institutional Environment, Community Government, and Corporate Governance: Understanding China's Township-Village Enterprises," *Journal of Law, Economics and Organization* 14(1) (1998): 1–23; Jean Chun Oi, *Rural China Takes Off:*

Institutional Foundations of Economic Reform (Berkeley: University of California Press, 1999); Jean Oi and Andrew Walder, eds., *Property Rights and Economic Reform in China* (Stanford, Calif.: Stanford University Press, 1999).

30. Susan Shirk provides an insightful analysis of how China's political structure facilitates the making of reform polices in *The Political Logic of Economic Reform in China* (Berkeley: University of California Press, 1993). For a discussion of industrial organizational structure and its effects on China's reform, see Yingyi Qian and Chenggang Xu, "Why China's Economic Reforms Differ: The M-form Hierarchy and Entry/Expansion of the Nonstate Sector," *Economics of Transition* 1(2) (1993): 135–170; Jeffrey Sachs and Wing Thye Woo, "Structural Factors in the Economic Reforms of China, Eastern Europe, and the Former Soviet Union," *Economic Policy* 18 (1994): 102–145.

31. See John McMillan, John Whalley, and Lijing Zhu, "The Impact of China's Economic Reforms on Agricultural Productivity Growth," *Journal of Political Economy* 97 (1989): 781–807; Justin Yifu Lin, "Rural Reforms and Agricultural Growth in China," *American Economic Review* 82 (1) (1992): 34–51. Jean Oi argues that the alignment of the interests of local governments with new rural industries produced the political coalition critical to the rapid growth of the manufacturing industries in rural China. Oi, *Rural China Takes Off*.

32. See Naughton, *Growing Out of the Plan.*

33. Lardy, *China's Unfinished Economic Revolution*; Christoph Duenwald and Jahangir Aziz, "The Growth-Financial Development Nexus," in Tseng and Rodlauer, eds., *China: Competing in the Global Economy*, 52–67; James Daniel et al., "Medium-Term Fiscal Issues," in Tseng and Rodlauer eds., *China: Competing in the Global Economy.*

34. Sachs and Woo, "Structural Factors in the Economic Reforms"; Jeffrey Sachs and Wing Thye Woo, "Understanding China's Economic Performance," *Working Paper No. 1793* (Cambridge, Mass.: Harvard Institute for International Development, 1997).

35. Young, "The Razor's Edge."

36. Jeffrey Sachs, Wing Thye Woo, and Xiaokai Yang, "Economic Reforms and Constitutional Transition," Social Science Research Network Electronic Paper Collection, Social Science Electronic Publishing Inc., papers. ssrn.com/paper.taf?abstract_id+254110.

37. For a few representative works that evaluate China's approach, see Wu Jinglian, "Zhongguo gaige de huigu yu qianzhan"; Fan Gang, *Jianjin gaige de zhengzhi jingjixue fenxi;* Zhao Renwei, "Dui woguo jingji gaige ershinian de ruogan sikao," 9–16; Li Jingwen, "Zhongguo jingji fazhan qianli fenxi yu yuce" (An Analysis and Forecast of China Economic Develop-

ment Potential), *Zhongguo shehui kexue jikan* (*Chinese Social Science Quarterly*) 26 (1999): 32–44; DRC, "Zhongguo jingji fazhan de jieduan xing bianhua, mianlin de wenti he fazhan de qianjing" (Changes in the State of the Chinese Economy, Its Problems and Prospects for Development), *Jingji yaocan* (*Important Economic Reference*) 1303 (August 29, 2002): 2–24.

38. DRC, "Zhongguo jingji fazhan de jieduan xing bianhua," 11.

39. Wu cites that the state-owned sector, which in the late 1990s contributed one-third of China's GDP, and used about two-thirds of the capital. Wu Jinglian, "Zhongguo gaige de huigu yu qianzhan," 2.

40. Fan Gang, *Jianjin gaige de zhengzhi jingjixue fenxi*, 165–167.

41. *Renmin ribao* (*People's Daily*), October 21, 2003, 1.

42. Wu Jinglian's views were summarized in a news story, www.chinanews. com.cn, March 4, 2001.

43. The interview with Wu was printed on www.chinanews.com.cn, March 1, 2003.

44. Roland, *Transition and Economics*, 12–13.

45. A big-bang approach is defined as incorporating not just stabilization, but also liberalization, privatization, and major institutional reforms. See the World Bank, *The World Development Report 1996: From Plan to Market* (Washington, D.C.: World Bank, 1996).

46. Alvaro Martínez and Javier Diaz, *Chile: The Great Transformation* (Washington, D.C.: Brookings Institution Press, 1996).

47. *Zhongguo caizheng nianjian 2002* (*Fiscal Yearbook of China*) (Beijing: Zhongguo caizheng zazhishe, 2002), 394.

48. www.chinanews.com.cn, October 20, 2003, and June 3, 2004. *Dangzheng ganbu wenzhai* (*Digest for Party and Government Officials*) 6 (2002): 48.

49. www.chinanews.com.cn, June 25, 2004.

50. Mary Gallagher, "Reform and Openness: Why China's Economic Reforms Have Delayed Democracy," *World Politics* 54(3) (2002): 338–372.

51. Yasheng Huang, *Selling China: Foreign Direct Investment During the Reform Era* (New York: Cambridge University Press, 2003).

52. Dickson, *China's Red Capitalists*.

53. The argument for the section on the predatory state was initially developed in Minxin Pei, "Rotten from Within: Decentralized Predation and Incapacitated State," in T. V. Paul, John Ikenberry, and John Hall, eds., *The Nation-State in Question* (Princeton, N.J.: Princeton University Press, 2003), 321–349.

54. See Chalmers Johnson, *MITI and the Japanese Miracle* (Stanford, Calif.: Stanford University Press, 1982); Stephan Haggard, *Pathways from the Periphery: The Politics of Growth in the Newly Industrialized Countries* (Ithaca, N.Y.: Cornell University Press, 1990); Robert Wade, *Governing the Market:*

Economic Theory and the Role of Government in East Asian Industrialization (Princeton, N.J.: Princeton University Press, 1990); Alice H. Amsden, *Asia's Next Giant: South Korea and Late Industrialization* (New York: Oxford University Press, 1989).

55. See the World Bank, *The East Asian Miracle: Economic Growth and Public Policy* (New York: Oxford University Press, 1993).

56. Wade, *Governing the Market*, 372–373.

57. See Barry Sautman's "Sirens of the Strongman: Neo-Authoritarianism in Recent Chinese Political Theory," *The China Quarterly* 129 (1992): 72–102.

58. Zhao Ziyang recalled this conversation when he was interviewed by a respected veteran Chinese journalist, Yang Jisheng, on October 29, 1996, in his residence in Beijing. Although Zhao himself was rumored to be an advocate of neoauthoritarianism in the late 1980s, Zhao told Yang that he did not know this concept or its main intellectual proponent at the time, a researcher in the CCP Central Committee's Secretariat called Wu Jiaxiang. See Yang Jisheng, *Zhongguo gaige niandai de zhengzhi douzheng (Political Struggle During the Reform Era in China)* (Hong Kong: Excellent Culture Press, 2005), 589.

59. See Andrei Shleifer and Robert W. Vishny, *The Grabbing Hand: Government Pathologies and Their Cures* (Cambridge, Mass.: Harvard University Press, 1998).

60. Peter Evans, *Embedded Autonomy: States and Industrial Transformation* (Princeton, N.J.: Princeton University Press, 1995).

61. Ibid., 248.

62. Adam Przeworski and Fernando Limongi, "Political Regimes and Economic Growth," *Journal of Economic Perspectives* 2(3) (1993): 65.

63. We may include South Korea, Singapore, Taiwan, Hong Kong, Malaysia, and Thailand. Outside East Asia, only Chile may qualify.

64. See Douglass North, *Structure and Change in Economic History* (New York: Norton, 1981), 20–32.

65. See Douglass North, *Institutions, Institutional Change and Economic Performance* (New York: Cambridge University Press, 1990); Thrainn Eggertsson, *Economic Behavior and Institutions* (Cambridge: Cambridge University Press, 1990). The institutionalist approach spurred a flurry of research on regime types and economic growth. The representative works include Martin McGuire and Mancur Olson, "The Economics of Autocracy and Majority Rule: The Invisible Hand and the Use of Force," *Journal of Economic Literature* 34 (1996): 72–96; Robert Barro, "Democracy and Growth," *Journal of Economic Growth* 1(1) (1996): 1–27; Robert Perotti, "Growth, Income Distribution, and Democracy: What the Data Say," *Journal of Economic Growth* 1(1) (1996): 149–187; Christopher Clague

et al., "Property and Contract Rights in Autocracies and Democracies," *Journal of Economic Growth* 1(1) (1996): 243–276.

66. The best example is the World Bank's *World Development Report 1997: The State and Development* (Washington, D.C.: World Bank, 1998).

67. North, *Structure and Change*, 20.

68. See Shleifer and Vishny, *The Grabbing Hand*.

69. Both North and Olson made this point. See North, *Structure and Change*, 21–24; Mancur Olson, "Dictatorship, Democracy, and Development," *American Political Science Review* 87(3) (1993): 567–576.

70. Susan Rose-Ackerman, *Corruption and Government: Causes, Consequences, and Reform* (Cambridge: Cambridge University Press, 1999), 114–121.

71. Olson, "Dictatorship, Democracy, and Development."

72. Eggertsson, *Economic Behavior and Institutions*, 323.

73. Margaret Levi, *Of Rule and Revenue* (Berkeley: University of California Press, 1988).

74. Olson, "Dictatorship, Democracy, and Development."

75. North, for example, saw agency costs as a serious constraint on the ruler's ability to take full advantage of his monopolist position. Eggertsson, *Economic Behavior and Institutions*, 324.

76. Andrei Shleifer and Robert Vishny, "Corruption," *The Quarterly Journal of Economics* 58(3) (1993): 599–617.

77. The theoretical distinction between predation and corruption can be hopelessly blurred in reality because of the agency problem. A fully disciplinary predatory state does not exist in practice. Diversion of revenues collected in the name of the state into the pockets of the agents is a common form of corruption. In theory, the degree of corruption in a predatory state heavily depends on the degree of centralization. In more centralized predatory state in which agents are tightly monitored, there should be less corruption or loss of the state's revenue.

78. See Paul Seabright, "Accountability and Decentralisation in Government: An Incomplete Contracts Model," *European Economic Review* 40 (1996): 61–75; Emanuela Carbonara, "Corruption and Decentralization," Universita di Bologna Dipartimento di Scienze Economiche WP 342/83, www.spbo.unibo.it/gopher/DSEC/vecchindex.htm.

79. David Wildasin, "Comments on 'Fiscal Federalism and Decentralization: A Review of Some Efficiency and Macroeconomic Aspects,'" in M. Bruno and B. Pleskovic, eds., *Annual World Conference on Development Economics, 1995* (Washington, D.C.: World Bank, 1996).

80. Van Rijckeghem and Beatrice Weder, "Corruption and the Rate of Temptation: Do Low Wages in the Civil Service Cause Corruption?" *IMF Working Paper WP/97/73* (Washington, D.C.: IMF, 1997).

81. Vito Tanzi, "Corruption, Arm's Length Relationships, and Markets," in Gianluca Fiorentini and Sam Peltzman, eds., *The Economics of Organized Crime* (Cambridge: Cambridge University Press, 1995), 161–180.

82. Shleifer and Vishny made this argument in "Corruption"; see also Olivier Blanchard and Andrei Shleifer, "Federalism with and without Political Centralization: China Versus Russia," *NBER Working Paper No. 7616,* www.nber.org/papers/w7616.

83. Carbonara and Seabright assume that local officials are constrained by the monitoring of civil society and an independent judiciary. In fact, Gurgur and Shah acknowledged that decentralization without strong judicial and political control mechanisms will lead to increased corruption.

84. Hellman, "Winners Take All," 203–234.

85. Michael McFaul, "State Power, Institutional Change, and the Politics of Privatization in Russia," *World Politics* 47(2) (1995): 210–243; Federico Varese, "The Transition to the Market and Corruption in Post-socialist Russia," *Political Studies* 45(3) (1997): 579–596.

86. Steven Solnick, "The Breakdown of Hierarchies in the Soviet Union and China: A Neoinstitutional Perspective," *World Politics* 48(2) (1996): 209–238.

87. See United Nations, *Human Development Report 1994* (New York: Oxford University Press, 1994).

88. Hellman, "Winners Take All." Also see Joel Hellman, Geraint Jones, Daniel Kaufmann, and Mark Schankerman, "Measuring Governance, Corruption, and State Capture," *World Bank Policy Research Working Paper No. 2312* (Washington, D.C.: World Bank, 2000); Ase Brodeland, Tatyana Koshechkina, and William Miller, "Foolish to Give and Yet More Foolish Not to Take—In-depth Interviews with Post-communist Citizens on Their Everyday Use of Bribes and Contacts," *Europe-Asia Studies* 50(4) (1998): 651–677.

89. See János Kornai, *The Political Economy of State Socialism* (Princeton, N.J.: Princeton University Press, 1990).

90. For a study of asset-stripping by state agents in China, see X. L. Ding, "The Illicit Asset Stripping of Chinese State Firms," *The China Journal* 43 (2000): 1–28.

91. Ibid.

92. X. L. Ding's investigation shows that Chinese managers have diverted a significant amount of state wealth into private overseas holdings. See Ding, "Informal Privatization Through Internationalization: The Rise of Nomenklatura Capitalism in China's Offshore Businesses," *British Journal of Political Science* 30(1) (2000): 121–146.

93. North, *Structure and Change,* 45–58.

2. Democratizing China?

1. The most detailed and perceptive analysis of the political aftermath of Tiananmen and the CCP's response to it is provided by Joseph Fewsmith, *China Since Tiananmen: The Politics of Transition* (New York: Cambridge University Press, 2001).

2. According to Pang Xianzhi, a senior official in the party's history research department, Deng initially raised the issue of political reform after his return to power mainly to avoid another Cultural Revolution. Wu Guoguang, *Zhao Ziyang yu zhengzhi gaige* (*Political Reform under Zhao Ziyang*) (Taipei: Yuanjing Publishing Co., 1997), 61.

3. Ibid. 486.

4. Deng Xiaoping, "Dang he guojia lingdao zhidu de gaige" (On the Reform of the System of Party and the State Leadership), *Deng Xiaoping wenxuan, 1975–1982* (*Selected Works of Deng Xiaoping*) (Beijing: Renmin chubanshe, 1983), 280–302.

5. Ibid., 283–300.

6. Ibid., 301.

7. Wu Guoguang, *Zhao Ziyang yu zhengzhi gaige*, 438.

8. Deng Xiaoping, "Zai tingqu jingji qingkuang huibao shide tanhua" (Remarks on the Domestic Economic Situation), *Deng Xiaoping wenxuan*, vol. 3 (*Selected Works of Deng Xiaoping*) (Beijing: Renmin chubanshe, 1993), 160.

9. Deng Xiaoping, "Guanyu zhengzhi tizhi gaige wenti" (On Reform of the Political Structure), *Deng Xiaoping wenxuan*, vol. 3, 176–177.

10. Ibid.

11. Ibid.

12. Deng Xiaoping, "Jiefang sixiang, shishi *qiushi*, tuanjie yizhi xiangqian kan" (Emancipate the Mind, Seek Truth From Facts and Unite As One in Looking to the Future), *Deng Xiaoping wenxuan, 1975–1982*, 134–135.

13. Wu Guoguang, a member of the task force, published his recollections of the task force's work in *Zhao Ziyang yu zhengzhi gaige*, which remains the most authoritative account of how China's ruling elites debated political reform. According to Wu, the Standing Committee of the Politburo decided in September 1986 to set up the task force. Its mandate was to produce a document on political reform before June–July 1987; it was to be discussed and approved at the 7th plenum in August–September 1987 and made public at the 13th Congress in October 1987. Wu Guoguang, *Zhao Ziyang yu zhengzhi gaige*, 20–21.

14. Ibid., 20.

15. Ibid., 20, 158–159.

16. Ibid., 73, 86, 102–114.

17. Ibid., 86.

18. Ibid., 210. In the Chinese original, *dangzheng fenkai* can mean the separation of the party from the government.

19. Bao Tong argued that *dangzheng fenkai* would enhance the leadership and authority of the party, establish a normal political order, and increase administrative efficiency. Wu Guoguang, *Zhao Ziyang yu zhengzhi gaige*, 139.

20. Ibid., 150.

21. Ibid., 161–162.

22. Ibid., 259, 304, 339.

23. Ibid., 159, 274.

24. Ibid., 263–265.

25. Ibid., 163, 286–288, 314, 286, 388–389.

26. Ibid., 297, 290.

27. Ibid., 161–162, 214.

28. Ibid., 58.

29. Ibid., 91–92.

30. Ibid., 385.

31. Ibid., 153.

32. Ibid., 386. Zhao was open-minded. He endorsed the assertiveness displayed by the NPC in the passage of two laws. "It takes time to get a good deed done. This time, the NPC was not a rubber stamp on the passage of the Bankruptcy Law and the Mining Law. This has made the laws better." Wu Guoguang, *Zhao Ziyang yu zhengzhi gaige*, 275.

33. Ibid., 384, 394, 443, 422.

34. Fewsmith, *China Since Tiananmen*.

35. Zhao's comments were revealed by his family friend, Wang Yangsheng, in an article in memory of Zhao, published in *Mingpao,* January 30, 2005, A4.

36. See Tanner, *The Politics of Lawmaking in Post-Mao China*; Dowdle, "The Constitutional Development and Operations of the National People's Congress," 1–123.

37. The docility of the NPC is fully described in Kevin O'Brien, *Reform without Liberalization: China's National People's Congress and the Politics of Institutional Change* (New York: Cambridge University Press, 1990).

38. Ibid.

39. Ying Songnian and Yuan Shuhong, *Zouxiang fazhi zhengfu (Toward a Government of Rule of Law)* (Beijing: Falü chubanshe, 2001), 410.

40. Stanley Lubman, "Bird in a Cage: Chinese Law Reform After Twenty Years," *Northwestern Journal of International Law and Business* 20 (2000): 383–423.

41. Tanner, *The Politics of Lawmaking in Post-Mao China*.

42. *Falü yu shenghuo* (*Law and Life*) 10 (2003): 2.

43. Ying and Yuan, *Zouxiang fazhi zhengfu*, 394–395.

44. www.chinanews.com.cn, April 18, 2004.

45. *Shidai zhuren* (*Master of the Times*) 7 (1999): 23.

46. Dowdle, "The Constitutional Development and Operations of the National People's Congress," 2; *Renmin zhiyou* (*People's Friends*) 9 (1999): 16–17.

47. At the second session of the 9th Congress in 1999, 22 percent of the delegates voted against the reports of the two top judicial organs. The only instance in which a major work report was voted down by the legislative branch occurred in 2001 when Shenyang's People's Congress refused to endorse the work report of the city's corruption-plagued intermediate court. The incident shocked the country but had no real political impact.

48. See Young-Nam Cho, "From 'Rubber Stamps' to 'Iron Stamps': The Emergence of Chinese Local People's Congresses as Supervisory Powerhouses," *The China Quarterly* 171 (2002): 724–740.

49. Kevin O'Brien, "Agents and Remonstrators: Role Accumulation by Chinese People's Congress Deputies," *The China Quarterly* 138 (1994): 359–380.

50. *Minzhu yu fazhi* (*Democracy and Legal System*) 20 (2000): 7–9.

51. *Renmin zhiyou* 11 (1999): 10–11.

52. *NFZM,* January 23, 2001; www.chinanewsweek.com.cn, September 20, 2004.

53. *Renmin zhiyou* 8 (1999): 10–11.

54. *Renmin zhiyou* 10 (1999): 42.

55. CCP Liaoning POD, "Gaijin difang renda zhengfu lingdao banzi huanjie xuanju gongzuo de yanjiu baogao" (A Research Report on Improving the Work of Electing Local People's Congress and Administrative Leaderships), in *ZGYW 1999*, 688–689.

56. Hangzhou CCP Organization Department, "Shixian renda he zhengfu lingdao banzi huanjie xuanju wenti yanjiu" (A Study on the Issue of the Elections of the Leaderships of [Municipal and County] People's Congress and Governments), in *ZGYW 1997*, 277.

57. *Renda gongzuo tongxun* (*NPC Work Newsletter*) 15 (1997): 8.

58. *ZGYW 1999*, 693.

59. *ZGYW 1977*, 277, 280–289, 299.

60. *NFZM,* February 20, 2003.

61. Dowdle, "The Constitutional Development and Operations of the National People's Congress," 2.

62. *Renda gongzuo tongxun* 24 (1998): 11.

63. *NFZM*, April 3, 2003.
64. Liu Zhi et al., *Shuju xuanju: Renda daibiao xuanju tongji yanjiu* (*Election Data: A Study of the Elections of People's Congress Deputies*) (Beijing: Zhongguo shehui kexue chubanshe, 2001), 337.
65. Liu Zhi et al., *Shuju xuanju*, 340, 350, 366.
66. Barrett McCormick, "China's Leninist Parliament and Public Sphere: A Comparative Analysis," in Barrett McCormick and Jonathan Unger, eds., *China After Leninism: In the Footsteps of Eastern Europe or East Asia?* (Armonk, N.Y.: M. E. Sharpe, 1996), 29–53.
67. Kevin O'Brien, "Chinese People's Congress and Legislative Embeddedness: Understanding Early Organizational Development," *Comparative Political Studies* 27 (1) (1994): 80–109.
68. Among the most important works on this subject are Potter, *Domestic Law Reforms in Post-Mao China;* Lubman, *China's Legal Reforms;* Lubman, *Bird in a Cage;* and Randall Peerenboom, *China's Long March toward Rule of Law* (New York: Cambridge University Press, 2002); Jianfu Chen, Yuwen Li, and Jan Michiel Otto, eds., *Implementation of Law in the People's Republic of China* (The Hague: Kluwer Law International, 2002).
69. Peerenboom, *China's Long March*, 6–8, 558.
70. Yuwen Li, "Court Reform in China: Problems, Progress and Prospects," in Chen, Li, and Otto, eds., *Implementation of Law*, 55–83.
71. Deng Xiaoping, "Jiefang sixiang," 136.
72. William Alford, "Seek Truth from Facts—Especially When They Are Unpleasant: America's Understanding of China's Efforts at Law Reform," *Pacific Law Review* 8(177) (1990): 181.
73. Cai Dingjian, "Development of the Chinese Legal System since 1979 and Its Current Crisis and Transformation," *Cultural Dynamics* 11(2) (1999): 135–166.
74. William Alford, "Double-edged Swords Cut Both Ways: Law and Legitimacy in the People's Republic of China," *Daedalus* 122(2) (1993): 45–69.
75. Lubman, *Bird in a Cage*, 298.
76. Lubman, "Bird in a Cage," 383–423.
77. See Gong Xiangrui, ed., *Fazhi de lixiang yu xianshi* (*The Ideal and Reality of the Rule of Law*) (Beijing: Zhongguo zhengfa daxue chubanshe, 1993); also see Minxin Pei, "Citizens v. Mandarins: Administrative Litigation in China," *The China Quarterly* 152 (1997): 832–862; Kevin O'Brien and Lianjiang Li, "Suing the Local State: Administrative Litigation in Rural China," *The China Journal* 51 (2004): 75–95; for a study of commercial disputes in China, see Minxin Pei, "Legal Reform and Secure Commercial Transactions: Evidence from China," in Peter Murrell, ed., *Assessing the*

Value of Law in Transition Economies (Ann Arbor: University of Michigan Press, 2001), 180–210.

78. Of the 220,000 judges in the country in 2003, 82,764 had college degrees and 3,774 had graduate degrees. www.chinanews.com.cn, April 4, 2003.

79. *Renmin sifa* (*People's Judiciary*) 9 (2001): 8; *NFZM,* July 11, 2002; *Renmin sifa* 5 (1999): 19.

80. Calculated from data supplied by *ZGFLNJ,* various years.

81. Lawyers Committee for Human Rights, *Lawyers in China: Obstacles to Independence and the Defense of Rights* (New York: Lawyers Committee for Human Rights, 1998).

82. *Minzhu yu fazhi* 2 (1999): 13.

83. www.chinanews.com.cn, April 4, 2003.

84. *Renmin sifa* 5 (1999): 16.

85. Among the institutional flaws listed by He and Zhang were the appointment of nonjudges to head local courts; the interference by presidents of courts and chiefs of tribunals in cases they do not preside over; the strange practice of rendering judgments without trying the cases by trial committees; the lack of independence between superior and subordinate courts; the courts' dependence on local budgets; the overlapping of courts' jurisdictions with local governments' jurisdictions (a source of local protectionism); and the court's weak enforcement capacity. He and Zhang offered many reform proposals. www.chinanews.com.cn, December 4, 2004.

86. For example, proposed court reforms, summarized in the Supreme People's Court's Five-Year Program to Reform the System of People's Courts issued in October 1999, did not deal with the fundamental institutional flaws in the legal system. Instead, these measures focused on trial procedures, reorganization of the internal structures of courts, personnel management of the courts, and improved supervision.

87. Li, "Court Reform in China."

88. *Renmin sifa* 6 (1999): 31.

89. For an excellent discussion of how these institutional flaws weaken judicial independence, see Cai Dingjian, "Fayuan zhidu gaige zhouyi" (On Reforming the Court System), *Zhanlüe yu guanli* 1 (1999): 97–101.

90. In one basic-level court in Jiangsu, of the fifteen members of the trial committee, two were high school graduates and two had only a middle-school education. *Renmin sifa* 2 (2001): 21.

91. *Renmin sifa* 5 (1999): 20.

92. Jianfu Chen, "Mission Impossible: Judicial Efforts to Enforce Civil Judgments and Rulings in China," in Chen, Li, and Otto eds., *Implementation of Law,* 85–111.

93. Cai Dingjian singled out corruption as one of the most serious problems in China's legal system. See Cai, "Development of the Chinese Legal System," 135–166.

94. www.chinanews.com.cn, January 26, 2004.

95. www.chinanewsweek.com.cn, April 19, 2004.

96. www.chinanews.com.cn, August 21, 2004; October 10, 2004; December 19, 2004.

97. See Donald C. Clarke, "Power and Politics in the Chinese Court System: The Enforcement of Civil Judgments," *Columbia Journal of Asian Law* 10 (1996): 1–92.

98. Even the inflated official enforcement rate (percentage of judgments actually executed) fell from 75 percent in 1995 to 68 percent in 1997. Chen, "Mission Impossible," 85–111.

99. Cai Dingjian, "Fayuan zhidu gaige zhouyi."

100. This sentiment was reflected in an article written by the division chief of the research office of the Supreme People's Court. He asked two important questions: why did some "seriously unqualified" individuals become judges and even obtain senior judicial appointments? and why have courts degenerated into a local bureaucracy solely interested in pursuing local interests? He concluded that China's judicial system requires "major surgery." See Jiang Huiling, "Zhongguo sifa zhidu xuyao dong dashoushu" (China's Judicial System Requires Major Surgery), www.caijing.com.cn, August 20, 2004.

101. One of the most enthusiastic promoters of village elections, Wang Zhenyao, expressed this view in his "Zhongguo de cunmin zizhi yu minzhuhua fazhan daolu" (The Road for Villagers' Self-government and Democratization in China), *Zhanlüe yu guanli* 2 (2000): 99–105; also see Kevin O'Brien and Lianjiang Li, "Accommodating 'Democracy' in a One-Party State: Introducing Village Elections in China," *The China Quarterly* 162 (2000): 465–489; Pastor and Tan, "The Meaning of China's Village Elections," 490–512.

102. Lianjiang Li, "The Empowering Effect of Village Elections in China," *Asian Survey* 43(4) (2003): 648–662.

103. O'Brien, "Villagers, Elections, and Citizenship in Contemporary China," 407–435.

104. Allen Choate, "Local Governance in China: An Assessment of Villagers Committees" (The Asia Foundation, Working Paper no. 1, 1997).

105. Xiao Tangbiao et al., "Zhongguo xiangcun shehui zhongde xuanju" (Elections in China's Rural Society) *Zhanlüe yu guanli* 5 (2001): 49–59.

106. Jean Oi and Scott Rozelle, "Elections and Power: The Locus of Decision Making in Chinese Villages," *The China Quarterly* 162 (2000): 513–539.

107. Bjorn Alpermann, "The Post-Election Administration of Chinese Villages," *The China Journal* 46 (2001): 45–67.

108. Wang Zhenyao, "Zhongguo de cunmin zizhi yu minzhuhua fazhan daolu."

109. *Renmin zhiyou* 1 (1999): 5.

110. Tianjian Shi, "Election Reform in China" (mimeo, Department of Political Science, Duke University, 2004).

111. Hu Rong, "Jingji fazhan yu jingzhengxing de cunweihui xuanju" (Economic Development and Competitive Elections of Villagers' Committees), www.people.com.cn/GB/14576.

112. Shi, "Election Reform in China."

113. Hu Rong, "Jingji fazhan yu jingzhengxing de cunweihui xuanju."

114. Shi, "Election Reform in China."

115. The most stringent standard means that the leading group of the village election must be directly elected by the villagers, that candidates must be nominated by villagers only, that candidates must be chosen by all villagers in a popular vote (*haixuan*), and elections must feature multicandidates for the villagers' committee. Shi, "Election Reform in China."

116. Shi, "Election Reform in China."

117. Xiao Tangbiao et al., "Zhongguo xiangcun shehui zhongde xuanju."

118. Ibid., 54, 57.

119. John James Kennedy, "The Face of 'Grassroots Democracy' in Rural China," *Asian Survey* 42(3) (2002): 456–482.

120. Hu Rong, "Jingji fazhan yu jingzhengxing de cunweihui xuanju."

121. Xie Ziping, "Fujiansheng 2000 niandu cunweihui xuanju diaocha shuju fenxi baogao" (A Report on Analysis of the Data on the Elections of Villagers' Committees in Fujian Province in 2000), www.chinarural.org.

122. Cao Ying, "Jilinsheng cunweihui xuanju shuju fenxi baogao" (A Report on Analysis of the Data on the Elections of Villagers' Committees in Jilin Province), www.chinarural.org.

123. Wu Miao, "Cunweihui xuanju zhiliang de lianghua fenxi: Yi Fujiansheng 9 shi 2000 niandu cunweihui huanjie xuanju tongji shuju wei jiju" (A Quantitative Analysis of the Quality of Village Elections Based on Data on the Villagers' Committee Elections in Nine Cities in Fujian Province in 2000), www.chinarural.org.

124. Liu Xitang, "Hunansheng 1999 niandu 40 ge xian cunweihui xuanju shuju fenxi baogao" (A Report on Analysis of the Data on the Elections in 40 Counties in Hunan Province in 1999), www.chinarural.org.

125. See Oi and Rozelle, "Elections and Power"; Alpermann, "The Post-Election Administration of Chinese Villages."

126. Such instances were reported in *Minzhu yu fazhi* 23 (2000): 31–33.

127. *NFZM*, September 12, 2002.

128. *Zhongguo gaige (nongcunban)* (*China Reform*, rural edition) 2 (2003): 18.

129. *Zhongguo gaige (nongcunban)* 2 (2003): 15.

130. David Zweig, "Democratic Values, Political Structures, and Alternative Politics in Greater China" (Washington, D.C.: U.S. Institute of Peace Peaceworks no. 44, 2002), 45.

131. *NFZM*, August 22, 2002.

132. Tony Saich and Xuedong Yang, "Innovation in China's Local Governance: 'Open Recommendation and Selection,'" *Pacific Affairs* 76 (2) (2003): 185–208.

133. Yu Keping, *Zhongguo difang zhengfu chuangxin* (*Innovations by Local Governments in China*) (Beijing: Shehui kexue wenxian chubanshe, 2002), 42.

134. *Zhongguo gaige (nongcunban)* 9 (2002): 6.

135. www.chinanewsweek.com.cn, November 22, 2004.

136. Melanie Manion, "Chinese Democratization in Perspective: Electorates and Selectorates at the Township Level," *The China Quarterly* 163 (2000): 764–781.

137. Tanner argues that the Chinese state's repressive capacity has declined since reform. See Murray Scot Tanner, "Cracks in the Wall: China's Eroding Coercive State," *Current History* (September 2001): 243–249.

138. Pei, "Is China Democratizing?" 78.

139. *The Washington Post* reported a chilling story of a political study group at Peking University that was penetrated by the secret police through its informants. *The Washington Post*, April 23, 2004, A01. Another story in *The Washington Post* described the experience of a Chinese college student who published witty political satires on the Web. She suspected that the government sent a spy to befriend her and obtain all the information about her contacts. She was later detained. *The Washington Post*, December 18, 2004, A01. The disclosure about recruiting informants in Jiangxi was made in Jiangxi Gong'anting, *Jiangxi gong'an nianjian 2001* (Public Security Almanac of Jiangxi) (Nanchang: Jiangxi gong'an nianjian chubanshe, 2002), 332.

140. For an example of the sophistication of these methods, see the Ministry of Public Security's directive on April 5, 2000, "Gong'anbu guanyu gong'an jiguan chuzhi quntixing zhi'an shijian guiding" (The Ministry of Public Security's Regulations on Dealing with Collective Public Security Incidents). It details the rules of engagement. *Shanghai gong'an nianjian 2001* (Shanghai Public Security Almanac) (Shanghai: Xuelin chubanshe, 2001), 346–351.

141. Ministry of Public Security, *Zhongguo gong'an nianjian 2000* (Beijing: Qunzhong chubanshe, 2001), 211.

142. Pang Qigui, "Chuzhi quntixing zhi'an shijian de jiben duice" (Basic Counter-measures for Dealing with Collective Public Security Incidents), in *Renmin gong'an (People's Public Security)* 2 (2002): 26–27.

143. See James Tong, "Anatomy of Regime Repression in China: Timing, Enforcement Institutions, and Target Selection in Banning the Falungong, July 1999," *Asian Survey* 42(6) (2002): 795–820.

144. Shanthi Kalathil and Taylor Boas, *Open Networks, Closed Regimes* (Washington, D.C.: Carnegie Endowment for International Peace, 2003), 1–12.

145. Guobin Yang, "The Co-Evolution of the Internet and Civil Society in China," *Asian Survey* 43(3) (2003): 405–422.

146. Kalathil and Boas, *Open Networks,* 13–42; Eric Harwit and Duncan Clark, "Shaping the Internet in China: Evolution of Political Control over Network Infrastructure and Content," *Asian Survey* 41(3) (2003): 377–408.

147. Kalathil and Boas, *Open Networks,* 40.

148. Michael Chase and James Mulvenon, *You've Got Dissent!* (Santa Monica, Calif.: Rand Corp., 2002), 89.

149. The number of Internet users was reported in *The Washington Post,* May 24, 2004, A01.

150. Ministry of Public Security, "Guanyu jiaqiang gonggong xinxi wangluo anquan jiancha gongzuo de yijian" (Views on Strengthening the Security and Monitoring of Public Information Networks), in *Zhongguo gong'an nianjian 2000,* 319.

151. Ibid., 320–322.

152. Ibid.

153. *The Washington Post,* May 24, 2004, A01.

154. Beijing Public Security Bureau, *Beijing gong'an nianjian 2001* (Beijing: Zhongguo renmin gong'an daxue chubanshe, 2001), 115, 116.

155. Beijing Public Security Bureau, *Beijing gong'an nianjian 2003* (Beijing: Zhongguo renmin gong'an daxue chubanshe, 2003), 114–115.

156. Beijing Public Security Bureau, *Beijing gong'an nianjian 2001,* 116.

157. Ministry of Public Security, *Zhongguo gong'an nianjian 2000,* 213.

158. *Xinwen Zhoukan* 18 (May 24, 2004), www.chinanewsweek.com.cn; www.chinanews.com.cn, April 28, 2004.

159. Kang Xiaoguang pointed out that the co-optation of the intelligentsia by the CCP critically weakened societal opposition after 1989. See Kang Xiaoguang, *Zhongguo: Gaige shidai de zhengzhi fazhan yu zhengzhi wending (China: Political Development and Political Stability in the Era of Reform)* (Beijing: Tsinghua University, 2003).

160. Jonathan Unger and Anita Chan, "Corporatism in China: A Developmental State in an East Asian Context," in McCormick and Unger, eds., *China After Leninism,* 95–129.

161. CCP COD, Propaganda Department, and State Education Commission, "Guanyu xinxingshi jiaqiang he gaijin gaodeng xuexiao dangde jianshe he sixiang zhengzhi gongzuo de ruogan yijian" (Some Suggestions on Strengthening and Improving the Party-Building and Ideological Political Work in Higher-Education Institutions under the New Conditions), *Zhonghua renmin gongheguo zhongyao jiaoyu wenxian, 1991–1997 (Important PRC Documents on Education)* (Hainan: Hainan chubanshe, 1998), 3546–3547.

162. Beijing Higher Education Bureau, *Beijing gaodeng jiaoyu nianjian, 1995* (Beijing: Beijing gaodeng jiaoyu chubanshe, 1995), 74–76.

163. Sichuan CCP POD, "Sichuansheng dixian dangzheng lingdao banzi nianqinghua jincheng diaocha baogao" (An Investigation of the Progress of Making Prefect and County Leadership Younger in Sichuan), in *ZGYW 1997,* 8.

164. *Dangjian yanjiu (Party-Building Research)* 2 (1995): 32.

165. *BYTNB* 6 (2003): 29–30.

166. *ZGYW 2000,* 90.

167. State Education Commission, "Guanyu shishi kuaishiji youxiu rencai peiyang jihua (renwen shehui kexue) de tongzhi" (Announcement on the Training of Outstanding Scholars in [Humanities and Social Sciences] for the Next Century), *Zhonghua renmin gongheguo zhongyao jiaoyu wenxian, 1991–1997,* 4185–4186.

168. www.chinanews.com.cn, May 28, 2004.

169. Meng Jianzhu, "Xinxingshi xia jiaqiang minjian zuzhi dangjian gongzuo de sikao yu tansuo" (Some Thoughts and Experiments on the Work to Strengthen Party-Building Inside Civic Groups in the New Situation), *Zhonggong zhongyang dangxiao baogaoxuan (Selected Reports of the Chinese Communist Party Central Party School)* 16 (2000): 17–28.

170. Yu Yunyao, "Buneng xishou shiyin qiyezhu rudang" (Private Entrepreneurs Must Not Be Admitted into the Party), *Dangjian yanjiu* 9 (1995): 4.

171. One example of the confusion over the political status of private entrepreneurs was an article published in April 2000 by Zhang Dejiang, the party chief of Zhejiang. In his article, published in the CCP's major journal on party-building, Zhang wrote, "The ban against admitting private entrepreneurs into the party must be made explicit. On this issue, the Central Committee issued explicit rules a long time ago, but there is quite a bit of confusion among some party leaders in some places over this issue." Zhang Dejiang, "Jiaqiang feigongyouzhi qiye

dangjian gongzuo xu yanjiu jiejue de jige wenti" (Several Issues on Intensifying the Work of Building the Party in Non-State Firms That Need
to Be Studied and Resolved), *Dangjian yanjiu* 4 (2000): 14.

172. See chapter 5.
173. Dickson, *Red Capitalists in China;* www.chinanews.com.cn, February 19,
2003.
174. *BYTNB* 3 (2003): 20.
175. www.chinanews.com.cn, February 19, 2003.
176. "Chinese Capitalists Gain New Legitimacy," *The Washington Post,* September 29, 2002, A01.
177. "For China's Local Bigwigs, New Money Means Power," *The Washington
Post,* July 7, 2002, A01.
178. Dickson, *Red Capitalists in China,* 116–141. *The Washington Post,* July 7,
2002, A01.

3. Rent Protection and Dissipation

1. The government's monopoly over cotton procurement was partially
ended in 1999. DRC, "Mianhua liutong tizhi yanjiu" (A Study of the
Cotton Procurement System), *DRC diaocha yanjiu baogao* 17 (2000):
1–27.
2. Between 1992 and 1999, annual policy losses incurred by SOEs in the
grain procurement system averaged 24 billion yuan. Li Hongmin,
"Liangshi liutong tizhi gaige haixu jinyibu shenhua" (The Reform of
the Grain Procurement System Needs Deepening), *Jingji yanjiu cankao*
(*Economic Research and Reference*) 28 (2001): 27. SOEs pooled their operating losses into policy losses. Enjiang Cheng, "Market Reforms and Provision of Credit for Grain Purchases in China," *The China Quarterly* 151
(1997): 633–654.
3. OECD, *China in the World Economy.*
4. Ibid.
5. Thomas P. Lyons, "Feeding Fujian: Grain Production and Trade,
1986–1996," *The China Quarterly* 155 (1998): 512–545.
6. See Yuk-shing Cheng and Shu-ki Tsang, "The Changing Grain Marketing System in China," *The China Quarterly* 140 (1994): 1080–1104.
7. OECD, *China in the World Economy,* 66.
8. Cheng and Tsang, "The Changing Grain Marketing System."
9. A poll of 708 peasants in Jiangxi in 1993 showed that only 22 percent
preferred the government-mandated quota system. Chen Xin, Zhou
Xianhua, and Deng Shengping, "Nongcun zhengce yao luoshi shichang

jingji pan youxu" (Implement Agricultural Policy and Look Forward to an Orderly Market Economy), *Diaoyan shijie* (*Investigation and Research Forum*), March 25, 1993, 8.

10. Cheng and Tsang, "The Changing Grain Marketing System."

11. Zhou Zhangyao and Chen Liangbiao, "Cong 'baoliang fangjia' dao 'tijia dinggou,'" (From "Guarantee Quantity but Liberalize Prices" to "Raise Prices and Mandate Procurement"), *Gaige* (*Reform*) 5 (1995): 58; Ma Kai, "Ruhe renshi xianxing liangshi gouxiao zhengce" (How to Understand the Current Policies on Purchase and Sale of Grain), *Gaige* 2 (1996): 11.

12. OECD, *China in the World Economy*, 63–64.

13. Zhou and Chen, "Cong 'baoliang fangjia' dao 'tijia dinggou,'" 57.

14. Wang Laibao and Fan Weili, "1999 nian liangshi liutong tizhi gaige zongshu" (A Summary of the Reform of the Grain Procurement System in 1999), *Jingji yanjiu cankao* 22 (2000): 4–5; DRC, "1999 nian liangmian liutong tizhi gaige" (The Reform of the Procurement Systems for Grain and Cotton in 1999), *DRC diaocha yanjiu baogao* 11 (2000): 3.

15. DRC, "Mianhua liutong tizhi yanjiu," 5–10.

16. After 1998, the dual-track pricing system again became a one-track single price system. The SOEs purchased grain directly from peasants at a government-set protected price and sold to consumers at a loss. The losses were made up by the budget. Li Hongmin, "Liangshi liutong tizhi gaige haixu jinyibu shenhua," 26–29.

17. In 2001, the government fully liberalized the grain purchase system in the eight provinces that were net consumers of grain; in 2002, liberalization was extended to the provinces in which grain production and consumption were in balance (such as Yunnan, Chongqing, and Guangxi). But the government retained the same monopoly system in grain-producing provinces. Ding Zhengjing, "Liangshi liutong gaige yu nongye zhengcexing jinrong zhineng dingwei" (Reform of the Grain Purchase System and the Definition of the Financial Function of Agricultural Policy), *Zhongguo nongye jingji* (*China Agricultural Economics*) 10 (2003): 72.

18. The figure on accumulated losses is from *Nanfang zhoumo*, August 28, 2003, www.nanfangdaily.com.cn/zm/20030828/. In the reform era, the average cycle of shortage and glut was about three to four years, as was the case in 1985–1988, 1989–1993, and 1994–1998. For example, in the 1994–1998 cycle, prices initially rocketed in 1994 but collapsed in 1996. Yuan Yongkang and Song Ze, "Jianquan tiaokong jiage binggui jingying fangkai" (Improve Macro-Control, Unify Prices, and Liberalize Markets), *Gaige* 2 (1997): 41.

19. In the early 1980s, for example, the government's commitment to

purchase surplus grain from farmers at higher prices caused a glut; budgetary subsidies to grain almost tripled from 1978 to 1984. Cheng and Tsang, "The Changing Grain Marketing System," 1090.

20. Yuan and Song, "Jianquan tiaokong jiage binggui jingying fangkai," 43.

21. Li Hongmin, "Liangshi liutong tizhi gaige haixu jinyibu shenhua," 27.

22. Yuan and Song, "Jianquan tiaokong jiage binggui jingying fangkai," 46.

23. Li Hongmin, "Liangshi liutong tizhi gaige haixu jinyibu shenhua," 29.

24. Yuan and Song, "Jianquan tiaokong jiage binggui jingying fangkai," 44.

25. One researcher claimed that private agents controlled half the procurement market and they had developed cozy ties with SOEs. Li Hongmin, "Liangshi liutong tizhi gaige haixu jinyibu shenhua," 30.

26. In May 2004, the State Council approved in principle a draft regulation on grain procurement and marketing that would liberalize the market fully, but the details were not made public. www.chinanews.com.cn, May 19, 2004.

27. Mike Peng and Bing Zhang, "Telecom Competition, Post-WTO Style," *The China Business Review* 27(3) (2000): 14; DRC, "Zhongguo dianxinye jingzheng fenxi" (An Analysis of Competition in China's Telecom Sector), *DRC diaocha yanjiu baogao* 80 (2003): 11–12; *ZGTJZY 2000,* 130.

28. www.chinanews.com.cn, January 15, 2004.

29. Institute of Industrial Economics, Chinese Academy of Social Sciences (CASS), "Zhongguo zhengfu guanzhi gaige chutan" (A Preliminary Study of Reforming China's Regulatory System), *Jingji yanjiu cankao* 76 (1998): 26; Peng and Zhang, "Telecom Competition."

30. Zhang Weiying and Sheng Hong, "Cong dianxinye kan Zhongguo de fan longduan wenti" (Antimonopoly in China: The Case of Telecom), *Gaige* 2 (1998): 68.

31. Eric Harwit and Jack Su, "A Telecom Newcomer Challenges the MPT Monopoly," *The China Business Review* 23(3) (1996): 22; Zhang and Sheng, "Cong dianxinye kan Zhongguo de fan longduan wenti," 70.

32. In 1994, a reorganization of MPT separated its telecom business from its postal service. As a result, China Telecom, the national monopoly, was formed, however China Telecom remained as part of MPT. "Chinese Telecoms: Into the Crucible," *Economist* 361 (8246) (November 3, 2001), 67.

33. Zhang and Sheng, "Cong dianxinye kan Zhongguo de fan longduan wenti," 71–73; Lynn Crisanti, "Untangling China's Datacom Networks," *The China Business Review* 24(2) (1997): 40.

34. Institute of Industrial Economics, CASS, "Zhongguo zhengfu guanzhi gaige chutan," 26.

35. Zhang and Sheng, "Cong dianxinye kan Zhongguo de fan longduan wenti," 71.

36. China Mobile was separated from China Telecom in 1998. The data presented for the paging market are for 1998. Peng and Zhang, "Telecom Competition," 12.

37. DRC, "Zhongguo dianxinye jingzheng fenxi," 12.

38. Peng and Zhang, "Telecom Competition," 18.

39. Kenneth DeWoskin, "The WTO and the Telecommunications Sector in China," *The China Quarterly* 167 (2001): 630–654.

40. In 1999, China Telecom (HK) became China Mobile (HK).

41. Tom Holland, "The Perils of Privatization," *Far Eastern Economic Review*, June 22, 2002, 55.

42. DRC, "Zhongguo dianxinye jingzheng fenxi," 11.

43. Ibid., 7–8.

44. Li Zhong (with the State Planning Commission), "Woguo dianxin tizhi gaige de huigu yu zhanwang" (A Review and Prospective Look at Reforming China's Telecom System), *Jingji yanjiu cankao* 43 (2000): 5.

45. Crisanti, "Untangling China's Datacom Networks," 38.

46. Ted Dean, "The Data Communications Market Opens Up," *The China Business Review* 28(1) (2001): 22–24.

47. For example, China ranked sixty-third (out of eighty-two countries rated) in terms of competition in the telecom service industry. Its score was 3.41, out of a possible score of 7 (well below the mean score of 4.53). This placed China behind India (4.65, ranked 42), Russia (3.56, 58), Indonesia (4.08, 51), Thailand (4.47, 44), Hungary (4.79, 38), the Czech Republic (4.68, 40), and the Philippines (4.83, 37). China was ahead of Vietnam (2.74, 74), Ukraine (3.14, 67), and Romania (3.22, 66). China scored poorly on "overall infrastructure quality" as well. With a score of 3.41, China was below the mean of 4.2 and ranked 50 (out of eighty-two countries). It was behind Hungary (4.27, 40), the Czech Republic (4.83, 29), and Thailand (4.77, 30), although it was above India (2.83, 64), Russia (3.12, 59), Indonesia (2.75, 66), and the Philippines (2.28, 76). The costs of service were also higher in China. The mean cost of a three-minute local call was US$9.36 (weighted against each country's per capita GDP). On this score, such a call cost US$12.31 in China, giving it a ranking of 60. China ranked behind the Philippines (free, 1), Ukraine ($1.27, 8), Russia ($1.94, 9), Indonesia ($6.67, 43), India ($7.55, 45), Hungary ($7.71, 48), the Czech Republic ($9.63, 54), and Thailand ($11.68, 58). China's ranking was above that of Vietnam ($12.73, 61) and Romania ($17.36, 71). The costs of a three-minute off-peak local cellular call in China were also higher than in most countries. The mean cost, weighted against GDP, was $0.68 in the eighty-two countries. With such a call costing $1.09, China was ranked 68, behind Russia ($0.03, 1), the

Czech Republic ($0.14, 19), Hungary ($0.25, 34), Indonesia ($0.48, 44), and the Philippines ($0.68, 54). Such a call was more expensive in Vietnam ($1.21, 71), India ($1.71, 76), and Ukraine ($2.07, 78). Soumitra Dutta et al., eds., *The Global Information Technology Report 2002–2003* (New York: Oxford University Press, 2003), 285–304.

48. One example was the MII's decision not to reform the rate structure in the mobile phone market out of fear that such reform would cause a plunge in the share prices of China Mobile (HK). China Telecom raised its monopoly long-distance rates before its IPO in 2002 to boost its business prospects.

49. Lardy's *China's Unfinished Economic Revolution* provides the most comprehensive description and analysis of the weakness of China's banking sector. OECD's survey of the Chinese economy in 2002 paints a gloomy picture of its banking sector. See OECD, *China in the World Economy*, 233–268.

50. State Planning Commission, "Zhongguo ziben shichang de peiyu he fazhan zhengce yanjiu" (A Study of the Policy of Developing Capital Markets in China), *Jingji yanjiu cankao* 5 (2001): 3. Researchers at the IMF also agreed that the pace of financial deepening in China during the reform era was impressive. See Jahangir Aziz and Christoph Duenwald, "Growth-Financial Intermediation Nexus in China," *IMF Working Paper No. 194*, (Washington, D.C.: International Monetary Fund, 2002).

51. Lardy, *China's Unfinished Economic Revolution*, 95.

52. For a description of the evolution of the banking system, see Minxin Pei, "The Political Economy of Banking Reforms in China: 1993–1997," *Journal of Contemporary China* 7(18) (1998): 321–350.

53. Wu Jinliang, "Guanyu jiakuai jinrong tizhi gaige de shexiang" (Ideas on Accelerating the Reform of the Financial System), *Gaige* 5 (1993): 93–97.

54. Ibid.

55. The government also allowed joint-stock banks and Minsheng to be listed on the domestic stock markets.

56. The performance of the four AMCs was mixed. They used both debt-for-equity swaps (taking stakes in indebted SOEs) and sale of impaired assets to dispose of the 1.4 trillion yuan in NPLs. As of 2003, about 35 percent of the NPLs was disposed of, with a cash recovery rate of 17 percent. *The Wall Street Journal*, January 15, 2004, A12. But the real recovery rate was likely lower. In Orient Asset Management (tied to BOC), the real recovery rate was only 12 percent, not the 19 percent it reported. The rate of disposing of bad assets was too slow, and at the current rate, could take fifteen years. *Xinwen zhoukan*, August 4, 2003. www.chinanewsweek.com.cn. The debt-equity swap was also deferring the real costs of the bailout to the future be-

cause NPLs were transferred at par value and the valuation of equity in SOEs was unrealistic. In addition, debt-equity swaps had no impact on corporate restructuring. See Edward Steinfeld, "Market Visions, Market Illusions: Debt-Equity Conversion and the Future of Chinese State Sector Reform," *CLSA Emerging Markets* (2000).

57. www.chinanews.com.cn, January 12, 2004.

58. *The Financial Times,* January 16, 2004, 16.

59. *Caijing (Business and Finance Review),* January 11, 2004, www.caijing.com.cn.

60. The bail-out costs could balloon further if the NPLs in rural and urban credit cooperatives are written off. These small financial institutions were in even weaker conditions than the SCBs. In 2001, according to the Ministry of Agriculture, liabilities exceeded assets by 236 billion yuan for all the RCCs. The bailout of RCCs would cost 200 billion yuan. *Caijing,* August 8, 2003, www.caijing.com.cn.

61. Hu Shuli, "Zaitan jinrong gaige burong ciyi" (Once More, Financial Reform Broods No Delay or Doubts), *Caijing,* July 31, 2003. www.caijing.com.cn.

62. Lardy, *China's Unfinished Economic Revolution*; Man-Kwong Leung and Vincent Wak-Kwong Mok, "Commercialization of Banks in China: Institutional Changes and Effects on Listed Enterprises," *Journal of Contemporary China* 9 (23) (2000): 41–52.

63. Genevieve Boyreau-Debray, "Financial Intermediation and Growth: Chinese Style," *World Bank Policy Research Working Paper No. 3027* (Washington, D.C.: World Bank, 2003).

64. Aziz and Duenwald, "Growth-Financial Intermediation Nexus in China."

65. Boyreu-Debray, "Financial Intermediation and Growth."

66. Justin Lin and Zhou Hao, "Gaige jinrong zhengce he tizhi shi woguo jingji zouru liangxing xunhuan" (Reforming Financial Policy and System to Make China's Economy Enter a Virtuous Cycle), *Gaige* 2 (1993): 97–105.

67. Genevieve Boyreau-Debray and Shang-Jin Wei, "Can China Grow Faster? A Diagnosis on the Fragmentation of the Domestic Capital Market" (Washington, D.C.: IMF, 2004).

68. One private conglomerate, Delong Group, successfully bought stakes in four city commercial banks in three provinces in 2002. With 10 to 40 percent of the shares, Delong was able to control management in two city commercial banks. *Caijing,* March 20, 2003, 39–54.

69. Through the SCBs and other nonprivate banks, the state controlled 90 percent of the banking market (excluding RCCs). Ding Ling and Chen Ping, "Yinhang longduan, xinyong weiji he jinrong gaige" (Banking Monopoly, Credit Crisis, and Financial Reform), *Gaige* 2 (2000): 90.

70. *The Wall Street Journal,* January 15, 2004, C16.

71. *The Financial Times,* January 10, 2004, www.ft.com.

72. Li Xinxin, "Cong dongya jinrong weiji kan woguo de jinrong yinhuan" (A Look at China's Financial Risks from the Perspective of the East Asian Financial Crisis), *Gaige* 3 (1998): 32; M. K. Leung, D. Rigby, and T. Young, "Entry of Foreign Banks in the People's Republic of China: A Survival Analysis," *Applied Economics* 35 (2003): 23.

73. James Barth, Rob Koepp, and Zhongfei Zhou, "Disciplining China's Banks," *The Milken Institute Review* 6(2) (2004): 88.

74. In 1999, the International Finance Corporation of the World Bank (which invested in Minsheng Bank) paid US$22 million for a 5 percent stake in Bank of Shanghai (previously known as the Shanghai City Cooperative Bank); HSBC paid $65 million for an 8 percent stake in Bank of Shanghai.

75. *The Wall Street Journal,* December 30, 2003, B5.

76. Zhou Xiaochuan, "Wenbu tuijin lilu shichanghua gaige" (Steadily Promoting the Reform in the Marketization of Interest Rates), *Caijing,* January 11, 2004. www.caijing.com.cn.

77. Pei, "The Political Economy of Banking Reforms in China," 325–326.

78. www.chinanews.com.cn, November 17, 2003. The SCBs' share of the outstanding loans was calculated from the data released by the government on January 11, 2004; www.chinanews.com.cn. In terms of assets in all financial institutions in 2001, the four SCBs accounted for 65 percent; the joint-stock banks accounted for 12 percent; urban credit cooperative and city commercial banks had 5 percent; and RCCs had 9 percent. Cem Karacadag, "Financial System Soundness and Reform," in Tseng and Rodlauer, eds., *China Competing in the Global Economy,* 153. Foreign banks had only 1 percent of the assets in the financial system in 2001. *China Banking Outlook: 2003–2004* (New York: Standard & Poor's, 2003), 15.

79. Y. C. Richard Wong and M. L. Sonia Wong, "Competition in China's Domestic Banking Industry," *Cato Journal* (Spring/Summer 2001): 31.

80. Yu Liangchun and Ju Yuan, "Longduan yu jingzheng: Zhongguo yinhangye de gaige he fazhan" (Monopoly and Competition: The Reform and Development of China's Banking Sector), *Jingji yanjiu* (*Economic Research*) 8 (1999): 54.

81. Wong and Wong, "Competition in China's Domestic Banking Industry," 28.

82. www.chinanews.com.cn, September 8, 2003; the NPL ratio for the SCBs was for September 2003, www.chinanews.com.cn, December 2, 2003.

83. The government reported that, using China's less stringent three-category classification, the NPL ratio for the SCBs at the end of 2003 was 16.8 percent; the ratio for city commercial banks was 12.8 percent. www.chinanews.com.cn, January 11, 2004.

84. Joel Baglole, "Opening Up Private Banks," *Far Eastern Economic Review* September 18, 2003, 49.

85. www.chinanews.com.cn, December 2, 2003.

86. Chen Zhiqiang, "Woguo zhongxia qiye fazhan ji guoyou shangye yinhang jinrong fuwu zhuangkuang de diaocha" (An Investigation of the Development of Medium and Small-Sized Firms and the Status of Financial Services Provided by State Commercial Banks in China), *Gaige* 1 (1999): 54.

87. Wong and Wong, "Competition in China's Domestic Banking Industry," 32.

88. DRC, "Minying qiye rongzhi xianzhuang diaoyan baogao" (An Investigative and Research Report on the Status of Financing Private Firms), *DRC diaocha yanjiu baogao*, April 18, 2001, 15.

89. Pei, "The Political Economy of Banking Reforms in China," 327.

90. DRC, "Minying qiye rongzhi xianzhuang diaoyan baogao," 8.

91. Boyreau-Debray, "Financial Intermediation and Growth," 30–31.

92. State Planning Commission, "Jiang Zhe zhongxiao qiye rongzi yu jinrong jigou fazhan diaocha baogao" (An Investigative Report on the Financing of Medium and Small Firms in Jiangsu and Zhejiang and the Development of Financial Institutions), *Jingji yanjiu cankao* 1662 (2002): 2–17.

93. OECD, *China in the World Economy*, 242.

94. *China Banking Outlook 2003–2004*, 6.

95. At the end of 2002, China had 1,215 listed companies, with a market capitalization of 4.27 trillion yuan (almost 40 percent of GDP); the float was only one-third of the total shares, implying a significantly smaller market capitalization. State Planning Commission, "Zhongguo ziben shichang de peiyu he fazhan zhengce yanjiu," 8–11.

96. Ibid., 5.

97. Ibid., 11.

98. Of the sixty-three banks included in the Fortune Global 500 in 1999, China's ICBC and BOC were considered the least efficient and profitable. Feng Zongxian, Tan Yi, and Guo Genglong, "Woguo yinhangye guoji jingzhengli fenxi" (An Analysis of the International Competitiveness of China's Banking Sector), *Gaige* 4 (2000): 86. On bank profitability, see Lardy, *China's Unfinished Economic Revolution*, 100–115.

99. See Lardy, *China's Unfinished Economic Revolution*, 92–100; Pei, "The Political Economy of Banking Reforms in China," 335.

100. *China Banking Outlook 2003–2004*, 32.

101. *Xinwen zhoukan*, August 4, 2003, www.chinanewsweek.com.cn.

102. *Caijing*, July 31, 2003, www.caijing.com.cn.

103. "Recapitalization Still Necessary for China's Banks Despite Lower Impaired Asset Ratio," *China Banking Outlook 2003–2004*, 8.

104. David Lague, "The Great Kaiping Bank Robbery," *Far Eastern Economic Review*, May 30, 2002, 26–29.

105. Xie Ping and Lu Lei, "Zhongguo jinrong fubai yanjiu: Cong dingxing dao dingliang" (Studying Financial Corruption in China: From Qualitative to Quantitative Approach), *Bijiao* (*Comparative Studies*) 8 (2003): 15.

106. X. L. Ding, "Systemic Irregularity and Spontaneous Property Transformation in the Chinese Financial System," *The China Quarterly* 163 (2000): 655–675.

107. Cao Haili, "Liu Jinbao beiqisu" (Liu Jinbao Was Indicted), *Caijing*, November 29, 2004, 107.

108. Lague, "The Great Kaiping Bank Robbery," 26–29.

109. *The Financial Times*, March 15, 2002, www.ft.com.

110. *Nanfang dushibao* (*Southern Metropolitan News*), June 26, 2002, www.nanfangdaily.com.cn/ds/20020626/.

111. *Caijing*, July 31, 2003, www.caijing.com.cn.

112. Xie and Lu, "Zhongguo jinrong fubai yanjiu," 1–45.

113. Ibid., 15.

114. Xie and Lu report wide variations between regions. Regions with more active private sectors and higher levels of development had lower bribery premiums. For example, the premium for firms was lower in eastern China (1.5 percent) and southern China, but higher in northern China (6.3 percent). The premium for individual farmers was the highest in northern China (8.7 percent) and the lowest in eastern China (2.8 percent). Ibid., 17–18.

115. Ibid., 17 and 26.

116. OECD, *China in the World Economy*, 235; *China Banking Outlook 2003–2004*, 28.

117. OECD, *China in the World Economy*, 247–263.

118. Paul Heytens, "State Enterprise Reforms," in Tseng and Rodlauer, eds., *China: Competing in the Global Economy*; OECD, *China in the World Economy*, 163–192.

119. DRC, "Guanyu Zhongguo shichanghua jincheng de yanjiu" (A Study of China's Marketization), *DRC diaocha yanjiu baogao* 112 (2002): 3.

120. Ibid., 4.

121. *ZGTJNJ 2002*, 423; *ZGTJNJ 1988*, 311.

122. *ZGTJNJ 1988*, 304; *ZGTJNJ 2002*, 424.

123. DRC, "Guanyu Zhongguo shichanghua jincheng de yanjiu," 5.

124. Thomas Rawski, "China's Move to Market: How Far? What Next?" www.pitt.edu/~tgrawski/paper99.

125. Wai jingmaobu gongping maoyiju yu Beijing shifan daxue jingji yu ziyuan guanli yanjiusuo Zhongguo shichang jingji fazhan yanjiu ketizu, "Zhongguo shichang jingji fazhan baogao" (Report on the Development of a Market Economy in China), *Zhanlüe yu guanli* 6 (2002): 12.

126. Gu Haibing, "Zhongguo jingji shichanghua de chengdu panduan" (An Estimate of the Level of Marketization in China), *Gaige* 1 (1995): 86–87.

127. Ibid., 85.

128. DRC, "Guanyu Zhongguo shichanghua jincheng de yanjiu," 7.

129. Ibid., 7; Gu Haibing, "Zhongguo jingji shichanghua de chengdu panduan," 85.

130. DRC, "Guanyu Zhongguo shichanghua jincheng de yanjiu," 7.

131. Rawski, "China's Move to Market." Also see Rawski, "Will Investment Behavior Constrain China's Growth?" (mimeo, University of Pittsburgh, September 2002).

132. DRC, "Guanyu Zhongguo shichanghua jincheng de yanjiu," 9.

133. Fan Gang et al., "Zhongguo ge diqu shichanghua xiangdui jincheng baogao" (A Report on the Relative Progress in China's Regions), *Jingji yanjiu* 3 (2003): 16.

134. See Chen Zongsheng et al., *Zhongguo jingji tizhi shichanghua jincheng yanjiu* (*A Study of the Progress of the Marketization of the Economic System in China*) (Shanghai: shanghai renmin chubanshe, 1999).

135. Yin Wenquan and Cai Wanru, "Woguo difang shichang fenge de chengyin he duice" (Fragmentation of Local Markets in China: Causes and Corrective Measures), *Jingji yanjiu* 6 (2001): 3–12. State Planning Commission, "Dapo difang shichang fenge jianli quanguo tongyi shichang" (End Market Fragmentation and Establish an Integrated National Market), *Jingji yanjiu cankao* 27 (2001): 9.

136. www.peopledaily.com.cn, February 22, 2003. Minxin Pei's analysis of 141 commercial disputes adjudicated in Chinese courts in the 1990s found that local firms had a 3 to 1 win ratio vis-à-vis nonlocal firms. See Minxin Pei, "Does Legal Reform Protect Economic Transactions? Commercial Disputes in China," in Peter Murrell, ed., *Assessing the Value of Law in Transition Economies* (Ann Arbor: University of Michigan Press, 2001), 180–210.

137. Young, "The Razor's Edge: Distortions and Incremental Reform in the People's Republic of China."

138. Zheng Yusheng and Li Chonggao, "Zhongguo difang fenge de xiaolu sunshi" (Efficiency Losses Caused by Fragmentation of Local Markets in China), *Zhongguo shehui kexue* (*Social Sciences in China*) 1 (2003): 64–72.

139. *BYTNB* 7 (2001): 49.

140. State Planning Commission, "Qiche shichang de difang baohu zhuangkuang ji duice yanjiu" (A Study on Local Protectionism in the Automobile Market and Policy Prescriptions), *Jingji yanjiu cankao* 27 (2001): 39.

141. State Planning Commission, "Dapo difang shichang fenge jianli quanguo tongyi shichang," 14.

142. Boyreau-Debray and Wei, "Can China Grow Faster?"

143. State Planning Commission, "Dapo difang shichang fenge jianli quan-guo tongyi shichang," 5–7.

144. DRC, "Zhongguo difang baohu chengdu yanjiu" (A Study of the Degree of Local Protectionism in China), *DRC diaocha yanjiu baogao* 46 (2003): 3–16.

145. State Planning Commission, "Dapo difang shichang fenge jianli quan-guo tongyi shichang," 7–8. Qi Lüdong, *Zhongguo xiandai longduan jingji yanjiu* (*A Study of the Economics of Contemporary Monopolies in China*) (Bei-jing: Jingji kexue chubanshe, 1999), 150.

146. DRC, "Dangqian Zhongguo shichang fayu quexian dui qiye jishu jinbu de yingxiang" (Flaws in the Development of the Markets in China and Their Impact on the Technological Progress of Firms), *DRC diaocha yan-jiu baogao* 103 (1999): 14.

147. DRC, "Dangqian Zhongguo shichang fayu quexian dui qiye jishu jinbu de yingxiang," 7.

148. For example, China's CR4 (the concentration ratio of the largest four producers) in 1984 was 17 percent for automobiles, 15 percent for cigarettes, 17 percent for plate glass, and 2 percent for cement. In the United States, the CR4 in 1982 was 97 percent for automobiles, 90 percent for cigarettes, 78 percent for plate glass, and 31 percent for cement. In India, the CR4 ratio in 1968 was 57 percent for automobiles, 64 percent for plate glass, and 60 percent for cement. Qi Lüdong, *Zhongguo xiandai longduan jingji yanjiu,* 146–148.

149. DRC, "Zhongguo shichang fayu de jiben tezheng jiqi cunzai wenti" (Ba-sic Characteristics and Existing Problems in the Development of Mar-kets in China), *DRC diaocha yanjiu baogao* 102 (1999): 7.

150. DRC, "Dangqian Zhongguo shichang fayu quexian dui qiye jishu jinbu de yingxiang," 12–13.

151. World Bank, *World Development Report 1996: From Plan to Market,* 33.

152. China scored 5.5, compared with Croatia (6.2), the Czech Republic (6.8), Estonia (7.4), Hungary (6.9), Latvia (6.6), Lithuania (6.2), Poland (6.0), the Slovak Republic (6.0), Russia (5.0), Ukraine (4.6), Al-bania (5.7), Bulgaria (5.2), Romania (4.6), India (6.1), Mexico (6.2), South Africa (6.8), the Philippines (6.7), and Brazil (5.7). Economic Freedom Index, www.fraserinstitute.ca/.

4. Transforming the State

1. Some of the materials in this chapter are drawn from Pei, "Rotten from Within," 321–349.

2. See Sun, *Corruption and Market in Contemporary China*; Zengke He, "Corruption and Anti-Corruption in Reform China," *Communist and Post-Communist Studies* 33 (2000): 243–270; Ting Gong, "Forms and Characteristics of China's Corruption in the 1990s: Change with Continuity," *Communist and Post-Communist Studies* 30 (3) (1997): 277–288; Xiaobo Lu, *Cadres and Corruption: The Organizational Involution of the Chinese Communist Party* (Stanford, Calif.: Stanford University Press, 2000).

3. The surveys were conducted in urban areas from 1995 to 1999. Corruption was ranked as the third most important issue from 1995 to 1997; it rose to be the second most important issue in 1998; it became the most important issue in 1999. Xu Xinxin, "1998–1999: Zhongguo shimin de guanzhu jiaodian yu weilai yuqi" (Chinese Urban Residents' Focus Issues and Future Expectations in 1998–1999), in Ru Xin et al., eds., *SHLPS 1999*, 87; Yuan Yue, "1998–1999: Zhongguo chengshi xintai zonghe pingjia" (A Comprehensive Evaluation of the Sentiments of Urban Residents in China in 1998–1999), in RuXin et al., *SHLPS 1999*, 103.

4. *Liaowang* (*Outlook*), August 7, 2000, 27.

5. Sichuan CCP Organization Department, "Sichuansheng dangzheng lingdao banzi chengyuan sixiang zhengzhi suzhi zhuangkuang diaocha baogao" (An Investigative Report on the Status of the Ideological and Political Caliber of Prefect and County Party and Government Officials in Sichuan Province), in *ZGYW, 1999*, 24.

6. news.xinhuanet.com/legal/2004–02/17, February 17, 2004.

7. news.xinhuannet.com/legal/2004–01/05, January 5, 2004.

8. For a study of administrative downsizing in China during the reform era, see Kjeld Erik Brodsgaard, "Institutional Reform and the *Bianzhi* System in China," *The China Quarterly* 170 (2002): 361–386.

9. It is notable that in the official data the growth of government personnel was no longer reported after 1990. But press reports and internal Chinese studies continue to portray a bloated and growing state bureaucracy into the 1990s.

10. A vice minister of the CCP Organization Department said in May 2001 that the Chinese government has 41 million "cadres." *Zhongguo qingnianbao* (*China Youth Daily*), May 19, 2001.

11. *ZGTJNJ 2003*, 129.

12. The national data for 1990 show that the number of people employed by the state was more than 9 million. But Table 4.2 shows that the total number of personnel in various government agencies (excluding those in the central government) was about 7.5 million. It is likely that the discrepancies are caused by different accounting methods used in arriving at these numbers. The lower number, given by the Office of the Central

Government's Staffing Commission, does not include personnel employed in law enforcement agencies (the police, prosecutors, the judiciary, and the People's Armed Police) and the armed forces.

13. The practice of hiring substitute cadres is officially sanctioned. Wu Jie, *Zhongguo zhengfu yu jigou gaige* (*Government and Institutional Reform in China*) (Beijing: Guojia xingzheng xueyuan chubanshe, 1999), 434.

14. *ZGTJNJ 2003*, 285.

15. Ibid., 281.

16. Calculated based on the salary costs data given in *ZGTJNJ 1979, 1999.*

17. *ZGTJNJ 2003*, 285–286.

18. Zhongyang jigou bianzhi weiyuanhui bangongshi (Office of the Central Government's Staffing Commission), *Zhongguo xingzheng gaige da qushi* (*Major Trends in China's Administrative Reform*) (Beijing: Jingji kexue chubanshe, 1993), 62.

19. Wang Chengyao, "Shilun shuifei fenliu gaige" (On the Reform to Separate Taxes from Fees), *Shuiwu* (*Taxation Research*) 10 (1998): 35.

20. At the local level, anecdotes of lavish spending by government officials abound. For example, an official study shows that, in 1998, in one of the poorest provinces, Anhui, each township government spent more than 100,000 yuan, and each village spent more than 10,000 yuan on entertainment-related expenses. In the same year, each township mayor (or party secretary) spent more than 100,000 yuan on automobile and cell phone expenses. *Neibu canyue* (*Internal Reference*), June 23, 2000, 16.

21. Not all off-budget revenues were illegal. The amount here referred to tax and fee incomes levied by local authorities in violation of the rules of the central government. State General Administration of Taxation, "Guanyu woguo feigaishui wenti de yanjiu" (A Study on the Issue of Converting Fees into Taxes in China), *Jingji yanjiu cankao* 86–87 (1998): 8.

22. Calculation based on data in *ZGTJNJ 1998*, 283.

23. The experience of Anhui province is typical. According to an official study of fifteen township governments conducted by the provincial government in 1998, funding of excess township government personnel was provided by fees and fines collected by these governments. Township government officials hired within the quota system had their salaries fully paid out of the fiscal revenues of the county and township governments. Staff hired outside the quota were supported by off-budget revenue. Office of Rural Economy, Anhui Provincial Government, "Xiang (zheng) jigou gaige sizhai bixing" (Reforming the Administration of Township Governments Is Inevitable), *Dangjian yanjiu neican* (*Party-Building Internal Reference*) 1–2 (1999): 13–16.

24. *Jingji yanjiu cankao* (July 24, 1998): 9.

25. Fiscal decentralization in China has been extensively studied and singled out by many scholars as the principal cause of a wide range of policies and behavioral patterns adopted by local governments. See World Bank, *China: Revenue Mobilization and Tax Policy* (Washington, D.C.: World Bank, 1990); Christine Wong, "Central-Local Relations in an Era of Fiscal Decline—the Paradox of Fiscal Decentralization in Post-Mao China," *The China Quarterly* 128 (1991): 691–714; Wang and Hu, *Zhongguo guojia nengli baogao*; Christine Wong et al., *Fiscal Management and Economic Reform in the People's Republic of China* (Hong Kong: Oxford University Press, 1995); Le-Yin Zhang, "Chinese Central-Provincial Fiscal Relations, Budgetary Decline and the Impact of the 1994 Fiscal Reform: An Evaluation," *The China Quarterly* 157 (1999): 115–141; Yasheng Huang, *Inflation and Investment Controls in China: The Political Economy of Central-Local Relations During the Reform Era* (New York: Cambridge University Press, 1996).

26. In his assessment of China's 1994 fiscal reforms, Pak Lee concludes that the 1994 reforms did little to strengthen the fiscal capacity of the central state. Lee, "Into the Trap of Strengthening State Capacity: China's Tax Assignment Reform," *The China Quarterly* 164 (2000): 1007–1024.

27. The estimate for revenues not counted by the Chinese official budget was obtained from Zhang, "Chinese Central-Provincial Fiscal Relations," 124.

28. *ZGTJNJ 2003*, 288.

29. *Zhongguo caizheng nianjian 1999*, 476.

30. *ZGTJNJ 2003*, 281, 288.

31. *Zhongguo caizheng nianjian 1999*, 477; *Zhongguo caizheng nianjian 2002*, 388.

32. *Zhongguo caizheng nianjian 1999*, 476.

33. State General Administration of Taxation, "Guanyu woguo feigaishui wenti de yanjiu."

34. Wen Shengtang, "2000 nian fan fubai douzheng" (Anti-Corruption Fight in 2000), in Ru Xin et al., eds., *SHLPS 2001*, 275.

35. The best example is the largest corruption scandal in Beijing's history. Its executive vice mayor, who alone controlled the capital's off-off-budget accounts, was accused of diverting several billion yuan of the city government's funds into various illegal schemes and the pockets of numerous mistresses. He committed suicide in the spring of 1995 after he was tipped off of his impending arrest.

36. *ZGTJNJ 1991*, 223; *ZGTJNJ 1995*, 223; *ZGTJNJ 1998*, 277.

37. This estimate is arrived at by comparing the official figure for total aggregate revenue in 1979, which was about 40 percent of GDP, with the estimated total aggregate revenue in the late 1990s, which included budget revenues, off-budget revenues, and off-off-budget revenues, and

which was about 30 percent of GDP. See State General Administration of Taxation, "Guanyu woguo feigaishui wenti de yanjiu," 8.

38. Ministry of Finance, "Xianji caizheng weiji jiqi duice" (The Fiscal Crisis of County Governments and Solutions), *Caizheng yanjiu* (*Fiscal Research*) 5 (1996): 55–59.

39. www.chinanews.com.cn, February 16, 2004.

40. Yasheng Huang, "Administrative Monitoring in China," *The China Quarterly* 143 (1995): 828.

41. Minxin Pei, "Civic Associations in China: An Empirical Analysis," *Modern China* 2 (1998): 285–318.

42. www.chinanews.com.cn, June 25, 2004.

43. www.people.com.cn, December 13, 2004.

44. news.xinhuanet.com/newscenter/2003–08/26, August 26, 2003.

45. Shanxi Provincial CCP Organization Department, "Guanyu jianli jianquan ganbu guanli jiandu jizhi wenti yanjiu baogao" (A Report on Establishing and Improving the Mechanisms for Supervising and Monitoring Cadres), *Zhonggong zhongyang dangxiao baogaoxuan* 16 (2000): 9, 523.

46. Sichuan CCP Organization Department, "Sichuansheng dangzheng lingdao banzi chengyuan sixiang zhengzhi suzhi zhuangkuang diaocha baogao," 33.

47. www.chinanews.com.cn, January 30, 2004.

48. news.xinhuanet.com/legal/2004–02/24.

49. *Fazhi ribao* (*Legal Daily*), April 16, 1998, 1.

50. *Zhongguo jijian jianchabao* (*Chinese Discipline Inspection Gazette*), January 28, 1997, 3.

51. *ZGFLNJ 1992*, 877.

52. Ibid.

53. *ZGFLNJ*, various years.

54. *ZGFLNJ 1991*, 939; *ZGFLNJ 2000*, 1212.

55. For the full text of the report, see *Zhongguo jijian jianchabao*, September 25, 1997, 1, 4.

56. Sun, *Corruption and Market*, 47.

57. *ZGFLNJ*, various years. The data for 2004 came from www.chinanews.com.cn, January 21, 2005.

58. Wu Guanzheng, "Work Report to the 3rd Plenum Meeting of the CDIC," www.chinanews.com.cn, February 22, 2004.

59. See note 10, chapter 1.

60. *Xuexi shibao* (*Study Times*), November 11, 2003.

61. *Caijing*, April 5, 2004, 16–17.

62. www.chinanews.com.cn, May 18, 2004.

63. www.chinanews.com.cn, May 22, 2004.

64. www.chinanews.com.cn, May 27, 2004.

65. *Dangzheng ganbu wenzhai* (*Digest for Party and Government Officials*) 1 (2002): 27.

66. www.caijing.com.cn/mag/preview.aspx?ArtID=4527. Lu was later extradited back to China and sentenced to death.

67. www.chinanews.com.cn, December 7, 2004.

68. news.xinhuanet.com/legal/2004–07/23, July 23, 2004.

69. www.chinanews.com.cn, December 13, 2004.

70. www.caijing.com.cn, September 30, 2004.

71. www.chinanews.com.cn, May 28, 2004.

72. www.chinanews.com.cn, September 10, 2002.

73. See X. L. Ding, *The Decline of Communism in China* (New York: Cambridge University Press, 1994); Yan Sun, *The Chinese Debate over Socialism* (Princeton, N.J.: Princeton University Press, 1997); Andrew Nathan, *China's Transition* (New York: Columbia University Press, 1997), 174–197.

74. *Zhongguo dangzheng ganbu luntan* (*Chinese Party and Government Officials' Forum*) 1 (2000): 32.

75. Sichuan CCP POD, "Sichuansheng dixian dangzheng lingdao banzi nianqinghua jincheng diaocha baogao," 24–25.

76. Ibid., 21–39.

77. Ibid., 25.

78. www.chinanews.com.cn, July 14, 2004.

79. www.xinhuanet.com, July 14, 2004.

80. Yu Jianrong's research on the criminalization of rural governments in the late 1990s shows that the phenomenon of local mafia states is probably widespread in China. See Yu, "Nongcun hei'e shili he jiceng zhengquan tuihua" (Evil Forces in Rural Areas and the Degeneration of Rural Governments), *Zhanlüe yu guanli* 5 (2003): 1–14.

81. A representative collection of corruption cases is *Dangqian jingji lingyu weifa weiji dianxing anli pingshi* (*Comments on and Analysis of Current Representative Illegal and Rule-Breaking Cases in the Economic Area*) (Beijing: Zhonghua gongshang lianhe chubanshe, 1996). *ZGFLNJ* also contains a small collection of major corruption cases in its annual issue.

82. See an interview with Liu at www.jcrb.com/ournews/asp/readNews.asp?id=128509 on December 9, 2002.

83. www.chinanews.com.cn, October 10, 2004; www.people.com.cn, August 25, 2004.

84. Awww.jcrb.com/zyw, May 24, 2003.

85. A*NFZM*, August 22, 2002.

86. A*NFZM*, February 20, 2003.

87. A*Nanfangwang* (*Southnet*), February 27, 2002, quoted on www.jcrb.com.cn.

88. www.chinanews.com.cn, February 25, 2002.

89. www.chinanews.com/cn, February 18, 2003.

90. www.jcrb.com/ournews/asp, November 5, 2002.

91. www.jcrb.com/ournews/asp, November 26, 2002.

92. www.chinanews.com.cn, July 4, 2003.

93. www.chinanews.com.cn, July 3, 2003.

94. For a detailed account of this case, see Zhang Xianhua et al., *Fengbao: Chachu Xiamen teda zousi an jishi* (*The Storm: A True Account of the Investigation and Resolution of the Super-Large Xiamen Smuggling Case*) (Beijing: Zuojia chubanshe, 2001).

95. Most of these cases were reported on the Web sites of www. jcrb.com and www.chinanews.com.cn; others were selected from official publications specializing in the coverage of corruption and law enforcement, such as *Minzhu yu fazhi* and *NFZM*.

96. www.chinanews.com.cn, July 3, 2003.

97. This case involved Xiamen's two deputy mayors, two deputy party secretaries, seven key law enforcement officials, 13 percent of the employees of the local customs agency, and the heads of the provincial branches of the three largest state banks.

98. Yan Sun also documented numerous cases of selling government appointments for personal gain. See Sun, *Corruption and Market*, 225–226.

99. *Renmin ribao,* June 19, 2001; www.chinanews.com.cn, November 29, 2001.

100. *NFZM,* August 22, 2002.

101. www.chinanews.com.cn, February 7, 2002.

102. *Renmin gong'anbao* (*People's Public Security News*), April 19, 2002.

103. www.chinanewsweek.com.cn, November 22, 2004.

104. Liu Haiqi, "Dahei bixu fanfu" (To Strike at Organized Crime, We Must Combat Corruption), *Zhongguo jiancha* (*Supervision in China*) 6 (2001): 48–49; www.chinanews.com.cn, January 22, 2002.

105. The criminal gang in Dong'an county in Hunan operated from 1993 to 2000; the local mafia state in Bangzhou, Hunan, thrived during 1997–2001; Liu Yong's group in Shenyang survived for eight years (1992–2000); the Zhou family mafia in Qianshan county in Jiangxi lasted twelve years (1990–2001).

5. China's Mounting Governance Deficits

1. Elizabeth Kopits and Maureen Cropper, "Traffic Fatalities and Economic Growth," *World Bank Policy Research Working Paper No. 3035* (Washington, D.C.: World Bank, 2003).

2. *ZGTJNJ*, various years.

3. www.chinanews.com.cn, February 24, 2003.

4. www.factbook.net/EGRF_Regional_analyses_AsiaPacific.htm.

5. *BYTNB* 10 (2002): 58.

6. *Zhongguo gonghui tongji ziliao 1998 (Chinese Labor Union Statistics)* (Beijing: Zhongguo gonghui tongji ziliao chubanshe, 1998), 309.

7. www.chinanews.com.cn, February 24, 2003.

8. www.laborsta.ilo.org.

9. Zhu Yichang, "Woguo anquan shengchan jiandu guanli tizhi jidai gaige" (China's System of Managing and Enforcing Workplace Safety Urgently Needs Reform), *Jingji yaocan (Important Economic Reference)* 55 (2002): 20.

10. *NFZM*, August 1, 2002. Coal mine accidents claimed 5,798 lives in 2000, 6,399 in 1999, and 5,670 in 2001. Wu Xiaoli, "Guanyu meikuang anquan jiancha zhifa gongzuo de xianzhuang yu jianyi" (On the Status of Inspection of Enforcement of Safety Rules in Coal Mines and Policy Recommendations), *Jingji yaocan* 42 (2002): 34.

11. *NFZM*, May 29, 2003. A government inspection of illegal coal mining operations in Guizhou in 2003 found that "a significant number of local officials" were investors in these mines. www.chinanews.com.cn, June 16, 2003. In a mining disaster in Nandan county in Guangxi in 2001, the county's party secretary and other local officials accepted large bribes from the mine owner in exchange for permission to operate in violation of safety regulations. Eighty-one miners died when the mine was flooded. www.jcrb.com, June 20, 2002.

12. *NFZM*, July 4, 2002.

13. World Bank, *World Development Indicators 2001* and *World Development Indicators 2002* (Washington, D.C.: World Bank); UNESCO Institute for Statistics, available at www.uis.unesco.org/ev.php?URL_ID=5187&URL_DO=DO_TOPIC&URL_SECTION=201.

14. *BYTNB* 12 (2001): 11.

15. UNESCO, *Education for All: Is the World on Track?* (Paris: UNESCO, 2002); Table 1.1 in the UNDP, *Human Development Report 2005* at www.undp.org.np/publications/hdr.2005.

16. James Heckman, "China's Investment in Human Capital," *NBER Working Paper No. 9296* (Cambridge, Mass.: National Bureau for Economic Research, October 2002).

17. Su Ming, "Zhongguo nongcun jichu jiaoyu de caizheng zhichi zhengce yanjiu" (A Study of the Policy of Fiscal Support for Basic Education in Rural China), *Jingji yanjiu cankao* 25 (2002): 34–42.

18. Wang Guijuan, "Jiaoyu jinfei nali chule" (Where Did the Education Money Go?), *Gaige neican (Reform Internal Reference)* 10 (2002): 21–22.

19. Lu Wangshi, "Caizheng jiaoyu touru youguan wenti yanjiu" (A Study of Fiscal Spending on Education and Other Issues), *Jingji yanjiu cankao* 94 (2000): 22.

20. Quoted in *NFZM*, August 29, 2002.

21. For a brief survey of the decline of China's public health system, see Yanzhong Huang, "Mortal Peril: Public Health in China and Its Security Implications" (Washington, D.C.: Chemical and Biological Arms Control Institute, 2003).

22. World Health Organization, *The World Health Report 2000* (Geneva, 2000), 152–155. For low-income countries, government spending on public health in 1997–1998 was 1.26 percent of the budget; in China, the figure was 0.62 percent. *NFZM*, May 15, 2003.

23. An example of the inequality in the provision of healthcare is that 5 percent of the health expenditures are spent in the seven poorest provinces in the western region, whereas Shanghai, Beijing, Jiangsu, and Zhejiang account for 25 percent of the health spending. Ibid.

24. *Caijing*, www.caijing.com.cn, May 16, 2003.

25. The privatization of the rural healthcare system occurred in 1984 as a result of township fiscal reforms. *Caijing*, May 16, 2003, www.caijing.com.cn; *BYTNB* 4 (2001): 10; Wang Yanzhong, "Shilun guojia zai nongcun yiliao weisheng baozhang zhongde zuoyong" (On the Role of the State in Safeguarding Rural Healthcare), *Zhanlüe yu guanli* 3 (2001): 18–19.

26. Overall, rural areas account for only 30 percent of all healthcare spending. *BYTNB* 4 (2001): 13.

27. Wang Yanzhong, "Shilun guojia zai nongcun yiliao weisheng baozhang zhongde zuoyong," 17.

28. *BYTNB* 4 (2001): 8–11.

29. *NFZM*, May 15, 2003; www.chinanews.com.cn, December 3, 2004.

30. Ministry of Health, *Guojia weisheng fuwu yanjiu* (*National Health Service Research*), www.moh.gov.cn/statistics/ronhs98/index.htm; the 2003 data are from www.chinanews.com.cn, January 10, 2005.

31. *BYTNB* 4 (2001): 8; Wang Yanzhong, "Shilun guojia zai nongcun yiliao weisheng baozhang zhongde zuoyong," 17.

32. www.chinanews.com.cn, December 3, 2004.

33. *NFZM*, May 15, 2003.

34. www.chinanews.com.cn, May 17, 2003.

35. www.chinanews.com.cn, November 28, 2004.

36. The Chinese government's estimate placed the number of HIV-carriers at 850,000 in 2002. But a UN AIDS report in June 2002 offered a higher estimate of 1 million. And a CIA estimate contended that the number of infected was between 1 million and 2 million. See Nicholas Eberstadt,

"The Future of AIDS," *Foreign Affairs* 81(6) (2002): 22–45; National Intelligence Council, "The Next Wave of HIV/AIDS: Nigeria, Ethiopia, Russia, India, and China" (Washington, D.C., 2002); www.chinanews. com.cn, June 27, 2002.

37. Only about two hundred people in China could afford to pay for the antiviral treatment. The costs of treating half of China's AIDS patients and HIV-carriers were estimated to be 54.6 billion yuan. *NFZM,* November 28, 2002; *Gaige neican* 20 (2002): 47.

38. United Nations, "HIV/AIDS: China's Titanic Peril," Executive Summary of the Joint United Nations Program on HIV/AIDS (New York: United Nations, 2002).

39. For an analysis of the rise in poverty in China, see Azizur Rahman and Carl Riskin, eds., *Inequality and Poverty in China in the Age of Globalization* (Oxford: Oxford University Press, 2001).

40. Wei Zhong and B. Gustafsson, "Zhongguo zhuanxin shiqi de pinkun biandong fenxi" (Analysis of Changes in Poverty in China's Transitional Period), *Jingji yanjiu* 11 (1998): 64–68. A government audit found that from 1997 to the first half of 1999, 20 percent of the funds earmarked for poverty relief in the country's 529 most impoverished counties had been misappropriated by local government officials. *NFZM,* May 30, 2002.

41. *NFZM,* July 29, 2004.

42. www.chinanews.com.cn, January 27, 2003. In the first half of 2003, 21.68 million urban residents received poverty-relief payments. According to the government, 28.2 million rural residents were living in poverty in 2003, down from 49.6 million in 1998. www.chinanews.com.cn, June 20, 2003; June 25, 2003.

43. Wang Yanzhong, "Shilun guojia zai nongcun yiliao weisheng baozhang zhongde zuoyong," 17. The Chinese definition of poverty is less than 637 yuan in per capita income a year. www.chinanews.com.cn, July 17, 2004. World Bank data showed that the number of people living in extreme poverty was 376 million in 1990. The World Bank's estimates suggest that the official Chinese poverty rate may be too low. See World Bank, *World Development Indicators 2003,* 5. Based on the World Bank international poverty line ($1 per day), China lifted 14 million people out of poverty in the 1990s. But the overall poverty rate was 17.4 percent at the end of the decade. See Chen Shaohua and Wang Yan, "China's Growth and Poverty Reduction: Recent Trends between 1990 and 1999" *World Bank Policy Research Working Paper No. 2651* (Washington, D.C.: World Bank Institute, 2001).

44. See Elizabeth Economy, *The River Runs Black: The Environmental Challenge to China's Future* (Ithaca, N.Y.: Cornell University Press, 2004).

45. Qu Geping, "Guanzhu Zhongguo de shengtai anquan" (Pay Attention to China's Ecological Security), *Zhonggong zhongyang dangxiao baogao xuan* 1 (2002): 4–6.
46. www.chinanews.com.cn, March 14, 2003.
47. www.chinanews.com.cn, November 29, 2004.
48. Qu Geping, "Guanzhu Zhongguo de shengtai anquan," 6–7.
49. World Bank, *China 2020*, 77.
50. www.chinanews.com.cn, March 14, 2003.
51. Jie Zhenghua, "Dangqian de huanjing xingshi he zhanlüe duice" (Current Environmental Conditions and Strategic Solutions), *Zhonggong zhongyang dangxiao baogao xuan* 12 (2000): 4.
52. Zhang Jun and He Hanxu, "Zhongguo nongcun de gonggong chanpin gongji" (Provision of Public Goods in Rural China), *Gaige* 5 (1996): 52.
53. Center for Chinese Studies, Tsinghua University, "21 shiji: Zhongguo jinru huanbao shidai" (21st Century: China Enters the Era of Environmental Protection), *Jingji yanjiu cankao* 97 (2000): 8.
54. Wang Shaoguang and Hu Angang, *The Chinese Economy in Crisis: State Capacity and Tax Reform* (Armonk, N.Y.: M. E. Sharpe, 2001); Christine P. W. Wong, Christopher Heady, and Wing T. Woo, *Fiscal Management and Economic Reform in the People's Republic of China;* Ramgopal Agarwala, "China: Reforming Intergovernmental Fiscal Relations" *World Bank Discussion Paper No. 178* (Washington, D.C.: World Bank, 1992); Christine P. W. Wong, ed., *Financing Local Government in the People's Republic of China* (New York: Oxford University Press, 1997).
55. *ZGTJZY 2000*, 62.
56. Research Institute of the State Tax Administration, "Guanyu woguo shuishou fudan wenti zaiyanjiu" (A Second Look at the Issue of the Tax Burden in China), *Jingji yanjiu cankao* 17 (1998): 3.
57. The municipal governments' share of funds increased as well, but the authors of the study did not disclose the precise magnitude. They simply suggested that in 2001 municipal governments declared a surplus of more than 13 billion yuan. See Jia Kang and Bai Jingmin, "Jiceng caizheng kunnan zai nali" (What Are the Difficulties in Local Public Finance?), *Gaige neican* 15 (2002): 23.
58. Fan Liming and Wang Dongni, "Woguo difang caizheng zhichu jiegou shizheng fenxi" (An Empirical Analysis of the Structure of China's Local Fiscal Expenditures), *Gaige* 3 (2001): 72.
59. Xiang Huaicheng, "Dangqian de caizheng gongzuo yu caizheng gaige" (Current Fiscal Tasks and Reform), *Zhonggong Zhongyang dangxiao baogaoxuan* 4 (1999): 8.
60. *BYTNB* 11 (1999): 5.

61. Su Ming, "Woguo xianxiang caizheng wenti de fenxi yu zhengce jianyi" (The Problem of County and Township Finance: Analysis and Policy Recommendations), *Neibu cankao* 39 (2002): 19.

62. Su Ming, "Zhongguo nongcun jichu jiaoyu de caizheng zhichi zhengce yanjiu," 45.

63. He Xuefeng and Xiang Jiquan, "Huaijie cunji zhaiwu de ganga" (Resolving the Difficulties in Village Indebtedness), *Gaige neican* 11 (2002): 22–23.

64. He Junwei, "Xiangcun zhaiwu wenti de xianzhuang chengyin ji duice" (Township and Village Debts: The Status, Causes, and Policies), *Jingji yaocan* 45 (2002): 9.

65. www.chinanews.com.cn, November 29, 2004.

66. He Junwei, "Xiangcun zhaiwu wenti de xianzhuang chengyin ji duice," 10.

67. *BYTNB* 9 (2000): 14.

68. *BYTNB* 5 (2001): 37.

69. He Junwei, "Xiangcun zhaiwu wenti de xianzhuang chengyin ji duice," 9.

70. Quan Junliang, "Xiangcun yanzhong fuzhai de chengyin ji zhili" (The Causes of and Solution to the Heavy Debts Incurred by Townships and Villages), *Jingji yanjiu cankao* 114 (2000): 37–38.

71. Zhao Limin et al., "Jiakuai tuijin nongcun shuifei gaige de nandian he duice" (On the Difficulties and Policies in Accelerating the Implementation of Tax and Fee Reforms in the Countryside), *Jingji yanjiu cankao* 74 (2002): 34.

72. *BYTNB* 9 (2000): 23.

73. He Junwei, "Xiangcun zhaiwu wenti de xianzhuang chengyin ji duice," 10.

74. Zhao Shukai, a DRC researcher, argued that the collapse of public finance in rural areas is a principal cause of the increasing conflict between peasants and local governments. See Zhao Shukai, "Xiangcun zhili: Zuzhi he chongtu" (Rural Governance: Organization and Conflict), *Zhanlüe yu guanli* 6 (2003): 1–8.

75. Quan Junliang, "Xiangcun yanzhong fuzhai de chengyin ji zhili," 39.

76. In Xiangtan city in Hunan, 25 percent of township officials reported they would like to seek other positions. Chu Guoliang, "Xiangzhen zhengfu de caizheng heidong" (The Black Hole in the Finance of Township Governments), *Gaige neican* 5 (2002): 6.

77. Research Institute of the Ministry of Finance, "Xiangzhen caizheng chizi yu zhaiwu yanjiu baogao" (Research Report on the Deficits and Debts of Townships), *Jingji yanjiu cankao* 78 (2002): 2–8.

78. Samuel Huntington, "Social and Institutional Dynamics of One-Party Systems," in Huntington and Clement Moore, eds., *Authoritarian Politics in Modern Society: The Dynamics of Established One-Party Systems* (New York: Basic Books, 1970), 4, 9.

79. In village elections, individuals who have demonstrated economic success have a better chance of getting elected to villagers' committees. In Zhejiang province, 30 percent of villagers' committee members were successful wealthy peasants and private entrepreneurs. Fan Ping, "2003 nian Zhongguo nongmin fazhan de jiben zhuangkuang" (Rural Development in China in 2003: Basic Situation), in Ru Xin et al., eds., *SHLPS 2004*, 306–307.

80. The withdrawal by the Chinese state from providing critical social services has been extensively documented. See Li Junpeng, *Gonggong fuwuxing zhengfu* (Public Service Oriented Government) (Beijing: Peking University Press, 2004). For the decline of government-provided social services in the countryside, see Center for Economic Studies of the Ministry of Agriculture, *Zhongguo nongcun yanjiu baogao 2000* (Research Report on Rural China) (Beijing: Zhongguo caizheng chubanshe, 2001).

81. See Zhao Shukai, "Xiangcun zhili: Zuzhi he chongtu," 1–8.

82. This is evident in the collapse of the Communist Youth League in rural China. A survey conducted by the league's organization in Xiangtan city in Hunan in 1999 found that 90 percent of the villages did not have a league cell. Since the CCP recruits from the league, the collapse of the league does not bode well for the party. See Huang Ren, "Jiceng tuan zuzhi mianlin de wenti burong hushi" (The Problems Faced by the League's Grassroots Organization Cannot Be Ignored), *Neibu canyue* (*Internal Reference*), October 27, 1999, 19–23.

83. Sichuan CCP POD, "Zhendui pinkun diqu tedian jinyibu jiaqiang nongcun jiceng zuzhi jianshe" (Target the Special Characteristics of Poor Areas and Further Strengthen the Building of Rural Grassroots Organizations), *Dangjian yanjiu neican* (*Party-Building Research Internal Reference*) 7 (1998): 11. Although there are no official data on how many CCP members have left the countryside for the cities, sociologists estimate that 120 million rural residents migrated to urban areas between 1978 and 2002. The CCP members account for 3.75 percent of the general rural population. Thus, at least 4.5 million CCP members have left the countryside. The actual number of CCP member migrants is likely much larger because brighter prospects in urban areas should attract more party members. The estimate of rural migrants is from Fan Ping, "2003 nian Zhongguo nongmin fazhan de jiben zhuangkuang," 304.

84. Shanxi CCP POD, "Guanyu dangyuan duiwu jiegou fenxi ji shutong dangyuan duiwu chukou wenti de diaoyan baogao" (An Investigative Research Report on the Structure of Party Members and the Issue of the Exit of Party Members), in *ZGYW*, 53.

85. *BYTNB* 7 (2001): 8.

86. The time of the survey was not identified. See Lu Xianfu, "Dangxian dangde jianshe de jige zhongda wenti" (Several Major Issues in Party-Building Today), *Lilun dongtai* (*Theoretical Development*) 1531 (2001): 13.

87. Li Jing and Cheng Wei, "Tingchan bantingchan qiye dangyuan guanli qingkuang diaocha" (An Investigation into the Management of Party Members in Enterprises That Have Ceased or Partially Ceased Operation), *Dangjian yanjiu* (*Party-Building Research*) 2 (1998): 38.

88. Shanxi CCP POD, "Guanyu dangyuan duiwu jiegou fenxi ji shutong dangyuan duiwu chukou wenti de diaoyan baogao," 53.

89. Other than trying to assert its control, the CCP's motives for trying to penetrate the private sector remain puzzling because Bruce Dickson's research shows that Chinese private entrepreneurs do not constitute a threat to the party. See Dickson, *Red Capitalists in China.*

90. Li Li'an, "Zai feigongyouzhi qiyezhong kaizhan dangjian gongzuo zhi wojian" (My Views on Implementing Party-Building Efforts in Non–State-Owned Enterprises), *Dangjian yanjiu neican* (*Internal Research Reference on Party-Building*) 4 (2002): 1.

91. In Guangdong's 7,301 civic associations, the party had cells in only 1.3 percent of them in 2000; the party had only one cell in Beijing's 1,140 private clinics and hospitals. In Beijing's private service firms, only 1.8 percent of the employees were CCP members. Institute of Party-Building Research of the CCP COD, ed., "Shehui zhongjie zuzhi dangjian gongzuo qingkuang diaocha" (Investigation of the Status of the Party-Building Work in Intermediating Social Organizations), *Dangjian yanjiu neican* 7 (2002): 8.

92. Shanghai CCP POD reported that only 3 percent of the wholly-owned foreign firms in the city had party organizations. Shanghai Municipal CCP School, "Xin jingji zuzhi dangjian gongzuo de xianzhuang yu qianzhan," *Dangjian yanjiu neican* 6 (2001): 11. In Shenzhen, only 4 percent of the foreign-invested firms had party cells. Li'an, "Zai feigongyouzhi qiyezhong kaizhan dangjian gongzuo zhi wojian," 1.

93. Lu Xianfu, "Dangxian dangde jianshe de jige zhongda wenti," 10.

94. *ZGTJNJ 2003*, 127.

95. For a description of the erosion of the party's ideological values, see chapter 4.

96. The time of the survey was not disclosed. Lu Xianfu, "Dangxian dangde jianshe de jige zhongda wenti," 14.

97. Ha'erbin CCP Municipal Organization Department, "Guanyu tuijin dangzheng lingdao ganbu nengshang nengxia wenti de yanjiu baogao" (A Research Report on Improving the System of Promotion and Demotion of Party and Government Officials), in *ZGYW 1998, part I,* 365.

98. Anhui CCP POD, "Tuijin dangzheng lingdao ganbu nengshang nengxia wenti yanjiu baogao" (A Research Report on Improving the System to Promote and Demote Party and Government Officials), in *ZGYW 1998, part I*, 335.

99. Sichuan CCP POD, "Sichuansheng dixian dangzheng lingdao banzi nianqinghua jingcheng diaocha baogao," *ZGYW 1997*, 20.

100. Yu Yunyao, "Mianxiang xin shiji de Zhongguo gongchandang" (The Chinese Communist Party Faces the New Century), *Zhonggong zhongyang dangxiao baogaoxuan* 1 (1998): 15.

101. www.people.com.cn, May 31, 2001.

102. Beijing CCP Municipal Organization Department, "Beijingshi dangyuan duiwu jiegou fenxi ji shutong dangyuan duiwu chukou wenti yanjiu" (A Study on the Structure of Party Members and the Issue of the Exit of Party Members in Beijing), *ZGYW 2000*, 229–232.

103. Ha'erbin CCP Municipal Organization Department, "Guanyu tuijin dangzheng lingdao ganbu nengshang nengxia wenti de yanjiu baogao," 365.

104. Jilin CCP POD, "Guanyu bu chengzhi dangzheng lingdao ganbu xia de wenti de diaocha yu sikao" (An Investigation and Some Thoughts on Demoting Incompetent Party and Government Officials), *ZGYW 1998, part I*, 399.

105. Zeng Qinghong, "Wei shixian 10/5 qijie de fazhan mubiao tigong zuzhi baozheng he rencai zhichi" (Provide Organizational and Talent Support for the Development Goals of the 10th 5-Year Plan), *Zhonggong zhongyang dangxiao baogaoxuan* 16 (2000): 9.

106. Sichuan CCP POD, "Sichuansheng tuijin dangzheng lingdao ganbu nengshang nengxia wenti diaoyan baogao" (An Investigative Research Report on the Issue of Promoting and Demoting Party and Government Officials in Sichuan Province), *ZGYW 1998, part 1*, 298.

107. Changsha CCP Municipal Organization Department, "Ganbu xia nan wenti yanjiu" (A Study of the Difficulty in Demoting Cadres), *Dangjian yanjiu neican* 5 (1997): 7.

108. DRC, "Cunji zuzhi de kunjing" (The Plight of Village Institutions), *DRC diaocha yanjiu baogao* 169 (1999): 1–19.

109. *Zhongguo gaige, nongcun*, 2 (2003): 47.

110. Sichuan CCP POD, "Sichuansheng dangzheng lingdao banzi chengyuan sixiang zhengzhi suzhi zhuangkuang diaocha baogao" (An Investigative Report on the Status of the Ideological and Political Caliber of Prefect and County Party and Government Officials in Sichuan Province), *ZGYW 1999*, 25–26.

111. Xu Xuehai et al., "Shehui jingji guanxi xinbianhua yu dangzheng jiguan ganbu duiwu jianshe wenti tanwei" (New Changes in Socio-

economic Relations and Some Tentative Thoughts on the Building of the Ranks of Party and Government Officials), *Shehui kexue zhanxian* (*Social Sciences Gazette*) 1 (2000): 230.

112. Murray Scot Tanner provides an extensive analysis of the rising social unrest in China in "China Rethinks Unrest," *The Washington Quarterly* 27 (3): 137–156.

113. The data cited here are from No. 4 Research Institute of the Ministry of Public Security, "Woguo fasheng quntixing shijian de diaocha yu sikao" (A Study and Reflection on Collective Incidents in China), *Neibu canyue* August 10, 2001, 18. Lu Xueyi, "Nongcun yao jingxing di'erci gaige" (Rural Areas Need Another Reform), in Ru Xin et al., eds., *SHLPS 2004*, 190.

114. Yu Jianrong, "Nongmin youzuzhi kangzheng jiqi zhengzhi fengxian" (Organized Resistance by Peasants and Its Political Risks), *Zhanlüe yu guanli* 3 (2003): 1–16.

115. *BYTNB* 2 (2000): 8–12; *BYTNB* 1 (2001): 40–42.

116. The most informative description is Li Changping's *Wo xiang zongli shuo shihua* (*I Told the Premier the Truth*) (Beijing: Guangming ribao chubanshe, 2002). Li was a party secretary in a Hubei township. In his book, he described political decay and economic difficulties in rural China in the most stark terms.

117. No. 4 Research Institute of the MPS, "Woguo fasheng quntixing shijian de diaocha yu sikao," 21.

118. Shen Zelin, "Yingxiang dangqian nongcun wending fazhan de zhuyao yinsu" (The Main Factors That Affect Rural Stability and Development), *Shehuixue* (*Sociology*) 2 (2001): 52.

119. Peasant protests against local governments' expropriation of land replaced tax revolts as the focus of rural discontent in the first decade of the new century. See Xiaolin Guo, "Land Expropriation and Rural Conflicts in China," *The China Quarterly* 166 (2001): 422–439. Yu Jianrong's study found that, of the 22,304 viewers' calls to China Central TV, complaints about land issues totaled 15,312, making the land issue the most salient rural problem. See Yu Jianrong, "Tudi wenti yichengwei nongmin weiquan kangzheng de jiaodian" (The Land Issue Has Become the Focus of the Peasants' Resistance and Struggle in the Defense of Their Rights) (Beijing: Institute of Rural Development, Chinese Academy of Social Sciences, 2004).

120. Zhang Xuhong, "Woguo nongmin shouru de xianzhuang yu duice" (Peasant Income in China: The Current Status and Policy Options), *Jingji yanjiu cankao* 62 (2001): 18.

121. *NFZM*, March 29, 2002; *ZGTJZY 2000* (China Statistical Abstract), 84. Rural income is augmented by income from nonagricultural produc-

tion, with about 30 percent of rural income in 1999 derived from wage income of migrant laborers. www.chinanews.com.cn, January 19, 2003.

122. For an analysis of the constraints on increasing rural income, see Project on Peasant Income, "Zengjia nongmin shouru de shida zhiyue" (Ten Major Constraints on Increasing Peasant Income), *Zhongguo nongcun yanjiu* (*China Rural Research*) 6 (2002): 1–12.

123. Wang, Hu, and Ding, "Jingji fanrong beihou de shehui buwending," 27.

124. Li Changping, *Wo xiang zongli shuo shihua*, 21.

125. Cui Xiaoli, "Woguo nongcun shuifei zhengshou cunzai de wenti ji gaige jianyi" (Collection of Taxes and Fees in China's Rural Areas: Existing Problems and Recommendations for Reform), *DRC diaocha yanjiu baogao* 54 (2002): 5.

126. See Thomas Bernstein and Xiaobo Lu, *Taxation Without Representation* (New York: Cambridge University Press, 2003). Another notable source of tensions is the dispute between the peasantry and the government over land acquisitions by the state. In Hunan, disputes over land acquisitions and compensation were among the top eight issues that triggered peasant petitions to government. *BYTNB* 1 (2002): 5–7.

127. Li Tianzi and Li Haifeng, "Jixu zhongshi jiejue nongmin fudanzhong de wenti" (Continue to Pay Attention to and Solve the Problem of Heavy Peasant Burdens), *Dangjian yanjiu neican* 6 (1999): 13–14.

128. The total amount in taxes and fees paid by the agrarian sector was about 10 percent of rural GDP, with 2.63 percent in taxes and 7.43 percent in authorized levies and fees. Illegal fees and levies amount to an additional 10 percent of rural GDP. Research Institute of the State Tax Administration, "Guanyu woguo shuishou fudan wenti zaiyanjiu," 20; Research Institute of the Ministry of Finance, "Xiangzheng caizheng chizi yu zhaiwu yanjiu baogao," 6.

129. Shen Zelin, "Yingxiang dangqian nongcun wending fazhan de zhuyao yinsu," 51.

130. See Thomas Bernstein and Xiaobo Lu, "Taxation Without Representation: Peasants, the Central and the Local States in Reform China," *The China Quarterly* 163 (2000): 742–763.

131. Li and Li, "Jixu zhongshi jiejue nongmin fudanzhong de wenti," 13–14.

132. Institute of Macroeconomic Research, State Planning Commission, "Zhongguo jumin shehui xintai genzong fenxi" (Tracking Analysis of the Social Sentiments of Chinese Citizens), in Ru Xin et al., eds., *SHLPS 2002*, 22.

133. Rural Survey Group, National Bureau of Statistics, "Nongcun jiceng gongzuo yu nongmin yiyuan diaocha" (A Survey of Basic Level Administration in Rural Areas and Sentiments of Peasants), *Zhongguo guoqing guoli* (*China's National Conditions and Power*) 11–12 (2001): 41.

134. Li Changping, *Wo xiang zongli shuo shihua,* 20.

135. *BYTNB* 10 (2002): 37.

136. Fan Ping, "Biandong zhong de Zhongguo nongcun yu nongmin" (Changing Chinese Villages and Peasants), in Ru Xin et al., eds., *SHLPS 2002,* 257. A DRC report disclosed that collecting taxes and fees consumed more than half the work time of officials of township and village governments. Cui Xiaoli, "Woguo nongcun shuifei zhengshou cunzai de wenti ji gaige jianyi," 8.

137. Rural Survey Group, National Bureau of Statistics, "Nongcun jiceng gongzuo yu nongmin yiyuan diaocha," 41.

138. A survey of ninety townships in fifteen provinces by the Ministry of Civil Affairs in 1992 found that almost two-thirds funded their payrolls through collection of illegal fees. In some counties, income from such fees covered more than half the payroll costs. Liu Shuming, "Kao feigaishui jiejue nongmin fudan guanyong ma" (Will Tax-for-Fee Reform Solve the Problem of Peasant Burdens?), *Zhongguo guoqing guoli* 11–12 (2001): 43.

139. *NFZM,* September 19, 2002.

140. Yu Jianrong, "Jinru nongcun jiceng zhengquan de hei'e shili" (Evil Forces That Have Penetrated Local Governments in Rural Areas), *Gaige neican* 10 (2002): 39–42.

141. Zhang Zhiming and Zhao Wenhao, "Jiceng dangde lingdao fangshi zhuanbian yi kebu ronghuan" (Changes in the Party's Governing Style at the Local Level Can No Longer Be Delayed), *Lilun dongtai* 1577 (2002): 23–24.

142. *BYTNB* 12 (2000): 39–40.

143. *BYTNB* 10 (2002): 37.

144. Ibid., 38.

145. Ray Yep, "Can 'Tax-for-Fee' Reform Reduce Rural Tension in China? The Process, Progress and Limitations," *The China Quarterly* 177 (2004): 42–70.

146. Liu Shuming, "Kao feigaishui jiejue nongmin fudan guanyong ma," 42.

147. In a poll of 2,001 residents in six cities in July 2000, 64 percent thought the country was very stable or quite stable, and only 9 percent thought it was unstable or quite unstable. Yang Yiyong and Zhang Benbo, "Zhongguo chengzhen jumin shehui xintai de diaocha baogao" (A Report on the Public Sentiments of Urban Residents in China), in Ru Xin et al., eds., *SHLPS 2001,* 28–29.

148. Yuan Yue, "1998–1999: Zhongguo chengshi shimin xintai zonghe pingjia" (A Composite Evaluation of the Sentiments of Chinese Urban Residents in 1998–1999), in Ru Xin et al., eds., *SHLPS 1999,* 101–102.

149. Yuan Yue et al., "2001 nian Zhongguo shimin shenghuo manyidu de diaocha" (A Survey of Life Satisfaction of Chinese Urban Residents in 2001), in Ru Xin et al., eds., *SHLPS 2002,* 40.

150. Institute of Macroeconomic Research, State Planning Commission, "Zhongguo jumin shehui xintai genzong fenxi," 19–20.
151. Tanner reached similar conclusions in his "China Rethinks Unrest."
152. Also mentioned as among the top three issues in the five-year period were environmental protection, education, healthcare reform, and social security (each issue was once mentioned the number three issue in the period); Yuan Yue et al., "2001 nian Zhongguo shimin shenghuo manyidu de diaocha," 45.
153. Sun Li and Zheng Weidong, "1998: Zhongguo shehui xingshi yu gaige de shehui xinli diaocha baogao" (A Report on the Social Psychology of the Conditions and Reform in Chinese Society in 1998), in Ru Xin et al., eds., *SHLPS 1999,* 56.
154. Institute of Macroeconomic Research, State Planning Commission, "Zhongguo jumin shehui xintai genzong fenxi," 22.
155. Guo Yan, "Laobaixing de xintai" (Public Sentiments), *Gaige neican* 3 (2002): 21–24.
156. Wang, Hu, and Ding, "Jingji fanrong beihou de shehui buwending," 29.
157. Ibid., 27.
158. *NFZM,* June 13, 2002: the number of registered unemployed urban workers in mid-2001 was 6.18 million, or 3.3 percent of the urban labor force. Lu Jianhua, "Shehui fazhan jincheng buru quanxin de kaifang jieduan" (The Process of Social Development Has Entered a Brand-New Phase of Opening), in Ru Xin et al., eds., *SHLPS 2002,* 9.
159. Mo Rong, "Jiuye: Xinshiji mianlin de tiaozhan yu xuanze" (Employment: Challenges and Choices for the New Century), in Ru Xin et al., eds., *SHLPS 2001,* 219.
160. About 40 percent had a lower-middle school education or less. The average age was thirty-nine, with about half between thirty-five and forty-five and almost a quarter forty-five and older. Mo Rong, "Jiuye xingshi yiran yanzhong" (The Employment Situation Remains Severe), in Ru Xin et al., eds., *SHLPS 2002,* 165, 167.
161. Li Peilin and Zhang Yi, "Zhongguo shouru chaju kuoda de houguo ji zhili duice" (Rising Income Inequality in China: Consequences and Policy Options), *Jingji yaocan* 51 (2001): 3.
162. Mo Rong, "Jiuye: Xinshiji mianlin de tiaozhan yu xuanze," 220.
163. Song Bao'an and Wang Yushan, "Changchun shi xiagang zhigong zhuangkuang de wenjuan diaocha" (A Survey of the Conditions of Laid-off Workers in Changchun), in Ru Xin et al., eds., *SHLPS 1999,* 274.
164. Lu Jianhua, "1998–1999: Zhongguo shehui xingshi fenxi yu yuce zong baogao" (A General Report on and Analysis of the Social Conditions in China in 1998–1999), in Ru Xin et al., eds., *SHLPS 1999,* 9.

165. Yan et al., "Tianjin shi xiagang zhigong zhuangkuang de wenjuan diaocha" (A Survey of the Conditions of Laid-off Workers in Tianjin); Song and Wang, "Changchun shi xiagang zhigong zhuangkuang de wenjuan diaocha"; Jiang Shuge et al., "Xiagang yu zaijiuye wenti jiqi chulu" (Lay-offs and Reemployment: Problems and Solutions), in Ru Xin et al., eds., *SHLPS 1999*, 259–260, 281, 314.

166. In a survey of 1,152 laid-off workers in Tianjin in October 1998, 38 percent said they cut down on their spending to make ends meet, 23 percent relied on help from family, 11 percent used savings, and 18 percent relied on friends and relatives. Yan et al., "Tianjin shi xiagang zhigong zhuangkuang de wenjuan diaocha," 259–260.

167. Ibid., 262.

168. Mo Rong, "Zhongguo jiuye xingshi yiran yanzhong" 182, 168; Mo Rong, "Jiuye: Xinshiji mianlin de tiaozhan yu xuanze," 218.

169. Yu Jianrong, "Zhuanxing Zhongguo de shehui chongtu" (Social Conflicts in a China in Transition) (Beijing: Institute of Rural Development, Chinese Academy of Social Sciences, 2004).

170. Yan et al., "Tianjin shi xiagang zhigong zhuangkuang de wenjuan diaocha," 259.

171. Jiang Shuge, et al., "Xiagang yu zaijiuye wenti jiqi chulu," 315.

172. Wang, Hu, and Ding, "Jingji fanrong beihou de shehui buwending," 30.

173. Song and Wang, "Changchun shi xiagang zhigong zhuangkuang de wenjuan diaocha," 282.

174. On worker unrest, see Marc Blecher, "Hegemony and Workers' Politics in China," *The China Quarterly* 170 (2002): 283–303; Yongshun Cai, "The Resistance of Chinese Laid-Off Workers in the Reform Period," *The China Quarterly* 170 (2002): 327–344; William Hurst and Kevin O'Brien, "China's Contentious Pensioners," *The China Quarterly* 170 (2002): 345–360.

175. Wang, Hu, and Ding, "Jingji fanrong beihou de shehui buwending," 31.

176. Human Rights Watch has a detailed account of this specific incident in its "Paying the Price: Worker Unrest in Northeast China" (New York: Human Rights Watch, 2002).

177. *ZGFLNJ 2003*.

178. Yu Jianrong, "Xinfang de zhiduxin queshi jiqi zhengzhi houguo" (The Institutional Flaws of Letters and Visits and Their Political Consequences) (Beijing: Institute of Rural Development, CASS, 2004).

179. *NFZM*, November 4, 2004.

180. According to Yu Jianrong's research, about 50 percent of the petitioners thought the central government's authority in rural areas was "very high and quite high." In comparison, only 2 percent said the county

government's authority was "very high or quite high." Yu Jianrong, "Xinfang de zhiduxin queshi jiqi zhengzhi houguo."

181. Ibid.

182. The July 2000 poll surveyed 2,001 residents in urban areas in six cities. Yang and Zhang, "Zhongguo chengzhen jumin shehui xintai de diaocha baogao," 31. The September 2001 poll included 1,999 residents in five provinces. Institute of Macroeconomic Research, State Planning Commission, "Zhongguo jumin shehui xintai genzong fenxi," 20.

Conclusion

1. China's growth during this period lagged behind the growth rates for Japan, Taiwan, and South Korea during comparable periods of economic take-off. Martin Wolf, "Why Is China Growing So Slowly?" *Foreign Policy* (January–February 2005): 50–51.

2. Thomas Rawski, "What's Happening to China's GDP Statistics?" (University of Pittsburgh, memo, 2001).

3. See Minxin Pei, *From Reform to Revolution: The Demise of Communism in China and the Soviet Union* (Cambridge, Mass.: Harvard University Press, 1994).

4. O'Donnell and Schmitter, *Transitions from Authoritarian Rule.*

5. See Robert Ross, "Beijing as a Conservative Power," *Foreign Affairs* 76(2) (1997): 33–44; Ezra Vogel, ed., *Living with China: U.S.-China Relations in the Twenty-first Century* (New York: Norton, 1997); James Shinn, ed., *Weaving the Net: Conditional Engagement with China* (New York: Council on Foreign Relations, 1996).

6. See Jack Goldstone, "The Coming Chinese Collapse," *Foreign Policy* 99 (1995): 35–53; Gordon Chang, *The Coming Collapse of China* (New York: Random House, 2001).

Acknowledgments

In the three years of research and writing, I have received generous support and encouragement from many individuals and organizations. Otherwise, *China's Trapped Transition* could not have been finished. I want to thank the Smith Richardson Foundation for a three-year grant that financed most of the research on the project. The Carnegie Endowment for International Peace has provided the most hospitable environment for conducting research. I am privileged to have a group of outstanding colleagues. In particular, I wish to thank Jessica Mathews, the president of the endowment, for her enthusiastic support. Tom Carothers, Paul Palaran, and George Perkovich at the Endowment have also been very generous with their help.

Much of the research was done at the Center for Chinese Studies at the Chinese University of Hong Kong, formerly known as the Universities Service Centre. Under Jean Hung's energetic and selfless leadership, the centre has become the most valuable resource for China specialists around the world. In the course of my research, Jean and her colleagues made me truly welcomed at the Centre and gave me all the logistical assistance essential to successfully complete the project.

I am very grateful to Bruce Dickson for his helpful comments on the manuscript.

At the Carnegie Endowment, I had the great fortune of being assisted by Seth Garz, Sara Kasper, Merritt Lyon, and Victorien Wu, four bright and hardworking junior fellows. Elizabeth Reiter, Savina Rupani, and Jennifer Yi also provided valuable administrative assistance during the preparation of the manuscript. I want to thank them for their dedication and contribution.

Parts of Chapters 1 and 4 draw on materials published in my "Rotten from Within: Decentralized Predation and Incapacitated State," in T. V. Paul,

G. John Ikenberry, and John Hall, eds., *The Nation-State in Question* (Princeton, N.J.: Princeton University Press, 2003). I thank Princeton University Press for permission to use the materials.

I also want to thank Kathleen McDermott of Harvard University Press for her patience, understanding, and encouragement.

My wife, Meizhou, and my two boys, Alexander and Philip, are owed special gratitude for tolerating my long research trips to Asia and frequent bouts of workaholic behavior that must have made their lives miserable.

The greatest debt I owe is to Samuel P. Huntington, my teacher and friend. His seminal work on political development and democratization and brilliant insights into the centrality of political institutions have inspired me ever since I took my first seminar with him in 1986. Sam's enduring influence is evident in the theoretical assumptions and analytical approaches of the book. And to Sam this book is dedicated.

Index

Harvard University Press is a member of Green Press Initiative (greenpressinitiative.org), a nonprofit organization working to help publishers and printers increase their use of recycled paper and decrease their use of fiber derived from endangered forests. This book was printed on 100% recycled paper containing 50% post-consumer waste and processed chlorine free.